Know How

Know How

Jason Stanley

OXFORD
UNIVERSITY PRESS

OXFORD
UNIVERSITY PRESS

Great Clarendon Street, Oxford OX2 6DP

Oxford University Press is a department of the University of Oxford.
It furthers the University's objective of excellence in research, scholarship,
and education by publishing worldwide in

Oxford New York

Auckland Cape Town Dar es Salaam Hong Kong Karachi
Kuala Lumpur Madrid Melbourne Mexico City Nairobi
New Delhi Shanghai Taipei Toronto

With offices in

Argentina Austria Brazil Chile Czech Republic France Greece
Guatemala Hungary Italy Japan Poland Portugal Singapore
South Korea Switzerland Thailand Turkey Ukraine Vietnam

Oxford is a registered trade mark of Oxford University Press
in the UK and in certain other countries

Published in the United States
by Oxford University Press Inc., New York

© Jason Stanley 2011

British Library Cataloguing in Publication Data

Data available

Library of Congress Cataloging in Publication Data

Data available

Typeset by SPI Publisher Services, Pondichery, India
Printed in Great Britain
on acid-free paper by
MPG Books Group, Bodmin and King's Lynn

ISBN 978–0–19–969536–2

Contents

Preface

A fact, as I shall use the term, is a *true proposition*. A proposition is the sort of thing that is capable of being believed or asserted. A proposition is also something that is characteristically the kind of thing that is true or false; that snow is white is a true proposition, that Barack Obama is President of the United States as I am writing these words is another. Facts in this sense are not only among the things we believe and assert; they are also the kinds of things we know.

The thesis of this book is that knowing how to do something is the same as knowing a fact. It follows that learning how to do something is learning a fact. For example, when you learned how to swim, what happened is that you learned some facts about swimming. Knowledge of these facts is what gave you knowledge of how to swim. Something similar occurred with every other activity that you now know how to do, such as riding a bicycle or cooking a meal. You know how to perform activities solely in virtue of your knowledge of facts about those activities.

This thesis may seem puzzling. Learning how to do something eventuates in a state that is intimately connected with action. In contrast, knowledge of a fact seems like the kind of thing that is characteristically acquired by reading a book. Learning facts seems to leave us only with abstract or theoretical knowledge of the world. Learning how to do something, by contrast, seems to leave us with skills in engaging with it.

If it is surprising that knowledge of a fact can so immediately yield knowledge of how to swim, ride a bicycle, or play a piano, it is only so because of false assumptions about what it is know a fact. These false assumptions lie behind the idea of knowledge of a fact as something that is by its nature inherently contemplative, rather than a state implicated directly in action. There are false assumptions about what it is to *act* on knowledge of facts, there are false assumptions about what it is to have *knowledge* of facts, and there are false assumptions about the *nature* of facts. In the course of establishing the thesis of this book, I will have to dispel all of these myths. To make it plausible that knowing how to do something is knowledge of facts, I must erect at least the skeleton of the correct view of factual knowledge.

Of course, when you learned how to swim, you didn't just learn any old fact about swimming. You learned a special *kind* of fact about swimming. The fact you learned is the proposition that answers a question – the question "How could you swim?" Knowing how to do something therefore amounts to *knowing the answer to a question*. To explain the kind of propositions that answer these kinds of questions, it will be necessary first to take a step back and investigate the genus of which knowing how to do something is a species. An account of what it is to know how to Φ must fit into a more general account of *knowing answers to questions*. For example, an account of knowing how to catch a fly ball must fit into a more general account of knowing *when* to catch a fly ball and knowing *where* to position one's glove in order to catch a fly ball. More generally, we need an account of what one might call *knowledge-wh*; knowledge where, knowledge when, knowledge how, knowledge why, etc. As we shall see, according to the best available theories, knowledge of facts is necessary and sufficient for knowledge-wh.

The outlines of an account of the special kind of facts that constitute knowledge how will emerge from this more general theory of what it is to know the answer to a question. But, as we shall see, the standard theories of knowledge-wh that we will explore are conceptually impoverished. They are not even sufficient to explain the kinds of facts that one learns when one learns *who someone is*, much less the kinds of facts that one learns when one learns how to do something. I show that a more sophisticated notion of proposition (and hence a more sophisticated notion of fact) is required for a full account of knowledge-wh. This more sophisticated notion of proposition is one that exploits ways of thinking, or "modes of presentation", of objects, as in the works of Gottlob Frege. It also explains why learning a fact is not always something one can do by reading a book. Some ways of thinking of objects cannot be acquired by mere description. I defend this conception of facts against well-known charges of obscurantism.

My aim is not just to sketch an account of factual knowledge and some of its sub-species. I also provide an account of the role such knowledge plays in guiding action. Skilled action is action that manifests an agent's knowledge how. A surgeon wields her scalpel with skill only if it is an exercise of her knowledge of how to do the procedure. Acting with skill is action that manifests an agent's knowledge of facts. A further goal of this book is to demonstrate that it is our capacity to learn and retain knowledge of facts that explains our capacity for skilled engagement with the world.

There is a widespread assumption that factual knowledge is by its nature solitary, purely reflective, and detached from decision and action. The result is the view, common throughout the human sciences, that factual knowledge is an idle wheel in explaining and evaluating behavior. This is the second book I have written in opposition to this assumption. The guiding idea of this work has been that the value of knowledge lies in its connection to action. Its aim is to exploit these connections to shed light on the nature of states of factual knowledge, while simultaneously revealing the explanatory richness behind the conception of rational animals as creatures who know.

The valuable philosophical work on the nature of attitudes towards questions in the 1960s and 1970s by figures such as Nuel Belnap, Sylvain Bromberger, and Jaakko Hintikka failed to leave a legacy in philosophy departments. For example, episte-mologists have, until very recently, neglected knowledge-wh. At least in the United States, philosophical work on the logic and nature of questions, and concomitant work on the content of states of knowledge-wh moved into linguistics and computer science departments, where it was carried on by formal semanticists. Because of their departmental affiliations, much of this work does not take the form of an account of the nature of such states, but is rather stated in the formal mode – as an analysis of the meanings of the *ascriptions* of such states, i.e. the analysis of the meanings of *sentences* of the form "X knows where to find an Italian newspaper", or "X knows who went to the party". As with so much in formal semantics, a great deal of this work is only by sociological accidental conducted in the formal mode. The work can equally well be taken as claims, in the material mode, about the nature of such states. Though I will follow the sociology in making claims about sentences that ascribe knowledge, most of my claims are intended as claims about the states themselves. Still, since our beliefs about states of knowledge how are affected both by properties of its characteristic ascriptions and by properties of the states themselves, there will be a necessary admixture of considerations in the pages that follow.

This work has been many years in the making. I started on this topic either in the spring or fall of 1998, when I sent my close friend Timothy Williamson one of the many interminable papers I was writing at that time on knowledge of meaning. In the paper, I was arguing that knowing the meaning of a term was a kind of propositional knowledge. In a footnote, I noted that Michael Devitt had argued that knowledge of meaning was knowledge how rather than propositional knowledge, and responded to Devitt's claim by pointing out that on all the extant semantic accounts of embedded questions, knowing how *was* a kind of propositional knowledge. Tim was working on a review of a book by A.W. Moore (Williamson 1999) in which he had sketched a version of a propositional view of knowing how, that knowing how to Φ is to know, of some way w, that w is the way to Φ (a view he had held for several years already). This was, I assured him, what would emerge from an account of the semantics of knowledge-wh generally. We immediately started work on a joint paper. Working separately, we met for a week in New York City in the spring of 1999 to formulate a complete draft (ironically, one whole day of work was spent in Fanelli's Café in Soho, long owned by the Noë family). Out of that, our joint paper "Knowing How" emerged.

It was always clear to me that ultimately the topic deserved a book. However, the issues required many years to settle, and other work intervened for both he and myself. One reason for the inordinate delay in writing a book is that I was hoping to plan the writing of the book so that Tim and I would be able to co-author it. Unfortunately, Tim's time has been occupied defending the view that he necessarily exists (and will never perish). Other vicissitudes of life also intervened to make such a joint venture impossible. Initially, this almost defeated my plans of writing the book, since I was and continue to be painfully aware of how much better the book would have been if we could have written it together. I owe him an immense debt for the work he did on formulating the view in the first place.

Except for my paper "Knowing (How)" (forthcoming), from which I have liberally borrowed, and perhaps five or six paragraphs in total excerpted from two previous papers, none of the other material in this book is previously published. I am grateful to the journal *Nous* for allowing me to use material from "Knowing (How)". I am also grateful to the many audiences who have sat through lectures on this material since 2005, including philosophy departments, linguistics departments, and cognitive science departments at the University of Barcelona, Brown University, Queen's University, University of Buenos Aires, Princeton University, and Rutgers University, and at conferences including the Southern Society for Philosophy and Psychology in Savannah, Georgia, Meaning, Understanding, and Knowledge at the University of Latvia, in Riga, Latvia, Semantics and Linguistic Theory 20 in Vancouver, British Columbia, the Oberlin Colloquium, at the APA Pacific Division, and at a Workshop on Knowing How at the University of Geneva, in Geneva, Switzerland. I am very grateful to the group of philosophers at St. Andrews University in Scotland, where I have presented a good portion of this material over the last five years, especially since I joined the faculty there as a quarter-time professorial fellow in 2007.

In the spring of 2009 I taught a graduate seminar on this material at Rutgers University, with the aim of completing a final version by that summer. But the penetrating comments and feedback I received from the graduate students in the seminar sent me back for a subsequent two years of revision. Because of the students in that seminar, the book is immeasurably better than it otherwise would have been. The help I received from graduate students at Rutgers was not limited to that semester. Carlotta Pavese has been a tireless (and fierce) critic and interlocutor over the last two years. I have been extraordinarily fortunate to have had the opportunity to work with her. Though in the end she has a different view than I do on the topic, working with her has taught me much about the strengths and weaknesses of my own.

I am grateful for discussion of the material to many people over the years. In addition to the graduate students at Rutgers, whose comments necessitated changes too numerous to mention, among the people whose comments (in whatever forum) have occasioned changes are Nomy Arpaly, Matthew Biro, Herman Cappelen, Taylor Carman, David Chalmers, Michael Devitt, Randy Gallistel, Rochel Gelman, Tamar Gendler, Ephraim Glick, Jereon Groenendijk, Katherine Hawley, John Hawthorne, James Higginbotham, Mark Johnston, Jeff King, Ernie Lepore, Sarah-Jane Leslie, Franck Lihoreau, Peter Ludlow, Robert Matthews, Sarah Moss, Jennifer Nagel, Stephen Neale, Alva Noë, Francois Recanati, Ian Rumfitt, Daniele Sgaravatti, Ernest Sosa, Robert Stalnaker, Jason Streitfeld, Matthew Stone, Eric Swanson, Njeri Thande, Brian Weatherson, David Wiggins, Crispin Wright, and Elia Zardini. In all of my trips to St. Andrews I spent many hours in intensive discussion with Yuri Cath about the issues in the book, from which I learned (and continue to learn) a great deal. He also provided a commentary on an earlier version of Chapter 1 at the Pacific Division APA, which helped me in revisions. Jeremy Fantl provided incisive comments on a later version of Chapter 1 at the Oberlin Colloquium. Though to my knowledge my colleague Martin Lin has not developed commitments on the topics in this book, he has been an invaluable sounding board for the ideas in it over the last few years. Discussions with Corine Besson and Aaron Zimmerman about the Lewis Carroll problem have been very useful to me during the process of completing Chapter 1. Finally, thanks are due to Matthew Benton for proof-reading the manuscript and compiling the index.

This book covers a wide diversity of topics. As a result, I have needed to draw on the expertise of many different academics. I did so by sending chapter drafts, or sections of chapter drafts, to relevant experts in different areas for feedback. I am grateful for the immense intellectual generosity of my colleagues in philosophy. Peter Railton and Timothy Williamson gave me comments on earlier versions of Chapter 1. Daniel Rothschild provided invaluable help with Chapter 2, correcting errors in the first draft. Jonathan Schaffer and Will Starr provided comments on later drafts that resulted in important changes. Richard Heck provided very useful comments on Chapters 3 and 4. Carlotta Pavese provided very useful comments on Chapters 3, 4, and 5. Susanna Siegel and Brian McLaughlin both read Chapter 7, and provided very useful comments. Sarah Garfinkel provided the most valuable help with that chapter. At the start of the process she provided me with extensive reading lists for the cognitive science literature on memory, and was subsequently always available for brainstorming sessions about this or that experimental result or theoretical distinction in the literature I was reading.

Ever since I sat in a seminar of his on action theory when I was teaching at Michigan, David Velleman has been my action theory guru. The notes I still have from that seminar helped me out at crucial points in thinking through the action theory related issues in this book, and he also kindly made himself available for consultations. His timely intervention on a confusion of mine prevented me from embarking on a thoroughly unwarranted multi-month tangent. Sarah Paul and Kieran Setiya were also generous over email in helping me to understand their respective views about knowledge of action.

It will be clear from the pages that follow that I am sympathetic with the views defended in Peter Railton's recent work on action, and David Chalmers' recent work on content. For personal reasons, I have spent a good deal of time back in Ann Arbor during the last three years. Conversations with Peter over that period have been enormously useful. David has been equally helpful. During the last eight months or so of working on this manuscript, I managed to have several extended conversations with him about the *de se* and Fregeanism generally. These conversations were of enormous use, and helped convince me that I needed to elaborate the version of Fregean content that it is one of this book's purposes to defend.

Since I arrived at Rutgers University I have also been speaking with Jerry Fodor at every possible opportunity. We have had numerous lengthy conversations about the thesis of this book. I have not made as clear as I should have in its pages how much Fodor's work over the decades has been motivated by thinking about the relation between knowing how and knowing that, and especially about the kinds of regress arguments discussed in the first chapter. I have learned an immense amount from these discussions, and discussions with Jerry have had a quite significant impact on my views.

In the last decade, the literature on the topic of knowledge how has exploded, with numerous valuable and important contributions. There has been no way to incorporate reactions to all of it within the confines of this book, especially since most of this literature was being produced during the finishing stages of this work. I have chosen to focus on developing my own picture, the one descended from my joint work with Williamson, leaving to my subsequent papers critical discussions of novel alternative pictures, such as those defended in recent and forthcoming work by John Bengson and Marc Moffett, as well as Berit Brogaard.

I have been very fortunate to have as a life-partner someone with the intellectual acuity to explain to me when the interest or persuasive power of my latest argument or idea relies essentially on unexplained philosophical jargon. My wife Njeri Thande's effect on my ideas, and especially the topics I have chosen to work on over the years, has been profound. More specifically for the project in this book, her lived experience as a cardiologist in training has helped me gain a better understanding of the central role knowledge of facts plays in guiding action.

My first book was written in the shadow of my father's death. This last one has been written in the dawn of my son's impending birth. During the final stages of its writing Njeri has been in her last year of her cardiology fellowship at the University of Michigan. Throughout her entire pregnancy she has woken up almost every day at five in the morning to exercise, before going in to perform procedures for ten hours a day. This has been an easy year compared to her previous ones, many of which were spent working 80-hour weeks with lives depending upon her ability to assimilate and make rapid decisions on the basis of the research she did the night before. I can count on one hand the number of times I have heard her complain about work in her seven-year career thus far as a doctor. She is a persistent reminder to me of the indomitable character of the human spirit. This book is dedicated, with love and admiration, to her.

1

Ryle on Knowing How

Humans are thinkers and humans are agents. There is a natural temptation to view these as distinct capacities, governed by distinct cognitive states. When we engage in reflection, we are guided by our knowledge of propositions. By contrast, when we engage in intelligent action, we are guided by our knowledge of how to perform various actions. If these are distinct cognitive capacities, then *knowing how to perform an action* is not a species of propositional knowledge.

There is an intuitive basis for the view that those who are chiefly skilled in action have fundamentally different cognitive virtues than those who are chiefly skilled at theoretical reasoning. There are different professions to which they are best suited, as well as different positions in the socio-economic hierarchy. For those inclined to dichotomies popular in turn-of-the-century Vienna, they may correlate with differences in gender and religion. That there is an important distinction between the kinds of states that guide us in action and the kind of states that guide us in reflection is orthodoxy in much of the most influential work in twentieth-century philosophy. For example, Martin Heidegger writes:

"Practical" behavior is not "atheoretical" in the sense of "sightlessness". The way it differs from theoretical behavior does not lie simply in the fact that in theoretical behavior one observes, while in practical behavior one *acts*, and that action must employ theoretical cognition if it is not to remain blind; for the fact that observation is a kind of concern is just as primordial as the fact that action has its own kind of sight. Theoretical behavior is just looking, without circumspection. (1962: 99)

But the most systematic attempt to prove what philosophers and laypersons typically assume, that what guides us in action is a distinct cognitive capacity from what guides us in reflection, is due to Gilbert Ryle, in his major work, *The Concept of Mind*.

However, there has been little interpretive evaluation of Ryle's arguments for the view that knowing how is not a species of knowing that. The lacuna is perhaps not surprising. *The Concept of Mind* is devoted to advancing Ryle's behaviorist views. It is not immediately evident how the topic of knowing how fits into this now unpopular agenda. Furthermore, Ryle's arguments – in particular, his different versions of the 'regress' arguments – are compressed and pose interpretive difficulties. But Ryle's actual arguments deserve systematic appraisal. The arguments have had a broad impact on the views of philosophers and psychologists, who both explicitly and implicitly follow Ryle in running together various correct conclusions about the relation between knowledge and intelligent action with incorrect conclusions about the relation between knowing how and knowing that. By a careful review of Ryle's arguments, we can avoid these errors, and thereby make way for the account of knowledge how that is to follow in subsequent chapters.

My principle purpose in this chapter is therefore to distinguish Ryle's correct insights about action from his incorrect conclusions about the relation between knowing how to do something and knowing that something is the case. In section 1, I explain why Ryle regarded his arguments for a non-propositional notion of knowing how as so central to his behaviorist program in the philosophy of mind. In section 2, I turn to an explication of the "regress" argument Ryle presents in *The Concept of Mind* for the conclusion that knowing how is not a species of knowing that. This argument is intended in the first instance as a criticism of the intellectualist thesis that an action is intelligent in virtue of being guided by propositional knowledge. I argue that the argument neither refutes the intellectualist thesis, nor establishes that knowing how is not a species of knowing that. However, as we shall see, it nevertheless has some important consequences for the study of practical reason. In section 3, I apply the morals of the discussion in section 2 to a contemporary attack on the intellectualist view of skilled action, due to Hubert Dreyfus. Sections 4 and 5 consist of discussions of related regress arguments against the intellectualist view of intelligent action that Ryle employs in earlier work, including his version of the Lewis Carroll problem. I conclude in section 6 by considering a series of linguistic arguments Ryle takes as evidence that knowing how to do something is not a kind of propositional knowledge, the resolution of which will pave the way for the subsequent chapter.

1.

Gilbert Ryle's aim in *The Concept of Mind* is to advance a behaviorist conception of most mental properties and states. As Ryle conceives of logical space, there are only two positions on the metaphysics of the mental: Cartesian dualism, according to which mental states are properties of unknowable non-material souls, and his favored view, according to which mental states are dispositions to behave. Throughout the book, the correct behaviorist conception of various fundamental mental categories is contrasted with the "occult" or "ghostly" conceptions of these categories advanced by the Cartesian. The chapter entitled "Knowing How and Knowing That" occurs very early in the book, directly after the first chapter, entitled "Descartes' Myth", and is clearly intended as a central part of his anti-Cartesian picture. The purpose of this section is to explain why the category of knowing how to do something plays such a central role in Ryle's anti-Cartesian project.

Cartesianism must be rejected, according to Ryle, because it would make it unknowable whether the central concepts of rational appraisal are applicable in individual cases:

According to the theory, external observers could never know how the overt behavior of others is correlated with their mental powers and processes and so they could never know or even plausibly conjecture whether their applications of mental-conduct concepts to these other people were correct or incorrect. (21)

The fact that Cartesianism makes the applicability of mental-conduct terms unknowable does not just raise epistemological problems. It threatens the very *meaningfulness* of such attributions. As Ryle continues:

It would then be hazardous or impossible for a man to claim sanity or logical consistency even for himself, since he would be debarred from comparing his own performances with those of others. In short, our characterizations of persons and their performances as intelligent, prudent, and virtuous or as stupid, hypocritical, and cowardly could never have been made.

In this passage, Ryle infers from the premise that one is debarred from comparing one's own performances with those of others (the supposed consequence of Cartesianism), to the conclusion that our mental state characterizations could not be made.

Some read Ryle here as making the merely epistemological point that Cartesianism would make our characterizations of mental states to others unjustified, by rendering propositions about the mental states of others unknowable. On this view, Ryle's critique of Cartesianism is not meant to have any metaphysical consequences. It is the merely epistemological charge that Cartesianism results in an untenable epistemology of the mental. However, it is hard to read this particular passage of Ryle as making a merely epistemological point. If mental-conduct terms were still meaningful on the Cartesian view, even if we could not verify whether or not they could be applied to an individual case, we could still *make* judgments about the mental states of others — it is just that those judgments would not be justified. But Ryle does not say that we could make judgments, but our judgments would never be justified — he says that such judgments "could never have been made". Ryle therefore here seems to take the unknowability of the applicability of mental-conduct terms to show that sentences containing mental-conduct terms fail to express propositions. Ryle's criticism of Cartesianism therefore presupposes a version of the verifiability theory of meaning — that a term is only meaningful if it is knowable whether or not it applies in particular cases. By making the applicability of mental-conduct concepts to others unknowable, the Cartesian renders them vacuous of content.[1]

In *The Concept of Mind*, Ryle seeks to lay out an alternative picture of mental states, one that makes it knowable whether they apply to particular agents, and therefore makes discourse about the mental meaningful by the lights of the view of meaning he assumes. He starts with knowing how, because knowing how to do something is

---

[1] The charge of verificationism here is not due to any historical point about Ryle's influences. Ryle himself was a critic of the verificationist principle (Ryle 1971a, b). The point is rather that in order to interpret the letter of his arguments against the Cartesian, Ryle must have adhered to some view of meaning that entailed it.

conceptually connected to the central concepts of rational appraisal. If knowing how is a matter of dispositions to behave, then we can know whether or not our applications of rationality and intelligence to people and their actions are correct. If we can know whether the applications of such mental-conduct concepts to other people are applicable, then mental-conduct terms are meaningful.

The behaviorist holds that a mental state is a disposition to behave. On this picture, the mental states of others are knowable through various manifestations in their behavior. The behaviorist view of mental states stands in opposition to the view that mental states are categorical states of the agent. Given the conceptual connections between knowing how and many important concepts in the theory of action, if Ryle can establish his behaviorist account of knowing how, then he can conclude that fundamental concepts of rational appraisal are behaviorist as well. It is because of the conceptual connections between knowing how to do something and intelligence that knowing how to do something plays such a central role in Ryle's philosophy.

The mental conduct concepts that principally concern Ryle in the chapter "Knowing How and Knowing That" are *intelligence* concepts, as they are predicates of actions. As Ryle (p. 25) writes, "The mental-conduct concepts that I choose to examine first are those which belong to that family of concepts ordinarily surnamed 'intelligence'. Here are a few of the more determinate adjectives of this family: 'clever', 'sensible', 'careful', 'methodical', 'inventive', 'prudent', 'acute', 'logical', 'witty', 'observant', 'critical', 'experimental', 'quick-witted', 'cunning', 'wise', 'judicious' and 'scrupulous'." Ryle's target is the view that an action has one of these properties in virtue of being controlled by one's apprehension of truths, i.e. one's knowledge of truths. Ryle's chief aim in the chapter is to show that the intelligence concepts are better understood in other terms.

The intelligence concept that occupies Ryle perhaps the most is the concept of *skill*. With this and closely related concepts, Ryle notes that the lure of the intellectualist view is particularly strong:

On the assumption of the antithesis between "physical" and "mental", it follows that muscular doing cannot itself be a mental operation. To earn the title "skilful", "cunning", or "humorous", it must therefore get it by transfer from another counterpart act occurring not "in the machine" but "in the ghost"; for "skilful", "cunning" and "humorous" are certainly mental predicates.

Here is Ryle, describing the roots of the non-behaviorist view of intelligence and rational action that he opposes (p. 26):

When we speak of the intellect, or better, of the intellectual powers and performances of persons, we are referring primarily to that special class of operations which constitute theorizing. The goal of these operations is the knowledge of true propositions or facts. Mathematics and the established natural sciences are the model accomplishments of human intellects. The early theorists naturally speculated upon what constituted the peculiar excellences of the theoretical sciences and disciplines, the growth of which they had witnessed and assisted. They were predisposed to find that it was in the capacity for rigorous theory that lay the superiority of men over animals, or civilized men over barbarians and even of the divine mind over human minds. They thus bequeathed the idea that the capacity to attain knowledge of truths was the defining property of a mind. Other human powers could be classed as mental only if they could be shown to be somehow piloted by the intellectual grasp of true propositions. To be rational was to be able to recognize truths and the connections between them. To act rationally was, therefore, to have one's non-theoretical propensities controlled by one's apprehension of truths about the conduct of life.

Ryle begins with knowing how in part because he seeks to show that an action is intelligent, not in virtue of being "controlled by one's apprehension of truths", but because it manifests an ability or a disposition:

When a person is described by one or other of the intelligence-epithets such as "shrewd" or "silly", "prudent" or "imprudent", the description imputes to him not the knowledge, or ignorance, of this or that truth, but the ability, or inability, to do certain sorts of things. (Ryle 1949: 27)

Similarly, on skilled action:

The cleverness of the clown may be exhibited in his tripping and tumbling . . . The spectators applaud his skill at seeming clumsy, but what they applaud is not some extra hidden performance executed 'in his head'. It is his visible performance they admire, but they admire it not for being an effect of any hidden internal causes but for being an exercise of a skill. Now a skill is not an act . . . To recognize that a performance is an exercise of a skill is indeed to appreciate it in the light of a factor which could not be separately recorded by a camera. But the reason why the skill exercised in a performance cannot be separately recorded by a camera is not that it is an occult or ghostly happening, but that it is not a happening at all. It is a disposition, or a complex of dispositions.

An action manifests skill in virtue of being a manifestation of the agent's knowledge of how to do it. If Ryle can show that knowing how to do something is identical to a disposition or an ability, then on the assumption that knowledge of a truth is neither a disposition nor an ability, he will have refuted the intellectualist view that actions have intelligence properties in virtue of guidance by propositional knowledge.[2]

Ryle employs the connections between knowing how and other states to give behaviorist solutions to classical philosophical problems connected with rational action. A characteristic example occurs in Ryle's chapter on the Will, where he seeks to show that various versions of the "Problem of the Freedom of the Will" are spurious. Ascriptions of praise and blame are conceptually connected to whether or not an

---

[2] Ryle does not confuse abilities with tendencies, i.e. abilities with what we might in a narrow sense of the term call "dispositions". Rather, Ryle uses the expression "dispositional" to cover abilities *and* tendencies. As Ryle (1949: 123) writes, "We can now come back to consider dispositional statements, namely statements to the effect that a mentioned thing, beast or person, has a certain capacity, tendency, or propensity, or is subject to a certain liability."

action was done voluntarily. Ryle exploits a dispositional account of knowing how to show that he can explain successfully when a person is at fault for an action. He does so by arguing that whether or not someone has done an action voluntarily is not a matter of "the occurrence or non-occurrence of any occult episode", which would be unknowable. Rather it is a matter of whether or not the person has the relevant knowledge how, a fact which, given Ryle's behaviorist conception of knowing how, is knowable. As he writes:

> If a boy has tied a granny-knot instead of a reef-knot, we satisfy ourselves that it was his fault by first establishing that he knew how to tie a reef-knot, and then by establishing that his hand was not forced by external coercion and that there were no other agencies at work preventing him from tying the correct knot. We establish that he could tie reef-knots by finding out that he had been taught, had had practice, usually got them right, or by finding that he could detect and correct knots tied by others, or by finding that he was ashamed of what he had done and, without help from others, put it right himself. That he was not acting under duress or in panic or high fever or with numb fingers, is discovered in the way in which we ordinarily discover that highly exceptional incidents have not taken place; for such incidents would have been too remarkable to have gone unremarked, at least by the boy himself.
>
> The first question which we had to decide had nothing to do with the occurrence or non-occurrence of any occult episode in the boy's stream of consciousness; it was the question whether or not he had the required higher-level competence, that of knowing how to tie reef-knots. We were not, at this stage, inquiring whether he committed, or omitted, an extra public or private operation, but only whether he possessed or lacked a certain intelligent capacity. What satisfied us was not the (unattainable) knowledge of the truth or falsity of a particular covert cause–overt effect proposition, but the (attainable) knowledge of the truth or falsity of a complex and partially general hypothetical proposition – not, in short, that he did tie a shadowy reef- or granny-knot behind the scenes, but that he could have tied a real one with this rope and would have done so on this occasion, if he had paid more heed to what he was doing. The lapse was his fault because, knowing how to tie the knot, he still did not tie it correctly. (71)

The role Ryle's behaviorist account of knowing how as a disposition to behave plays in his response to the worry facing the Cartesian is clear in this passage. On the Cartesian view of mental states, it is unknowable whether or not someone was at fault for doing something (and hence attributions of fault are meaningless). But on Ryle's account, it is knowable. Hannah is at fault for not doing X if she knows she is supposed to do X, knows how to do X, and was not prevented from doing X by exceptional circumstances. Since knowing how to do X is a matter of having a certain capacity, constituted by tendencies to behave in various circumstances, rather than knowing a proposition, it is knowable whether or not Hannah knows how to do X. So for Ryle, it is knowable whether or not Hannah was at fault for not doing X. The view that knowing how is nothing over and above an ability the presence of which is behaviorally detectable is crucial in this account of blame.

So, Ryle's adoption of a behaviorist account of knowing how seems motivated by the view that mental conduct terms are only meaningful if it is knowable whether or not they apply – or at the very least by the view that behaviorism is the only account that yields a satisfactory epistemology of intelligence and rationality. These considerations lead him to adopt a behaviorist account of knowing how, which he then uses to give behaviorist accounts of central concepts of rational appraisal such as intelligence, rationality, praise, and blame.

There are a number of well-known concerns about this program. First, Ryle assumes a theory of meaning that connects linguistic meaning to verifiability: a term is meaningful only if it is possible in principle to verify whether or not it applies to something. This verificationist principle about meaning is now universally rejected. Second, even if we prescind from the charge of verificationism, and read Ryle as arguing against Cartesianism via the view that Cartesianism results in an untenable epistemology of the mental, his argument is unpersuasive. No one thinks anymore that the only way to make the applicability of mental-conduct concepts knowable is to characterize them as dispositional properties. Suppose, for example, that believing that p is the categorical property of having a sentence in one's "belief box" that expresses that p. It is perfectly knowable whether or not an agent has this categorical property. There are behavioral effects of having it. Furthermore, presumably neuroscience can reveal their presence or absence. Skepticism about ascriptions of categorical properties of the mind/brain that explain the behavior of a given rational agent is no more plausible than skepticism about the ascription of categorical properties to a glass that explain its fragility. None of Ryle's principal motivations for rejecting an intellectualist account of knowing how survive scrutiny.[3]

In light of these difficulties with Ryle's program in *The Concept of Mind*, some recent scholars have tried to rehabilitate Ryle from the charge of behaviorism. The major source of evidence marshaled by those so inclined is that, in Ryle's characterizations of the dispositions that constitute mental states such as knowing how to ride a bicycle, he appeals to properties that have no obvious behaviorist definitions. For example, Julia Tanney writes:

Ayer goes on to say that for a behaviourist programme to succeed, it has to be shown that mental talk can be reformulated in such a way as to eliminate any reference to an inner life. And yet *The Concept of Mind* abounds with such references. Ryle concedes the existence of an inner mental life, when he says, for example, that "Much of our ordinary thinking is conducted in internal monologue or silent soliloquy, usually accompanied by an internal cinematograph-show of visual imagery" or that exercises of knowing-how "can be overt or covert, deeds performed or deeds imagined, words spoken aloud or words heard in one's head, pictures painted on canvas or pictures in the mind's eye." (2005a)[4]

---

[3] This is not to deny that there may be metaphysical arguments that mental states are not brain states (see Weatherson 2007: section 3). But to attribute such arguments to Ryle is a bit of a stretch. Furthermore, such arguments are just as often as not nowadays used in the defense of some form of Cartesianism.
[4] The passage is from the English version of Tanney (2005a). See also her entry on Ryle in the *Stanford Encyclopedia* (2005b), as well as Brian Weatherson (2007) for similar thoughts.

It is certainly true that when Ryle characterizes dispositions to behave, he does so partially in terms that seem manifestly inconsistent with behaviorism. For example, he tells us that one exercise of a multitrack disposition can be having "pictures in the mind's eye". On the orthodox interpretation of Ryle, it is hard to see how he can appeal at face value to such notions as "pictures in the mind's eye".

However, to take such references as evidence that Ryle was not committed to behaviorism would be a misinterpretation. Ryle's description of his Cartesian stalking horse is:

Besides being currently supplied with these alleged immediate data of consciousness, a person is also generally supposed to be able to exercise from time to time a special kind of perception, namely inner perception, or introspection. He can take a (non-optical) 'look' at what is passing in his mind. Not only can he view and scrutinize a flower through his sense of sight and listen to and discriminate the notes of a bell through his sense of hearing; he can also reflectively or introspectively watch, without any bodily organ of sense, the current episodes of his inner life. (1949: 14)

The view that there is a "mind's eye", which "can take a (non-optical) look" at pictures, is clearly a part of the "Official Theory" that Ryle wishes in no uncertain terms to reject.

So why does Ryle explicitly and knowingly adopt the idioms of the official theory in describing his views? There is no great mystery here; he is quite clear about the fact that he does not know how to describe the phenomena with vocabulary he can accept at face value. As he writes, remarking about his adoption of the Cartesian idioms in his chapter "Sensation and Observation":

I do not know the right idioms in which to discuss these matters, but I hope that my discussion of them in the official idioms may have at least some internal Fifth Column efficacy. (201)

He also adopts the official idioms of the Cartesian theory because he hopes that he can construe them in a non-literal way which makes them acceptable for the behaviorist. As he writes in his chapter entitled "Imagination":

The crucial problem is that of describing what is 'seen in the mind's eye' and what is 'heard in the head'. What are spoken of as 'visual images', 'mental pictures', 'auditory images' and, in one use, 'ideas' are commonly taken to be entities which are genuinely found existing and found existing elsewhere than in the external world. So minds are nominated for their theatres. But, as I shall try to show, the familiar truth that people are constantly seeing things in their minds' eye and hearing things in their heads is no proof that there exist things which they see and hear, or that the people are seeing or hearing. Much as stage-murders do not have victims and are not murders, so seeing things in one's mind's eye does not involve either the existence of things seen or the occurrence of acts of seeing them. (245)

Ryle's behaviorist metaphysics brings him to repudiate mental images. However, he rightly recognizes that he must explain the usefulness of the idioms that seem to commit us to them. Like many a philosopher who wishes to repudiate an ontology while reaping its useful benefits, he appeals to the notions of pretense and make-believe:

Similarly, there are not two species of murderers, those who murder people, and those who act the parts of murderers on the stage; for these last are not murderers at all. They do not commit murders which have the elusive attribute of being shams; they pretend to commit ordinary murders, and pretending to murder entails, not murdering, but seeming to murder. As mock-murders are not murders, so imagined sights and sounds are not sights and sounds. They are not, therefore, dim sights, or faint sounds. And they are not private sights or sounds either. There is no answer to the spurious question, "Where have you deposited the victim of your mock murder?" since there was no victim. There is no answer to the spurious question, "Where do the objects reside that we fancy we see?" since there are no such objects. (250–1)

So, Ryle adopts the "official vocabulary" of the Cartesian theory, not because he repudiates behaviorist metaphysics for such properties, but because he sees no easy way to avoid using it. He argues that he can use it, consistently with his behaviorist view of their actual objects, because he thinks he can explain away its apparent commitments by fictionalist means. In short, Ryle is making a sophisticated modern maneuver. He accepts that he is not able to produce behavioral analyses of some fundamental mental notions – he is not a *logical* behaviorist. But he hopes to avoid the need for such analyses, by construing the problematic talk in fictionalist terms. Just as it would be wrong to deny the label "nominalist" to someone who allows for number-talk when construed as a pretense, so it is wrong to say of Ryle that he is not a behaviorist, since he allows for mental-image talk when construed as a pretense.[5]

This is not to suggest that Ryle ends up with satisfactory accounts of the official idioms of the Cartesian theory, fictionalist or otherwise. Ryle himself declares, at the beginning of the chapter "Sensation and Perception", that he is "not satisfied" with the chapter. But it is odd to suggest, as certain commentators have, that Ryle is not a behaviorist about (e.g.) sensation and perception because he feels the need to appeal to talk that, taken at face value, is inconsistent with behaviorism. As I have tried to make clear, Ryle is painfully aware of the problem this raises for him. In his two chapters on the subject, Ryle struggles a great deal with the problem of explaining ways of talking like "having a tune running in one's head", "having a picture in one's mind's eye", or "silent soliloquy" in ways that would be acceptable to the behaviorist.[6] It is also clear

---

[5] Thus, Tanney (2005a: 19) is incorrect in maintaining that "Nor . . . is there any sign that Ryle wants to deny the 'reality' of mental processes, or, as a contemporary philosopher would say, that he is *fictionalist* or *instrumentalist* about them as has often been alleged of various forms of behaviorism." There are abundant signs that Ryle is just this.

[6] Brian Weatherson (2007) appeals to Ryle's comment that "silent soliloquy is a form of pregnant non-sayings" as evidence that Ryle was not a behaviorist. But Weatherson diminishes the surrounding context of this remark, which occurs in the midst of a particularly tortured attempt to explain why such a notion is acceptable to the behaviorist. The idea Ryle is trying to pursue here (albeit without much success) is that the non-behaviorist notion of silent soliloquy really boils down to "knowing what would have been said and how one would have said it" (270) both of which are acceptable to the behaviorist. Of course, as Ryle knows, silent soliloquy is more than this, and has no satisfactory explanation of that. But to suggest that Ryle is just

that he is not particularly happy with the result. But none of this shows that Ryle, at the stage at which he wrote *The Concept of Mind*, does not think of many of the most central mental properties in behaviorist terms.[7]

Ryle himself vigorously denied that he was a behaviorist. By the end of his career, he went so far as to call the doctrine a "Category-howler" of the same type as Cartesianism (1979: 17). In evaluating the accuracy of Ryle's self-conception, one must bear in mind that Ryle was a committed ordinary language philosopher, unreflectively and immediately hostile to analysis and reduction of any kind.[8] In the case of mental states, his hostility to reduction and analysis took the form of a denial that the dispositions that are mental states could ever be analyzed. For Ryle (1949: 56): "intelligent capacities are not single-track dispositions, but are dispositions admitting of a wide variety of more or less dissimilar exercises." Ryle invariably follows the introduction of a mental capacity by emphasizing at some length that there is no one particular subjunctive conditional that one can use to characterize it, one kind of behavior that is necessary and sufficient for its manifestation. But this does not show that Ryle is not a behaviorist, in a contemporary sense of the term. Ryle certainly thought that mental capacities were not identical to dispositions characterized in terms of a single natural kind of behavior, like squinting. But it is consistent with Ryle's persistent admonishments that he thought of each mental capacity as identical with a very lengthy and complex disjunction of purely physical behavioral dispositions. These disjunctions may be so lengthy and complex – perhaps they are even infinite disjunctions – that there is no hope of describing the disjunction of purely physical behavioral dispositions in a finite amount of time. Perhaps he also thought that there could be vagueness about whether some behavioral manifestation on an occasion counted as a manifestation of a mental capacity. But as we have learned from the literature on physicalism in the philosophy of mind over the past few decades, the view that Fs are identical with complex disjunctions and perhaps even infinite disjunctions of Gs is fully consistent with the view that Fs are nothing over and above Gs, even given the possibility of vagueness. And the view that mental capacities are nothing over and above purely physical behavioral dispositions is certainly worthy of the title of "Behaviorism".

Nevertheless, certainly by the end of his career, Ryle was not a behaviorist. The reason Ryle did not end up a behaviorist was that he found no successful way to

---

fine with non-behaviorist notions such as "having a tune running one's head", "having a picture in one's minds' eye", or "silent soliloquy" is to ignore the fact that much of *The Concept of Mind* is devoted to grappling with these notions in order to make them acceptable to the metaphysical behaviorist.

[7] Towards the end of *The Concept of Mind*, Ryle makes the behaviorist proclamation:

Those human actions and reactions, those spoken and unspoken utterances, those tones of voice, facial expressions and gestures, which have always been the data of all of the other students of men, have, after all, been the right and the only manifestations to study. They and they alone have merited, but fortunately not received, the grandiose title 'mental phenomena'. (320–1)

[8] One must also bear in mind Warnock's remark about *The Concept of Mind*, namely that "Ryle ... used to say that he was no authority on the exposition or explanation of that work" (Ryle 1979: x).

characterize *thinking* in behavioral terms. Ultimately, Ryle concluded that there was a kind of thinking, *theoretical* thinking, which was detached from action:

Besides and in sharp contrast with this very hospitable notion of thinking, as that using or misusing of our wits which is internal to or constitutive of all our specifically human actions and reactions, we have another very specific, almost professional, notion of thinking, namely as the reflecting that is done by the Thinker as distinct from the Agent, the thinking that deservedly ranks as, in high or low degree, theoretical thinking. Here we can speak, intelligibly enough, of the thinking of thoughts in some detachment from the momentary practical tasks or concerns of the thinker. This reflecting can be very crudely described as operating from and with propositions; and the thinking of these thoughts has indeed a certain chilly disengagement from the urgencies of the moment, as well as a certain impersonality. (1971d: 422)

Ultimately, Ryle concluded that theoretical thinking, "operating from and with propositions", with its "chilly disengagement from the urgencies of the moment", could not be characterized in terms of dispositions and capacities. In short, Ryle ended up repudiating behaviorism because he thought that *the thinking of thoughts* was behaviorally inert. It is, for Ryle, "operating from and with propositions" that is disengaged from action. We shall see that Ryle's assumption that grasping propositions is behaviorally inert in fact plays a role in some of his key arguments.

The fact that Ryle ultimately concluded that theoretical reflection was something genuinely over and above behavioral dispositions does not mean Ryle's project in *The Concept of Mind* was a failure. Take one of Ryle's most important intelligence concepts, the concept of *skill*. It is at least *prima facie* plausible that an action exhibits skill if and only if the action is a manifestation of the agent's knowledge how; at least it could be argued that there is no *other* kind of knowledge of the agent responsible for skilled performance. If knowing how to do an action is just a matter of having an ability or a complex of dispositions, and manifesting propositional knowledge is not, then doing something with skill is not having "one's non-theoretical propensities controlled by one's apprehension of truths about the conduct of life." So if Ryle can show that knowing how to do something is just a matter of having one's behavior manifest certain propensities, and that it is distinct from acting on one's propositional knowledge, he will have shown, for example, that acting with skill cannot be accounted for on intellectualist terms.

2.

Ryle's central purpose, in his chapter "Knowing How and Knowing That", is to establish that whether or not an action has a property in the family of intelligence properties is constituted by the exercise of dispositional states of the speaker. He can then put this conception of intelligence to use in subsequent chapters in his behaviorist solutions of various philosophical problems. But we have yet to look at his central argument for the conclusion that knowing how is constituted by dispositional states, and not by propositional knowledge.

Ryle's argument that knowing how is not a species of knowing that is indirect. The principal target of the argument is the intellectualist view of what it is for an action to have an intelligence property, according to which an action counts as having such a property, for example skill or cunning, in virtue of being guided by propositional knowledge, say of maxims or rules. The model Ryle no doubt has in mind is the Aristotelian conception of practical reasoning, where an action is done from intelligence if it is the result of a decision based on a practical syllogism, whose premises are maxims or rules. Ryle's principal target is this conception of action; it is supposed to follow from the falsity of this conception of intelligent action that knowing-how cannot be defined in terms of knowing-that:

"Intelligent" cannot be defined in terms of "intellectual" or "knowing *how*" in terms of "knowing *that*" ... (1949: 32)

Since it is not the case that an action has an intelligence property in virtue of being guided by propositional knowledge, Ryle concludes that actions have intelligence properties in virtue of being the product of knowing how, which is *a fortiori* not propositional knowledge.

So Ryle's argument is in the first instance directed against the intellectualist view that an action is intelligent if and only if it is guided by propositional knowledge. The view must be formulated so that its falsity allows Ryle to conclude that intelligent action is a matter of being guided by a non-propositional state of knowing how.

The argument Ryle uses against the intellectualist view of intelligent action takes the form of a regress. As Ryle writes:

The crucial objection to the intellectualist legend is this. The consideration of propositions is itself an operation the execution of which can be more or less intelligent, less or more stupid. But if, for any operation to be intelligently executed, a prior theoretical operation had first to be performed and performed intelligently, it would be a logical impossibility for anyone ever to break into the circle. (30)

There are two premises in Ryle's argument:

Premise 1:   The intellectualist view entails that "for any operation to be intelligently executed", there must be a prior consideration of a proposition.
Premise 2:   "The consideration of propositions is itself an operation the execution of which can be more or less intelligent, less or more stupid."

In ordinary vernacular, what it is for an action to be described as "intelligent" is different than what it is for an action to be described as "skilled" or "careful". But Ryle's argument against intellectualist explanations of intelligence properties applies fairly generally across them, despite these differences. For example, if we replace "intelligently executed" by "skillfully executed" in Premise 1, and "intelligent" and "stupid" by "skillful" and "unskilled", in Premise 2, the argument retains exactly the same plausibility as an argument against the intellectualist view that skillful action is action guided by propositional knowledge. Bearing this in mind, I will just give it using the property of intelligence.

The first premise in Ryle's regress argument is that the intellectualist view of intelligent action entails that any intelligent action must be preceded by a prior act of contemplating the proposition or maxim that guides the action. As he writes:

[The intellectualist point] is commonly expressed in the vernacular by saying that an action exhibits intelligence, if and only if, the agent is thinking what he is doing while he is doing it, and thinking what he is doing in such a manner that he would not do the action so well if he were not thinking what he is doing. This popular idiom is sometimes appealed to as evidence in favor of the intellectualist legend. Champions of this legend are apt to try to reassimilate knowing *how* to knowing *that* by arguing that intelligent performance involves the observance of rules, or the application of criteria. It follows that the operation which is characterized as intelligent must be preceded by an intellectual acknowledgment of these rules or criteria; that is, the agent must first go through the internal process of avowing to himself certain propositions about what is to be done ('maxims', 'imperatives', or 'regulative propositions' as they are sometimes called); only then can he execute his performance in according with those dictates. He must preach to himself before he can practice. The chef must recite his recipes to himself before he can cook according to them; the hero must lend his inner ear to some appropriate moral imperative before swimming out to save the drowning man; the chess-player must run over in his head all the relevant rules and tactical maxims of the game before he can make correct and skillful moves. To do something thinking what one is doing is, according to this legend, always to do two things; namely, to consider certain appropriate propositions, or prescriptions, and to put into practice what these propositions or prescriptions enjoin. (29)

According to Ryle, one who holds that an action is intelligent in virtue of being guided by knowledge of maxims or rules is committed to the thesis that any intelligent action must be preceded by a distinct action of "avowing to himself" that maxim or rule.

Ryle's second premise is that "the consideration of propositions is itself an operation the execution of which can be more or less intelligent, less or more stupid." In defense of this, Ryle writes:

Why does the hero not find himself calling to mind a cooking-recipe or a rule of Formal Logic? Perhaps he does, but then his intellectual process is silly and not sensible. Intelligently reflecting how to act is, among other things, considering what is pertinent and disregarding what is inappropriate. (31)

We are now in a position to formulate Ryle's regress against the intellectualist position. By the first premise, the intellectualist is committed to the view that each intelligent action is preceded by a prior action of considering a proposition. Since considering a proposition is something that can be done intelligently or stupidly, it is an intelligent action. So, acting intelligently requires a prior action of considering a proposition, and considering a proposition intelligently requires a prior action of considering a proposition intelligently. Presumably, if any of these prior actions is performed stupidly, then the original action will not be performed intelligently. But then acting intelligently requires the performance of an infinite number of prior actions, which is a vicious regress.

Ryle's argument against the intellectualist account of intelligent action gains its force from the first premise. As Ryle writes:

> To put it quite generally, the absurd assumption made by the intellectualist legend is this, that a performance of any sort inherits all its title to intelligence from some anterior internal operation of planning what to do. (31)

The chief problem with Ryle's argument is the implausibility of its first premise. It is based upon his claim that intellectualism about intelligent action entails that any intelligent action must be preceded by a distinct action of avowing to oneself a maxim or rule. But it is just *manifestly absurd* that all intelligent actions are preceded by distinct actions of self-avowals of propositions. If anything can count as a datum of phenomenology, it is that we often act intelligently without first avowing to ourselves any maxims or rules. If the intellectualist position has the absurd consequence that this datum of phenomenology is incorrect, then Ryle is in no need of a regress argument to dismiss it. Since the view that an action is intelligent in virtue of being guided by knowledge of maxims or rules does not seem manifestly absurd, one should wonder about Ryle's unsupported claim that it has this consequence.

Perhaps Ryle intended the intellectualist position to be, *by definition*, the view that "a performance inherits all its title to intelligence from some anterior internal operation of planning what to do". But if Ryle intended his target to be one that makes the first premise true by definition, then while he may have succeeded in his goal of undermining its plausibility, he will have fallen well short of his goal of refuting anything but a straw man position. The reasonable intellectualist about intelligent action will hold that an action is intelligent in virtue of being guided by propositional knowledge, but deny that this entails that intelligent action requires a prior act of self-avowing the propositional knowledge that guides one's actions. Without an argument against the reasonable intellectualist view, Ryle is in no position to draw any conclusions about the relationship between knowing how and propositional knowledge.

Ryle therefore needs an argument that the view that "intelligent performance involves the observance of rules, or the application of criteria" entails that "the operation which is characterized as intelligent must be preceded by an intellectual acknowledgment of these rules or criteria; that is, the agent must first go through the internal process of avowing to himself certain propositions about what is to be done ('maxims', 'imperatives', or 'regulative propositions' as they are sometimes called); only then can he execute his performance in according with those dictates." In short, Ryle needs an argument that the reasonable intellectualist view of intelligent action collapses into the unreasonable view of intelligent action. That is, Ryle needs an argument that an action is only guided by (or is a manifestation of) my propositional knowledge that p if it is preceded by a distinct intelligent act of contemplating the proposition that p. Is this true?

Ryle holds that on his view of intelligent action, there is no threat of regress. This is because, on Ryle's view, someone's action is intelligent if it is a manifestation of their knowledge how, which is not propositional knowledge. This escapes the regress, because someone can act on their knowledge how, without a prior act of considering a proposition. But if someone can act on their knowledge how, without a prior act of considering a proposition, then someone can act on their propositional knowledge, without a prior act of considering that proposition. According to Carl Ginet:

all that [Ryle] actually brings out, as far as I can see, is that the exercise (or manifestation) of one's knowledge of how to do a certain sort of thing need not, and often does not, involve any separate mental operation of considering propositions and inferring from them instructions to oneself. But the same thing is as clearly true of one's manifestations of *knowledge that* certain propositions are true, especially one's knowledge of truths that answer questions of the form "How can one ...?" or "How should one ...?" I exercise (or manifest) my knowledge *that* one can get the door open by turning the knob and pushing it (as well as my knowledge *that* there is a door there) by performing that operation quite automatically as I leave the room; and I may do this, of course, without formulating (in my mind or out loud) that proposition or any other relevant proposition. (1975: 6–7)

If one can directly manifest one's knowledge of *how* to open a doorknob, then one can equally well directly manifest one's knowledge *that* one can open the door by turning the knob. Ginet's point shows that the reasonable intellectualist view of intelligent action does not entail the unreasonable intellectualist view of intelligent action. My action of opening the door can be guided by, or be a manifestation of, my propositional knowledge that I can get the door open by turning the knob, without it being the case that I contemplate that proposition before I open the door. So Ryle's regress argument does not threaten the reasonable intellectualist position on intelligent action.

Ryle might try replacing his first premise with a weaker notion than is suggested by "contemplation".[9] Perhaps manifesting one's propositional knowledge requires at least a prior *triggering of relevant representations*. For example, manifesting one's propositional knowledge that one can open the door by turning the knob might require a prior triggering of a doorknob representation.[10] Replacing contemplating a proposition by triggering representations in Premise 2, we obtain:

Premise 2*:   The triggering of representations is itself an operation the execution of which can be more or less intelligent, less or more stupid.

[9] Thanks here to Brian Weatherson, who discussed related issues on his blog (at http://tar.weatherson. org/2006/07/22/ryle-on-knowing-how-and-knowing-that).
[10] Dreyfus and Kelly (2007: 49) claim that someone who acts on her belief that one leaves a room by opening a door must be "giving a thought" to the door. I am not sure what they mean by "giving a thought" to the door. If they mean by this an intentional action, then they are endorsing a strong reading of Ryle's first premise (which Dreyfus clearly does in other work, see section 3 below). If "giving a thought" is some kind of automatic process, then they are endorsing this weaker reading of Premise 1.

If Premise 2* is true, one can reinstate the regress concern. If triggering representations is something that can be done intelligently or stupidly, then triggering a representation requires a prior (intelligent) triggering of a representation in order to be done intelligently, and so on.

However, Ryle cannot replace the appeal to *self-avowing* or *contemplating a proposition* by a notion like *triggering representations*. Premise 2* is far less plausible than Premise 2. Triggering a representation can certainly be done *poorly* or *well*. But this does not show it can be done *intelligently* or *stupidly*. In the vocabulary of Fodor (1983), triggering representations is something done by an *input system* rather than a *central system*, by a module rather than a central processor. Since triggering representations is something we do automatically, replacing "contemplating a proposition" by "triggering a representation" in Premise 2 of the regress argument results in a manifest implausibility.[11]

Furthermore, if we were to grant Premise 2*, then the regress threatens *any* conception of intelligent action, including Ryle's favored one in terms of a non-propositional sense of knowing how. If manifesting one's propositional knowledge that one can open the door by turning the doorknob requires a prior triggering of a representation of the doorknob, why doesn't manifesting one's knowledge of how to open the door require a prior triggering of a representation of the doorknob? That is, if knowing that requires prior triggering of representations, why doesn't knowing how require prior triggering of representations? After all, the same intuition that would lead one to think one needs to trigger a representation of a doorknob before manifesting one's propositional knowledge that the door can be opened by turning the doorknob would also lead one to think that one needs to trigger a representation of a doorknob before manifesting one's knowledge of how to open the door. There is no *intuitive* asymmetry here between requirements on the manifestation of propositional knowledge and requirements on the manifestation of knowledge how (in essence, this is Ginet's point).

Weakening the first premise may expand the target to include the reasonable intellectualist position on intelligent action. But the resulting deflationary conception of contemplation results in a much more implausible second premise, thus undermining the regress argument. If we nevertheless grant the second premise, on some weakened notion of contemplation, then the regress argument threatens *any* conception of intelligent action, including Ryle's favored one.

Perhaps Ryle could say that the distinction between knowing how and knowing that is that manifesting propositional knowledge requires some kind of prior mental act, whereas manifesting knowing how does not require any prior mental act. But as Ginet brings out, there is no intuitive phenomenological difference of this kind between manifesting one's knowledge of how to open the door and manifesting

---

[11] This is essentially the criticism that Stanley and Williamson (2001: 415–16) make of the attempt to save Ryle's regress argument by considering a more deflationary sense of "contemplating a proposition". They reconstruct the regress argument in a way that is somewhat less faithful to Ryle's text than I have done above.

one's knowledge that one can open the door by turning the knob. Either manifestations of both propositional knowledge and knowing how require a prior mental act, or manifestations of neither propositional knowledge nor knowing how require a prior mental act. Simply stipulating that knowing how can be manifested in the absence of a prior mental act amounts to stipulating that knowing how cannot be defined in terms of knowing that, which is supposed to be the conclusion of the argument, rather than one of its premises.

In order to draw a conclusion about knowing how, Ryle draws an unwarranted distinction between manifesting propositional knowledge and manifesting knowing how. He assumes that manifesting propositional knowledge requires a prior mental act, such as the prior triggering of a maxim or a rule (this is the first premise of his regress argument). Second, he assumes that knowing how in contrast can be manifested *without there being any prior mental act whatever*. It is only because of this second assumption that he is able to conclude that knowing how is not a species of knowing that. The problem is that these assumptions draw an unwarranted asymmetry between manifesting propositional knowledge and manifesting knowledge how.

Ryle is operating with a metaphysical picture of knowing how according to which one's know how just is *constituted* by the fact that when one is so situated, one acts thus. On Ryle's picture of action, intentional actions are not the effects of inner categorical causes. Thus, his picture of knowing how coheres with his conception of intentional action. Ryle's metaphysical picture is widely regarded as implausible, since it involves ungrounded dispositions – that is, the possession of dispositions without any categorical basis. But that is not the crucial point. The point is rather that if this picture is plausible for knowing how, then, given the phenomenology of action, it is no less plausible for knowing that.

Suppose Ryle is right, and my state of knowing how to open a door is manifested simply by my being in front of a door and opening it. If so, then my state of knowing that the door opens by turning the knob is also so manifested. More neutrally, if I can act intelligently on my knowledge of how to open a door by twisting the knob without a prior mental act, then I can act intelligently on my knowledge that the door can be opened by twisting the knob, without a prior mental act. If Ryle is allowed to assume without argument that knowledge how can be manifested without any prior mental act – such as a consideration of a maxim or a rule, or a triggering of a representation – then the intellectualist should be allowed to assume that propositional knowledge can be manifested without any prior basis.

There is an obvious model of the manifestation of propositional knowledge that is akin to Ryle's picture of knowing how. Consider the functionalist conception of belief, according to which (Stalnaker 1987: 15), "[t]o believe that P is to be disposed to act in ways that would tend to satisfy one's desires, whatever they are, in a world in which P (together with one's other beliefs) were true." If the functionalist conception of belief is correct, manifesting a belief is manifesting a dispositional state – just like, for Ryle, manifesting one's knowing how is manifesting a dispositional state. On this conception of belief, manifesting one's propositional knowledge is a matter of mani-festing a dispositional state that constitutes a true belief, a state acquired (say) via a reliable source. This is a metaphysical picture of manifesting propositional knowledge akin to Ryle's metaphysical picture of manifesting knowing how. Of course there are objections to this conception of the manifestation of propositional knowledge, but they are the same as the objections to Ryle's conception of the manifestation of knowing how. The existence of this conception of belief demonstrates that Ryle is wrong to think that his preferred conception of action tells against the intellectualist view.

Conversely, suppose we reject Ryle's metaphysical picture of action, and endorse the view that intentional actions are the effects of inner categorical causes. If so, then we would be apt to regard manifestations of knowing how no less than knowing that as the effects of such inner categorical causes. As Jerry Fodor writes:

Here is the way we tie our shoes:
There is a little man who lives in one's head. The little man keeps a library. When one acts upon the intention to tie one's shoes, the little man fetches down a volume entitled Tying One's Shoes. The volume says such things as: "Take the left free end of the shoelace in the left hand. Cross the left free end of the shoelace over the right free end of the shoelace . . . etc."
   When the little man reads the instruction 'take the left free end of the shoelace in the left hand', he pushes a button on a control panel. The button is marked 'take the left free end of the shoelace in the left hand.' When depressed, it activates a series of wheels, cogs, levers, and hydraulic mechanisms. As a causal consequence of the functioning of these mechanisms, one's left hand comes to seize the appropriate end of the shoelace. Similarly, *mutatis mutandis*, for the rest of the instructions. (1968: 627)

In short, if *pace* Ryle, we accept that manifestations of propositional knowledge are the effects of inner categorical causes, we will also accept this for manifestations of knowing how. Ryle seeks to show that intentional actions are not causal effects of inner mental processes. But whether or not he succeeds in so doing is simply independent of any alleged distinction between knowing how and knowing that.

Ryle thinks that the regress principally raises a problem for the view that knowing how is a species of knowing that. He arrives at this conclusion because he thinks that manifesting one's propositional knowledge is something that must be preceded by a special action that the agent does – contemplating a proposition, whereas in contrast manifesting one's knowing how does not require such a special action on the part of the agent. But, as we have seen, there is no reason for this dichotomy. If one can manifest one's know how without a prior intelligent action, then one can manifest one's propositional knowledge without a prior intelligent action. One can only conclude that knowing how is not a species of knowing that from the regress argument if one combines it with the false view that there is an asymmetry between the conditions on the manifestation of knowing how to do something, and the conditions on the manifestation of knowing that something is the case.

Nevertheless, Ryle's argument does show *something*. But what it shows is consistent with the intellectualist view that an action is intelligent in virtue of being guided by propositional knowledge. For the intellectualist, what the argument shows is that the knowledge that we act on when we act intelligently sometimes is manifested *directly*, without a prior mental action.

Nomy Arpaly is particularly clear in her work that the sort of regress that Ryle gives does not pose a threat to the view that rational action is action guided by propositional attitude states:

the thought that deliberating, in order to be a rational action, would have to be the result of deliberation seems to threaten an infinite regress: before deliberating about my textbooks, I would have had to deliberate about deliberating about my textbooks, and before that deliberate about deliberating about deliberating, and so forth, in order for all these intellectual acts to prove to be rational. (2003: 57)

Arpaly concludes from this regress that:

every step I take in deliberation is informed in a non-deliberative way by beliefs and desires that do not participate in it. (Ibid.: 58)

In short, Arpaly's conclusion from this regress is not that deliberative behavior must be *uninformed*. Her conclusion is rather that deliberative behavior can be informed in a *non-deliberative way* by propositional attitude states.

In a series of recent papers, Peter Railton has exploited essentially Ryle's regress argument in favor of an account of normative guidance that the intellectualist about intelligent action can straightforwardly adopt. Railton concludes from the regress that "*all* action – including in particular paradigmatic premeditated intentional action – *has and must have* unpremeditated action at its source and core" (2009: 102). This is not an insignificant result. It threatens "any model of action that seeks to understand the distinctive operation of autonomous or rational agency in terms of some special sort of action on the part of the agent, whether the act is 'choosing one's reasons,' or 'endorsing certain reasons,' or 'identifying a certain reason,' or 'throwing one's weight behind one reason rather than another'" (ibid.: 103). But this result neither raises problems for the view that knowing how is a species of knowing that, nor for the view that acting intelligently is acting on the basis of reasons. The moral of Railton's work, and the proper moral of Ryle's regress argument, is that *acting on the basis of a reason* does not involve an action of "choosing one's reasons".[12]

Railton's employment of the regress argument is not, like Ryle's, directed against the view that acting intelligently is acting on the basis of reasons. Rather, in Railton's hands, the regress argument is exploited against certain views of *what it*

---

[12] Though it is not the main point of his discussion, Railton unfortunately also seems to follow Ryle in thinking that the regress has some bearing on the relation between knowing how and knowing that. As he writes: "Practical intelligence is largely a matter of know-how rather than knowledge-that or reasoning ability" (2009: 95). I do not think this comment is consistent with the central morals of his work.

is to act for a reason. Not only does he not challenge the view that acting intelligently is acting on the basis of reasons, much of the *point* of Railton's work is to show that behavior that is "automatized" can nevertheless be "norm-guided" and done for a reason:

The saxophonist's improvisations, the guard's jumping, the timely downshift, and wicked comment are clearly done for reasons, and, moreover, for reasons *as such.* (Ibid.: 97–8)

If intellectualism is false, it is not because of the regress argument. The regress argument does not undermine intellectualism – it only undermines certain models of what it is to be guided by a reason – in particular those models that require the agent to acknowledge the reason for acting explicitly and intelligently prior to acting on it.

Suppose, as some have urged (Hawthorne and Stanley 2008; Hyman 1999), that there is an important sense of "reason" according to which proper reasons for action are (or contain) propositional knowledge states.[13] If so, then an action is done for a proper reason only if it is guided by propositional knowledge. Ryle's regress argument shows that one must be able to act on the basis of reasons in this sense, without a prior conscious mental act. But this moral does not threaten the view that when an action is done for proper reasons, then it is guided by an agent's propositional knowledge. I may be guided by a norm of action, even when I do not self-consciously judge that I am.

As Ginet points out, when I open the door I am guided by my knowledge that one opens a door by twisting the doorknob, without self-consciously judging that my twisting the doorknob is a manifestation of my belief. In the same vein, Railton writes, describing a neurotic who obsessively checks whether her garden gate is locked:

Even Sylvia is showing remarkable automaticity in the very way she yields to her obsessions. After all, her anxiety and doubt have a very narrow focus: Is the gate locked? To perform a 'check' on this is possible only because it never occurs to her to question an enormous amount of apparent fact which she simply takes on trust from her perceptual experience and memory. Is her perception of size and shape, or her sensation of grasping the latch knob, veridical? Is her memory of where her house is located, or what it looks like, or even who she is, accurate? Such things she assumes 'blindly', without second-guessing, as she shuttles back and forth between gate and walkway. This vast body of unquestioning confidence – *default trust*, as I will call it – enables her to act intentionally, and for a reason. (2004: 186)

What Railton describes as the "enormous amount of apparent fact" that we take on trust from our perceptual experience and memory is, on my own view, simply the body of propositional knowledge that a well-functioning agent possesses. Railton's point is that we act on this body of knowledge quite automatically.[14]

---

[13] The claim in Hawthorne and Stanley (2008) is importantly different than the claim in Hyman (1999). Hyman argues that something is a reason only if it is known. According to Hawthorne and Stanley (2008), something *ought* to be a reason only if it is known.

[14] Railton himself is neutral on the view that what we act on is a body of *knowledge*.

Of course, one would want to know what it is to be guided by a reason, when the guidance is not accompanied by an act of reflecting on that reason. Railton's work again provides an answer, as he provides an elegant theoretical model of what it is for one's conduct to be guided by a norm. The model makes clear that normative guidance by a propositional attitude state does not require a distinct mental act of contemplating that norm:

Agent A's conduct C is guided by norm N only if C is a manifestation of A's disposition to act in a way conducive to compliance with N, such that N plays a regulative role in A's C-ing, where this involves some disposition on A's part to notice failures to comply with N, to feel discomfort when this occurs, and to exert effort to establish conformity with N even when the departure from N is unsanctioned and non-consequential. (2006: 13)

As we have seen above, it is natural to take states such as belief and desire as dispositional states of the agent. My conduct is guided by the belief (say) that one ought to stand a respectful distance from someone when speaking to them when my behavior on a particular occasion manifests the disposition to stand a respectful distance from my interlocutor when speaking to them, in the ways described in Railton's characterization of norm guidance.

Whether one accepts Railton's particular characterization of norm guidance or not, it should be clear that there are multiple theoretical models for explaining how one could, in Arpaly's terms, be "guided in a non-deliberative way" by one's propositional attitude states. That is, there are multiple theoretical models of how one could be guided in action by one's propositional attitudes at a time without having explicitly to consider the content of the propositional attitude in question.

Of course, there is certain *normative* pressure to think, *contra* Railton, that in order for an action to be done for a reason, an agent must need a prior action of endorsing or recognizing her reason for acting as a reason for acting. Perhaps, as Christine Korsgaard has urged, we need to distinguish between acting merely *in accordance* with a normative consideration from acting *on* a normative consideration (e.g. Korsgaard 1997, 2008a). If our action is merely *guided* by a reason, one might worry that acting in accordance with it does not amount to rational agency. As she puts the point:

If [guidance] is all there is to rational agency, then of course it does not involve the exercise of any specifically human power which we might identify with the faculty of Reason: it is just a way we describe certain actions from outside, namely, the ones that conform to rational principles or to the particular considerations we call "reasons". (2008a: 213)

Perhaps one might think that what is needed to bridge the gap between being merely guided by a reason, and acting on that reason, is an action by the agent of endorsing the reason as a reason, or at least an action of recognizing it as such. One way to view the moral of Ryle's regress argument − suggested by Arpaly and Railton − is that such a demand on rational agency is impossibly demanding. We must seek an explanation of rational agency that does not require acting on a reason to be accompanied by a prior action of endorsing the reason as a reason.

In the face of the regress threat, advocates of the view that rationally acting on a reason requires reflectively endorsing that reason as a reason may deny that reflective endorsement is itself an action. Perhaps it is just a state of the agent – such as the state of believing that the reason is a good reason for the action. This riposte is analogous to the response to Ryle's regress argument, considered above, of deflating the notion of *contemplating a proposition*. The concern with it here is that if endorsing or recognizing a reason as a (good) reason is just a state of the agent, rather than something the agent *does*, it is then hard to see how the agent is not *merely guided* by the reflective endorsement of the reason as a reason. If the concern is that mere guidance by a reason is not sufficient for rational agency, it is hard to see how that concern can be met by appeal to additional mere guidance.

Whatever we think of the ultimate fate of the view that rational action requires endorsing one's reason as a reason, it should be clear that *Ryle* is certainly in no position to impose any such requirement on intelligent action. After all, according to Ryle, intelligent action does not require any prior mental act that is performed intelligently. Whatever reason there is to impose a requirement that an agent reflectively endorse a fit between some maxim and her action in order for that action to be intelligent is a reason Ryle will have to reject. Ryle allows that an action can be intelligent without any prior deliberation or intelligent action – after all, this is his view of intelligent action. Yet he maintains that if intelligent action is action guided by propositional attitudes, then it can only be intelligent if it is accompanied by a prior intelligent action. Once it is pointed out to him that one can be guided by one's propositional attitudes without prior deliberation or intelligent action, he is in no position to object that that action can only be intelligent if it is preceded by a prior intelligent act, on pain of not making a distinction between merely acting in accordance with a normative maxim and acting on that normative maxim. To say that rational action is a matter of one's action manifesting a behavioral disposition is tantamount to an enthusiastic endorsement of the view that "mere guidance" is all there is to rational action.

Ryle's regress argument shows that if acting intelligently, or with skill, is acting on a reason, acting on a reason cannot demand a prior intelligent action of contemplation on the side of the agent. This is a powerful argument against an intellectualist account of intelligent action only if it is plausible that acting on a reason demands a prior intelligent action of contemplating the content of that reason. However, there is simply no justification for the thesis that acting on a reason requires a prior intelligent action of contemplating the content of that reason. There is no sound regress argument of the form Ryle envisaged that leads from the possibility of intelligent action to the rejection of the intellectualist view of its source.

Furthermore, insofar as there are mysteries attending to the notion of acting for a reason, appeal to knowing how does not help with them. It is no more nor less mysterious how intelligence can be conferred on an action in virtue of its being guided by a non-propositional notion of knowing how than it is how intelligence can be conferred on an action in virtue of that action being guided by a reason, with no attending distinct action of contemplation.

3.

As with Ryle, the rejection of the intellectualist view that intelligent or skilled action is due to guidance by propositional reasons is a major theme of Hubert Dreyfus's work. However, Dreyfus's central arguments against intellectualism suffer from the same failings as Ryle's. They presuppose a false view of what it is to act on one's propositional knowledge.

According to Dreyfus (2005), skilled action requires abandoning "detached rule following". Appropriately enough, Dreyfus focuses on the phenomenology of expertise in motivating his anti-intellectualist views. As Dreyfus writes:

phenomenology suggests that, although many forms of expertise pass through a stage in which one needs reasons to guide action, after much involved experience, the learner develops a way of coping in which reasons play no role ... In general, instead of relying on rules and standards to decide on or to justify her actions, the expert immediately responds to the current concrete situation. (Ibid.)

Dreyfus also raises specific problem cases for the view that skilled action is acting on the basis of reasons. A particularly extreme case involves the second baseman Chuck Knoblauch:

As second baseman for the New York Yankees, Knoblauch was so successful he was voted best infielder of the year, but one day, rather than simply fielding a hit and throwing the ball to first base, it seems he stepped back and took up a "free, distanced orientation" towards the ball and how he was throwing it – to the mechanics of it, as he put it. After that, he couldn't recover his former absorption and often – though not always – threw the ball to first base erratically – once into the face of a spectator. Interestingly, even after he seemed unable to resist stepping back and being mindful, Knoblauch could still play brilliant baseball in difficult situations – catching a hard-hit ground ball and throwing it to first faster than thought. What he couldn't do was field an easy routine grounder directly to second base, because that gave him time to think before throwing to first. I'm told that in some replays of such easy throws one could actually see Knoblauch looking with puzzlement at his hand trying to figure out the mechanics of throwing the ball. There was nothing wrong with Knoblauch's body; he could still exercise his skill as long as the situation required that he act before he had time to think. In this case we can see precisely that the enemy of expertise is thought. (2007: 354)

In short, Dreyfus makes his case that "the enemy of expertise is thought" by relying on two facts. First, the phenomenology of action suggests that we do not *consult* reasons before acting. Second, when experts do engage in a distinct mental action of consulting their reasons before acting, this actually impedes successful performance. These facts are supposed to entail that in skilled action, "one develops a way of coping in which reasons play no role".

It is clear from Dreyfus's arguments that he accepts a strong reading of Ryle's Premise 1. In other words, Dreyfus accepts that if the intellectualist account of skilled action were correct, a skilled action would have to be preceded by a distinct mental act of *consulting* the proposition that guides the action. Only with this additional assumption does the fact that an expert "immediately responds to the current concrete situation" have any bearing *at all* on the view that their action is guided by propositional knowledge. As we have seen in the previous section, there is simply no reason to accept this assumption. There is no reason to think that acting on our propositional knowledge requires a prior mental act of consulting a proposition. It is fully consistent with intellectualism about intelligent action that we act *directly* on our propositional knowledge. The phenomenology of expertise is only relevant to the evaluation of the intellectualist thesis if one accepts a highly implausible thesis about what it is to act on propositional knowledge.

Dreyfus's particular case involving Chuck Knoblauch also relies on the implausible assumption about acting on propositional attitude states like belief. As we have seen, both the phenomenology of action and good philosophical sense suggest that we can act directly on our propositional knowledge. Only mere novices have to engage in a separate and prior intelligent act of *consulting* the proposition that guides their action. And we do not need to consider esoteric cases involving chess or baseball to make this point. To return to Carl Ginet's point, "I exercise (or manifest) my knowledge *that* one can get the door open by turning the knob and pushing it (as well as my knowledge *that* there is a door there) by performing that operation quite automatically as I leave the room; and I may do this, of course, without formulating (in my mind or out loud) that proposition or any other relevant proposition." No normal person would have to formulate in her mind the proposition she acted upon in using a knob to open a door.

If the intellectualist is allowed to have reasonable views about what it is to act on a reason, then she has no problem whatsoever explaining what occurred with Chuck Knoblauch. The reason that Knoblauch's reflection impeded his action was not because his action was unguided. It was rather because he engaged in a *distinct* action of reflecting on a proposition before he acted. As I will argue in subsequent chapters, genuinely skilled action requires being directly guided by one's propositional knowledge – being guided automatically and without reflection. It is therefore little wonder that the fact that Knoblauch's engagement in a distinct prior action of reflecting on the proposition that guided his action impeded his performance. Once one drops the unwarranted assumption that acting on the basis of one's propositional knowledge requires such an act, one can see clearly why engaging in an act of considering one's reason before acting would impede performance.

Moreover, if one does adopt the manifestly implausible assumption that acting on belief requires a distinct action of contemplating or giving a thought to its content, there is no need to appeal to phenomenology to reject the view that skilled action is action guided by knowledge of truths. As Ryle demonstrated in *The Concept of Mind*, it follows from this assumption that no skilled action is possible at all.

4.

The argument Ryle gives in the second chapter of *The Concept of Mind* is not the only attempt of Ryle's to show that knowing how is not a species of knowing that. Ryle's earlier 1946 paper "Knowing How and Knowing That" largely overlaps with the second chapter of *The Concept of Mind*. Nevertheless, it contains distinct though related regress arguments. The first, like the regress argument in *The Concept of Mind*, is supposed to entail the falsity of the intellectualist view that intelligent action is action guided by propositional knowledge. The second argument, a version of the argument in Lewis Carroll's famous paper, "What the Tortoise Said to Achilles", is supposed to entail the falsity of the view that *epistemic justification* is entirely a matter of propositional knowledge. The purpose of the next two sections is to treat these objections in detail.

The first objection in Ryle (1946) arises from the thought that while propositional knowledge is inert, knowing how to do something is not inert.[15] As Ryle writes:

> If a deed, to be intelligent, has to be guided by the consideration of a regulative proposition, the gap between that consideration and the practical application of the regulation has to be bridged by some go-between process which cannot by the pre-supposed definition itself be an exercise of intelligence and cannot, by definition, be the resultant deed. This go-between application process has somehow to marry observance of a contemplated maxim with the enforcement of behavior. So it has to unite in itself the allegedly incompatible properties of being kith to theory and kin to practice, else it could not be the applying of the one in the other. For, unlike theory, it must be able to influence action, and unlike impulses, it must be amenable to regulative propositions. Consistency requires, therefore, that this schizophrenic broker must again be subdivided into one bit which contemplates but does not execute, one which executes but does not contemplate and a third which reconciles these irreconcilables. And so on forever. (1971c: 213)

Ryle's thought here is that knowing how to do something involves having dispositions to behave in certain ways. But there is no way to build in such requirements into the possession of knowledge of a proposition. Out of this conception of the inertness of propositional knowledge, Ryle mounts another regress argument. If knowledge of a proposition is supposed to guide our actions, one needs a go-between process to broker between the disposition to act and the proposition, and since this brokering is itself an action, one needs a distinct go-between process to broker between the disposition to follow the result of brokering, and the proposition that regulates the brokering.

This regress argument is a version of the regress argument we discussed in section 2. We have already seen persuasive ways to respond. Suppose we assume, with Ryle, that possession of propositional knowledge does not entail possession of dispositions – i.e. that propositional knowledge is inert. We still do not need to accept Ryle's argument. If we assume that brokering occurs between inert states of propositional knowledge

---

[15] As we have seen from Dreyfus's talk of "detached rule following", he shares Ryle's conception that propositional attitude states are behaviorally inert.

and behavior, it is not necessary to suppose that the brokering is a further intelligent action. The brokering can simply be automatic processing, a by-product of mental mechanisms. The brokering is then not something that is a further action of the agent. As Fodor writes:

> knowledge doesn't eventuate in behavior in virtue of its propositional content alone. It seems obvious that you need mechanisms to put what you know into action; mechanisms that function to bring the organization of behavior into conformity with the propositional structures that are cognized. (1983: 9)

The mechanisms of which Fodor speaks in this passage are the ones that do Ryle's job of brokering between propositional knowledge and action. But Fodor does not suppose that the operation of the mechanisms is under our rational control. If so, we do not need to break up the brokering into a bit that is propositional and another bit that does more brokering. As we have now seen in detail, the intellectualist picture that intelligent action is action guided by propositional knowledge is not undermined by the existence of automatic processes mediating between a bit of propositional knowledge and the action it guides.

One might think that the "mechanisms to put what you know into action" are themselves states of knowing how. But this cannot be correct. First, the mechanisms of which Fodor speaks take propositions and result in behavior. They themselves lack content. The mechanisms that put an outfielder's knowledge of how to field a fly ball into action, on Fodor's picture, mediate between the knowledge of how to field a fly ball, and the action. They themselves do not encode information about fielding fly balls. The mechanisms are presumably *general* mechanisms for mediating between epistemic states and action. In contrast, knowledge of how to (say) field a fly ball is baseball specific knowledge.

More importantly, *even if we assume that Ryle's conception of knowledge how is correct*, we still need to postulate mechanisms that mediate between states of the speaker, whether propositional or not, and action. Suppose that knowledge how is a complex of dispositions. There still need to be automatic mechanisms that mediate between dispositions (and abilities) and the manifestation or execution of these dispositions and abilities. The mechanisms that mediate between dispositions and the manifestation or execution of these dispositions cannot themselves be more dispositions and abilities. Postulating non-propositional standing epistemic states of the speaker does *nothing* to avoid the consequence that there are automatic mechanisms that mediate between standing epistemic states of the speaker and action. In short, the existence of such mechanisms is no argument whatsoever that some standing epistemic states of the speaker are not propositional.

Ryle assumes here that possession of propositional knowledge is *behaviorally inert*. In other words, Ryle assumes that the possession of propositional knowledge does not entail the possession of dispositional states. As we have seen, postulating non-propositional dispositional states does not help Ryle answer the regress he himself poses. But in this book, I will also challenge the assumption.

The way to challenge the assumption that propositional knowledge is behaviorally inert is by motivating a conception of propositional knowledge according to which propositional knowledge is not behaviorally inert. In short, ultimately the challenge to Ryle must take the form of an account of the nature of states of propositional knowledge. There is an easy way and a hard way to argue that the possession of propositional knowledge entails dispositions to act. The easy way is, as we saw in section 2, to argue for a functionalist conception of the state of belief. On such views, by its very nature, a belief is a state that has certain downstream effects on action. The hard way is to argue that the contents of propositional attitude states *themselves* are individuated by something like functional roles.

In Chapters 3 and 4, I will argue that there is independent motivation for a view of at least some of the constituents of propositions according to which they can only be entertained if one possesses certain dispositions. By the end of Chapter 4, it will become clear that this account of content entails that propositional knowledge is not inert.

5.

In his 1946 paper, Ryle exploits a version of the argument in Lewis Carroll's famous paper, "What the Tortoise Said to Achilles", in arguing that knowing how is not a species of knowing that. Ryle himself regarded the Lewis Carroll problem as a special version of the general sort of regress we discussed in the previous section.[16] But his version of the regress argument in this earlier work is directed against a different target. The purpose of Ryle's regress argument in *The Concept of Mind* is to refute the view that *intelligent action* is action under the direction of the right kinds of propositional states. The purpose of Ryle's version of the Lewis Carroll regress is to refute the view that *epistemic justification* is entirely a matter of having the right propositional states. The moral of both arguments is that propositional knowledge is not enough to explain intelligence, whether practical or theoretical. Ryle thinks that the full story for both intelligent action and epistemic justification requires the addition of knowing how, which is *a fortiori* not a kind of propositional knowledge.

Here is Ryle's version of the Lewis Carroll problem:

A pupil fails to follow an argument. He understands the premises and he understands the conclusion. But he fails to see that the conclusion follows from the premises. The teacher thinks him rather dull but tries to help. So he tells him that there is an ulterior proposition which he has

---

[16] Ryle writes: "To bring out these points I rely on variations of one argument. I argue that the prevailing doctrine leads to vicious regresses, and these in two directions. (1) If the intelligence exhibited in any act, practical or theoretical, is to be credited to the occurrence of some ulterior act of intelligently considering regulative propositions, no intelligent act, practical or theoretical, could ever begin . . ." (1971c: 213). This is a good description of the vicious regress argument we have discussed in the previous section. Ryle then goes on to give the Lewis Carroll problem as an example of it.

not considered, namely, that *if these premises are true, the conclusion is true*. The pupil understands this and dutifully recites it alongside the premises, and still fails to see that the conclusion follows from the premises even when accompanied by the assertion that these premises entail this conclusion. So a second hypothetical proposition is added to his store; namely, that the conclusion is true if the premises are true as well as the first hypothetical proposition that if the premises are true the conclusion is true. And still the pupil fails to see. And so on for ever. He accepts rules in theory but this does not *force* him to apply them in practice. He considers reasons, but he fails to reason. (This is Lewis Carroll's puzzle in 'What the Tortoise Said to Achilles'. I have met no successful attempt to solve it). (1971c: 216)

The moral of his version of the Lewis Carroll conundrum, according to Ryle, is that knowing how to apply a rule is not an instance of knowing that something is the case:

knowing [a rule of inference] is not a case of knowing an extra fact or truth; it is knowing how to move from acknowledging some facts to acknowledging others. Knowing a rule of inference is not possessing a bit of extra information but being able to perform an intelligent operation. Knowing a rule is knowing how. It is realized in performances which conform to the rule, not in theoretical citations of it. (Ibid.: 216–17).[17]

Why does Ryle think that his version of the Lewis Carroll case shows that knowing how is not a species of knowing that? Merely knowing truths does not "force" one to accept the conclusion of a valid inference. The dull pupil envisaged by Ryle knows all of the relevant truths, yet is not rationally forced to accept the conclusion. Ryle's point here seems to be that epistemic justification is not just a matter of knowing truths, but involves a non-propositional element. This non-propositional element is what Ryle calls *knowing how to perform the inference*. We are justified in accepting an inference only if we know the premises, and we know how to perform the inference. But the knowledge of how to perform the inference cannot just amount to knowledge of another premise – it must be something non-propositional, something that shows itself in our ability to reason according to that inference pattern.

Ryle's version of the case differs from Carroll (1895), and many subsequent discussions, in not focusing on a skeptic who doubts a rule of inference, whom it is our business to convince. Instead, Ryle focuses on someone who lacks the capacity to employ it. The issue in Ryle is – what does the pupil lack that we possess that makes it the case that he is not rationally forced (epistemically obligated) to perform the inference? The reason Ryle thinks the Carroll case is akin to the regress argument he later presents in *The Concept of Mind* is presumably because it can be presented as a

---

[17]   Brian Weatherson, on his blog (http://tar.weatherson.org/2006/07/22/ryle-on-knowing how), questions whether Ryle identified knowing how to F with the ability to F. Weatherson's point here has been accepted by subsequent commentators, who have introduced the term "Neo-Rylean" in papers as a name for the view that knowing how to F is to be equated with the ability to F. As Yuri Cath (forthcoming) also points out, here Ryle is clearly a neo-Rylean, since he explicitly identifies knowing how to perform an intelligent inference with being able to perform it.

similar vicious regress. If one thinks that what the pupil lacks is knowledge of a proposition, then one would think that epistemic justification requires that the pupil adds that proposition to his premises. But then the pupil would need to add another proposition to his premises, to justify his inference from the new premise set to the conclusion, and so on *ad infinitum*.

There are numerous ways to resist Ryle's use of the Lewis Carroll case to argue that knowing how is not a kind of knowing that. One response to Ryle's argument is to challenge the underlying conception of propositional knowledge, the assumption we discussed in the last section, that propositional knowledge is behaviorally inert. Why should one agree with Ryle that his dull pupil knows all the relevant truths? For example, does the pupil in fact know that if the premises are true, then the conclusion is true? As Paul Boghossian writes: "the idea that, in general, we come to grasp the logical constants by being disposed to engage in some inferences involving them and not in others, is an independently compelling idea. And the thought that, in particular, we grasp the conditional just in case we are disposed to infer according to MPP is an independently compelling thought" (2003: 240–1).[18] Boghossian's account of the mastery of logical constants is inconsistent with Ryle's assumption that propositional knowledge is behaviorally inert. If Boghossian is right, and the student does in fact know the conditional, then the pupil will be disposed to infer according to *modus ponens*. If the pupil is not disposed to infer according to *modus ponens*, then, *contra* Ryle, the pupil cannot know the proposition that if the premises are true, then the conclusion is true.[19]

One might however be convinced that various counterexamples to dispositional accounts of our mastery of basic logical concepts cannot be overcome, and on that basis reject them (e.g. Williamson 2003).[20] Ryle's use of Carroll's argument is nevertheless easily resisted. If one rejects dispositional accounts of our mastery of basic logical concepts, one will be attracted to some other account of the justification of our

---

[18] Boghossian argues that a dispositional account of mastery of primitive logical concepts can explain what he terms our "blind but blameless" employment of basic rules of inference – that is, why we are entitled to engage in basic logical reasoning, even in the absence of "reflectively appreciable support" (2003). On a dispositional account, one is so entitled because the disposition to reason in accord with the basic logical inferences is written into the possession conditions of basic logical concepts.

[19] Noë (2005: 285–6) suggests that a dispositional account of the mastery of some class of concepts is tantamount to agreeing with Ryle that knowing how is not a species of knowing that. This is false. To justify it, one would need to show that these dispositions are plausibly identical to states of knowing how, and furthermore states of knowing how that lack propositional content. But there are many dispositions I have that are simply not plausibly identified with states of knowing how – e.g. my disposition to have red visual phenomenology when visually presented with a red object. The dispositions that would yield concept-mastery on Boghossian's account seem to be dispositions of this latter kind, rather than states of knowledge how. Furthermore, if they are not, then there is no reason to deny that they too could be explained in terms of the possession of other, more primitive propositional knowledge states.

[20] Whether or not Boghossian is right about the specific case of the logical constants, I will argue in later chapters that he is surely right that the possession of propositional knowledge requires possession of certain dispositional states (see the end of Chapter 5). The important point for our purposes is Boghossian's insight that the possession of propositional knowledge has consequences for our behavioral dispositions.

employment of basic logical inference rules. For example, Ian Rumfitt (forthcoming) argues that one acquires knowledge by deduction from known premises only if one is *deductively competent* with the relevant correct deduction rules. According to Rumfitt, "deductive capacity cannot consist in knowledge of true propositions – whether those propositions are logical truths or propositions to the effect that this statement follows from these others – for a thinker could know the propositions while lacking any capacity to make deductions". Instead, "deductive capacity is an intellectual ability". According to Rumfitt, *mastery* of logical concepts does not require possession of reliable dispositions to infer according to the corresponding deduction rules. But *gaining knowledge* by deduction does.

However, in order to obtain a conclusion about knowledge how from Rumfitt's view, one would need an *independent* argument showing that the disposition to infer according to some deduction rules is identical to a kind of knowledge state, a state of knowing how to infer according to those rules. One would also need to demonstrate that, in addition to being a kind of knowledge state, it is one that lacks propositional content – that is, one would need to demonstrate that it is not a dispositional propositional knowledge state.

By analogy, consider externalist theories of knowledge of the reliabilist variety, according to which a true belief is an instance of knowledge in virtue of being produced by a process that reliably results in true beliefs. In many cases, the reliable processes themselves do not appear to be instances of *knowledge*. For example, the mechanism by which perception leads to true perceptual beliefs in a normal agent is not itself a kind of knowledge. As Rumfitt himself points out, his appeal to the disposition to infer according to *modus ponens* is supposed to play a similar role in his account of logical justification as reliable processes do for the externalist. If so, they are not knowledge states, or even abilities. They are *merely* dispositions.

Rumfitt might reply by arguing that deductive competence is not analogous with the mechanisms that undergird perceptual knowledge. Perhaps one might motivate this response by drawing distinctions between these sorts of dispositions and the kind of automatic mechanisms by which perception leads to true perceptual beliefs. Perhaps, for example, the dispositions to which Rumfitt appeals in his account of the justification of inferences are rational in some way that automatic mechanisms are not. However, this is only an argument for a non-propositional notion of knowing how if there is no proposition the grasp of which could yield the kind of dispositions Rumfitt appeals to in his account of justification. As Rumfitt recognizes, the propositional theory of knowing how that is defended in Stanley and Williamson (2001) and in this book is one such account.

Both of these accounts of the Lewis Carroll argument suppose that the moral of the Lewis Carroll case is that the subject lacks certain dispositions, without which the subject is not epistemically *forced* to draw an inference. The thought behind such response strategies is that the problem the Carroll examples poses is that no matter how many propositions the agent appears to grasp, they may nevertheless *fail to apply* the propositions to the specific case at hand. But if this is the problem raised by the Lewis Carroll case, it simply cannot be solved by appeal to a non-propositional account of knowing how, or mere dispositions. If one has some knowledge, whether propositional or non-propositional, how can there *not* be a possibility of failing to apply it when the time comes? The same point arises for mere dispositions. One can have all the dispositions one wants, but the exigencies of the situation may inhibit their manifestation.

In short, if the moral of the Lewis Carroll case is that there is a gap between standing epistemic states of the agent and the manifestation or application of those states on a particular occasion, appealing to more standing epistemic states of the agent, whether propositional or not, is no solution at all.

There are of course other accounts of what is missing in the Lewis Carroll case. For example, Timothy Williamson (2009) proposes a condition that he calls "safe derivation" as an account of the conditions under which "one makes a 'knowledgeable' connection" from the premises of an argument to its conclusion. But safe derivation does not require knowledge how – for example, in the case of an argument with no premises, an agent will have a safe derivation of the conclusion if and only if the agent knows that conclusion.[21] Or perhaps some other kind of external condition must be met in order for the inference to be justified, distinct from a reliable disposition, and if so, perhaps Ryle's dull pupil meets it – in which case, he is epistemically obligated to accept the conclusion, even though he in fact fails to draw it. Or perhaps Ryle's dull pupil is in an environment in which the external condition does not obtain (as with Carroll (1895), Ryle's case is under-described). Alternatively, perhaps the justification for drawing the inference is a non-inferential recognition of the fact that the conclusion follows from the premises, and Ryle's dull pupil lacks this quasi-perceptual capacity (see Boghossian 2003: 235). None of these other possible positions on what is missing in Ryle's dull pupil provide any support for the conclusion that what he lacks is non-propositional knowing how.

6.

We have seen that both of Ryle's regress arguments fail to establish that knowing how is not a species of knowing that. It remains to evaluate the last two considerations Ryle gives in favor of the thesis that knowing how is not a species of propositional knowledge. Both of these considerations are advanced in the second chapter of *The Concept of Mind*. The first is given early in the chapter:

---

[21] Both knowledge and safe derivation are explained in terms of elaborated models involving epistemic counterparts of formulas – knowing p requires safety (in Williamson's "no risk" sense) from the falsity of p and the falsity of all the formulas that are epistemic counterparts of p. Safe derivation forges an epistemic connection between the premises and conclusions of an inference, one sensitive to the epistemic counterparts of the premises and conclusions.

we never speak of a person believing or opining how . . . (28)[22]

The second "non-parallelism between the concept of knowing *that* and the concept of knowing *how*" (59) advanced by Ryle occurs later in the chapter. It is that:

We never speak of a person having partial knowledge of a fact or truth, save in the special sense of his having knowledge of a part of a body of facts or truths. A boy can be said to have partial knowledge of the counties of England, if he knows some of them and does not know others. But he could not be said to have incomplete knowledge of Sussex being an English county. Either he knows this fact or he does not know it. On the other hand, it is proper and normal to speak of a person knowing in part how to do something, i.e. of his having a particular capacity in a limited degree. An ordinary chess-player knows the game pretty well but a champion knows it better, and even the champion has still much to learn. (59)

So the two "non-parallelisms" are as follows. The first is that while we ascribe knowledge and belief with locutions such as "she knows that snow is white" and "she believes that snow is white", we do not say "she believes how to swim". The second is that propositional knowledge is not, as the linguists would say, *gradable* – it does not come in degrees (see Stanley 2005: ch. 3). On the other hand, *knowing how* does come in degrees. For example, we can speak of a person *partially* knowing how to do something, whereas we cannot speak of a person only *partially* knowing that something is the case.

In assessing the force of these considerations, it is worthwhile to return to another of Ryle's early statements of the intellectualist view of intelligent action he wishes to rebut:

both philosophers and laymen tend to treat intellectual operations as the core of mental conduct; that is to say, they tend to define all other mental-conduct concepts in terms of concepts of cognition. They suppose that the primary exercise of minds consists in finding the answers to questions and that their other occupations are merely applications of considered truths . . . (26)

According to the intellectualist, then, knowing how to do something is a matter of *knowing an answer to a question*. But if knowing how to do something is a matter of knowing an answer to a question, there is a smooth intellectualist explanation of both of the considerations that Ryle incorrectly thinks tell against the doctrine.

On the face of it, the English construction "John knows how to ride a bicycle" seems to contain what linguists call an *embedded question*. An embedded question is a clause headed by a question word, such as "who", "what", "why", "whether", "when", "where", or "how". The clause which "how" heads, in a sentence such as "John knows how to ride a bicycle", is not a *finite* clause – one marked for tense, but rather an *infinitive* clause. So a

[22] Ryle continues this by adding "and though it is proper to ask for the grounds or reasons for someone's acceptance of a proposition, this question cannot be asked of someone's skill at cards or prudence in investments." However, this second claim presupposes that knowing how to play cards is identical to skill at cards, which can hardly be presupposed in a consideration advanced in support of the thesis that knowing how is a skill, rather than propositional knowledge.

sentence such as "John knows how to ride a bicycle" appears, on its surface, to contain the verb "know", together with the embedded question construction "how to ride a bicycle". It seems therefore linguistically in a family with constructions like "John knows why to ride a bicycle", "John knows when to ride a bicycle", "John knows where to ride a bicycle", etc. (see Brown 1970; Stanley and Williamson 2001). Assuming that ascriptions of knowing how involve embedded questions provides a smooth explanation of both considerations raised by Ryle.

First, the verb "believe" does not grammatically take embedded questions. Ryle is correct to note that we cannot talk of "believing how". But we also cannot talk of "believing when", "believing where", or "believing why". The verb "believe" does not take embedded questions. So the hypothesis that sentences that ascribe knowing how contain embedded questions explains Ryle's first consideration. Unless Ryle is prepared to assert that no construction involving an embedded question can be defined in terms of knowledge that, his first consideration is therefore idle. But the situation is worse. It seems that what it is to know why to do something is to know an answer to the question "why do that?" Similarly, it seems that what it is to know when to do something is to know an answer to the question "When could (or should) you do it?" If sentences that ascribe knowing how contain embedded questions as well, then it would be natural to think of knowing how to do something as knowing an answer to the question "how could you do it?" But this is precisely the intellectualist position that is Ryle's target. As we have just seen, the intellectualist position provides a particularly smooth explanation of why we do not use the locution "believing how" – namely, "believes" does not take embedded questions.[23]

It is of course a difficult matter to say why "believes" and its cognates do not take embedded questions. But it is a difficult matter that has nothing whatsoever to do with the alleged distinction between knowing how and knowing that. Rather, it has to do with a distinction between questions and non-interrogative clauses. The intellectualist regards the occurrence of "how to ride a bicycle" in a construction like "John knows how to ride a bicycle" as introducing a question, and so patterning with other question constructions, such as "why to ride a bicycle" or "when to ride a bicycle". So the intellectualist smoothly predicts that "believes" should not take "how to ride a bicycle" as a complement. It can therefore hardly be a mark against intellectualism that its prediction is so well borne out by the facts.

The hypothesis also explains Ryle's second consideration. Ryle is of course right that propositional knowledge is not gradable (Stanley 2005: ch. 2). But we can speak of knowing an answer to a greater or lesser degree. As Lahiri (2002: 144) points out, one may utter "Bill partly knows where John went" if "Bill knows that John went to Santa Monica Boulevard and Vermont Avenue, but doesn't know that he also went to Silverlake." What is meant here is that John knows something that is a partial but not

---

[23] The verb "believe" does take free relative clauses, as in "I believe what John told me". But here "what John told me" is a definite description, rather than an embedded question.

complete answer to the question "where did John go?" One can also make sense of the idea of someone knowing where John went better than another person knows where John went. Given the semantics for questions I will introduce in the next chapter, it is not hard to define a sense in which one answer is a more informative answer than another answer (Groenendijk and Stokhof 1997: 1095). One can use this to give formal rigor to the idea of one person knowing the answer to a question better than another person – what they know is a better partial answer to the question than what the other person knows (for details, see Pavese and Stanley 2011).

As Pavese and Stanley (2011) show, there is a clear sense in which ascriptions of knowing how are gradable that goes beyond measuring the completeness of an answer one possesses. But *pace* Ryle, it does not amount to grading the knowledge itself. Ryle holds that when we utter (1), we are comparing their relative states of *knowing how* – it is this special cognitive relation of knowledge how that is being compared:

(1)   John knows how to play Chopin better than Mary does.

However, this is not what we are doing when we say that John knows how to play Chopin better than Mary does. Rather, we are comparing the *way* in which John knows how to play Chopin to the *way* in which Mary knows how to play Chopin, and declaring the first superior to the second. Recognizing this is only possible if one distinguishes the contribution of "know" from the contribution of "how" in such claims – in short if one recognizes that sentences ascribing knowledge of how to do something are embedded questions.

To see why an explanation of the gradability of knowing how requires rejecting Ryle's view of knowing how, compare (1) with (2):

(2)   John remembers how he played football better than Mary remembers how he played football.

This sentence is ambiguous between (3) and (4):

(3)   How John plays football is something he remembers better than Mary remembers.
(4)   The way in which John remembers playing football is a superior way to play football than the way in which Mary remembers John playing football.

In (3), we are comparing the memories, and in (4) we are comparing the ways of playing football. In contrast (1) lacks these two readings. The only meaning (1) has is the one analogous to (4) – the way known by John of playing Chopin is a superior way to play Chopin than the way known by Mary of playing Chopin. This is straightforwardly predicted by the hypothesis that sentences such as "John knows how to ride a bicycle" involve the propositional knowledge verb, together with an embedded question. Since the propositional knowledge verb is not gradable, the reading analogous to (3) is lacking. The reading analogous to (4) is present, because the embedded question in (1) involves quantification over ways.

Ryle also predicts that (1) is unambiguous. According to Ryle (1) is a way of comparing states of knowing how, as in (5) or (6):

(5)   *How to play Chopin is something John knows better than Mary.
(6)   *Playing Chopin is something John knows how better than Mary.

However, both (5) and (6) are nonsensical. In no sense are states of knowing how being compared in (1). Between the two competing hypotheses – the hypothesis that ascriptions of knowing how involve a single gradable cognitive state that relates persons to actions, and the hypothesis that ascriptions of knowing how such as (1) involve the propositional knowledge verb and an embedded question, only the latter can explain the evidence Ryle proffers for the former.[24]

In short, Ryle's two additional "non-parallelisms" between knowing how and knowing that only serve to strengthen the case for the intellectualist position that he seeks to refute. If knowing how to do something is a matter of knowing the answer to the question "how could you do it?" we should expect that one could compare answers. Similarly, as we have seen, if attributions of knowing how involve an embedded question, we should also expect that, as with other embedded questions, their complements cannot occur as complements of "believes". So Ryle's additional considerations are thoroughly unpersuasive.

Ryle's motivation for arguing that knowing how is not a species of knowing that was a desire to defend a behaviorist view of mental states. This motivation is less than compelling. His various regress arguments fail to raise a problem for the view that knowing how is a species of knowing that. Finally, the other considerations he adduces against the intellectualist position in chapter 2 of *The Concept of Mind* are, if anything, evidence for the view that knowing how to do something is a matter of knowing the answer to a question. If there is a persuasive argument for the view that knowing how is not a species of knowing that, it is not to be found in Ryle's work.

6.

According to Ryle, one knows how to do something if and only if one bears an intellectual relationship to an action type. Thus, for Ryle, knowing how to do something is not a species of knowing that something is the case. In contrast, Ryle's "intellectualist" holds that knowing how to do something amounts to *knowing the answer to a question*. In order to develop a proper intellectualist account of knowing how, it is therefore necessary to give an account of what it is to know the answer to a question, or (as I shall call it), *knowledge-wh*. We can then use the general account to develop an account of its various sub-species, including the state of knowing how to do something.

---

[24] See Pavese and Stanley (2011), for an extended discussion of Ryle's gradability objection.

2

Knowledge-wh

The kinds of ascriptions of knowledge that are most familiar from the literature in epistemology are ones that have the form ⌜X knows that p⌝. However, not all ascriptions of knowledge take this form. Consider, for example, the sentences in (1):

(1)   a. John knows whether Mary came to the party.
        b. John knows why Obama won.
        c. Hannah knows what Obama will do in office.
        d. Hannah knows who Obama is.
        e. Hannah knows what she is pointing at.
        f. Hannah knows how Obama will govern.
        g. Hannah knows why to vote for Obama.
        h. Hannah knows how to vote.

Part of the task of epistemology is to explain the nature of the states ascribed to agents by such sentences. In particular, one may wonder whether they ascribe states of the same *kind* as ascriptions such as ⌜X knows that p⌝. If so, then the task of explaining the nature of these states is no different from the task of epistemology as it has always been conceived — to say something informative about such states. The role of explaining the difference between the states ascribed in sentences such as (1), and the states ascribed by sentences such as "John knows that Obama is a Democrat", would fall within the purview of the theorist of content, who is tasked with explaining the distinction between different kinds of contents generally.

     The default assumption is that the ascriptions in (1) are ascriptions of the same kind as ascriptions of the form ⌜X knows that p⌝. After all, the same verb "know" occurs in all of these constructions. Furthermore, it is a stable cross-linguistic fact that most of the sentences in (1) are translated with the same verb used in translations of sentences of the form ⌜X knows that p⌝. This contrasts with the sort of ascriptions in (2):

(2)   a. John knows Bill.
        b. John knows the mayor of Boston.

In many languages, the translations of the sentences in (2) do not involve the verb that translates "know" in sentences like "John knows that snow is white". For example, in French, the verb used in knowledge attributions such as "John knows that snow is white" is "savoir", and the verb used to translate "know" in the sentences in (2) is "connaitre". "Savoir" is also used to translate the sentences in (1). Similarly, in German, the verb used in knowledge attributions such as "John knows that snow is white" is "wissen", which is also used in the translations of the sentences in (1). In contrast, the verb used to translate the sentences in (2) is "kennen".[1] Surely, if humans thought of the sort of state expressed by ascriptions of the form ⌜X knows that p⌝ and the verb "know" in sentences such as (1) as clearly distinct, there would be many languages in which different words were employed. The fact that we do not employ different words for these notions suggests they are at the very least intimately related concepts.

Of course, it could be that the fact that the same verb is used cross-linguistically for embedded question constructions as for attributions involving "that" clause complements is a kind of widespread error. Perhaps we have a single concept for propositional knowledge and the kind of knowledge ascribed in sentences such as (1), but science will reveal that in fact (say) propositional knowledge ascriptions and ascriptions of knowing-where or knowing-who are very different in kind. In short, perhaps the situation is similar to what happened with the concept corresponding to the expression "jade". Our single concept turned out to be a concept corresponding to two very different kinds, jadeite and nephrite. One concept of knowledge turns out upon further investigation to be fractured.

The default position should be that the sentences in (1) do ascribe the same kinds of states as ascriptions of the form ⌜X knows that p⌝. First, it seems that all of the sentences in (1) are synonymous with ascriptions that take the form ⌜X knows that p⌝. As we will see in detail in Chapter 5, infinitives in embedded question constructions such as (1) are ambiguous between a "could" reading and an "ought" reading. On the "could" reading of the infinitive "to move a disc", someone who *knows where to move a disc* in the Tower of Hanoi puzzle *knows that* she can move a disc to any peg that has a larger disc as its topmost disc. Similarly, suppose Open Market is open from noon to midnight. Someone *knows when to buy groceries at Open Market* if and only if she knows that she can buy groceries at Open Market between noon and midnight. As we shall later see, there are similar paraphrases available for the other ascriptions in (1). The existence of such paraphrases is easily explained if the occurrences of "know" in the sentences in (1) denoted the same relation as the verb that occurs in constructions of the form ⌜X knows that p⌝, and difficult to explain otherwise.

Of course, it may be that science will discover that our one concept of knowledge, like our previous concept of jade, answers to different kinds. But this does not show that the default position is that there are distinct kinds of knowledge. Even in the case of jade, the default position is that there was only one kind of jade. After all, we had a great deal of evidence that jadeite and nephrite were the same kind – they appeared to

---

[1] There are diagnostics for distinguishing the two readings of "know" in English. As I have pointed out elsewhere (2005: 38), the acquaintance sense of "know" is gradable, whereas the verb that takes "that"-complements is not (ibid.: ch. 2).

be the same. It took a definitive chemical discovery to undermine that default position. It should take a similar definitive scientific discovery to undermine the default position that all of the ascriptions in (1) ascribe the same kind of state as ascriptions of the form ⌜X knows that p⌝.

Nevertheless, constructions in (1) raise problems not raised by uncontroversial propositional knowledge ascriptions. In contrast with ascriptions of the form ⌜X knows that p⌝, philosophical work on the nature of knowledge ascriptions such as the ones in (1) has been sporadic, halting, and unsystematic. For example, for somewhat accidental reasons, much of the discussion in philosophy has been centered on ascriptions of the form of (1d) and (1e), ascriptions of *knowing-who* or *knowing-what*. The reason these constructions have been extensively discussed by philosophers is because of their putative connections to singular thought. For example, consider *de re attitude ascriptions*. A *de re* attitude ascription is a sentence in which a quantifier outside the scope of a propositional attitude verb binds a position within the scope of that verb. The following are examples:

(3)   a.   There is a politician in France whom John believes is a journalist.
      b.   Every teacher of Bill is such that John believes he is a spy.

Such sentences appear to have the function of attributing singular thoughts to agents. For instance (3a) appears to attribute to John a mental state which is about a particular person with whom he is acquainted. Some philosophers have connected the coherence of *de re* attitude ascriptions, such as "the man in the brown hat is someone whom John believes is a spy", to ascriptions of knowing-who, such as (1d). The thought was that an ascription of the form (3a) could only be true if the agent knows who the person in question is. For example (3a) could be true only if John knows who the politician is. For example, Jaakko Hintikka writes:

Let us consider the familiar distinction between "b knows that there is an individual x such that S[x]" and "b knows of some individual x that S[x]"... the contrast in question is roughly between "knowing that there is" and "knowing who or what". (1989a: 24–5)

Many philosophers other than Hintikka have also connected ascriptions of knowing-who or knowing-what to the capacity for singular thought about an object or a kind. Ascriptions of knowing-who and knowing-what thus became of philosophical interest derivatively, via their alleged connection to this much discussed topic (see e.g. Quine 1976: 863; Kaplan 1989a: 555). It is for this reason that Stephen Boer and William Lycan (1986) were able to devote an entire book to the subject of knowing-who.

The philosophical discussion about knowing-who and its connection to singular thought was not connected to a general theory of the nature of the states ascribed by the sentences in (1). But it is surely odd to disassociate discussions of knowing-who from the other states attributed by the sentences in (1). After all, "Hannah knows who Obama is" differs from "Hannah knows where Obama is" only in the replacement of "who" by "where". Presumably, the states ascribed by such sentences are very similar, if not the same. Considerations from the compositionality of meaning should lead us to seek an account of the meanings of question words such as "who", "where", "why", and "what" that, together with an account of "know", yields the meanings of the sentences in (1).

As early as the 1950s, philosophers were working on the semantic analysis of questions (e.g. Hamblin 1958). This topic remained a focus through the 1960s and 1970s, through the work not just of Hamblin and Hintikka, but also figures such as Sylvain Bromberger (1966) and Nuel Belnap (e.g. Belnap and Steel 1976). But the topic has remained *au courant* primarily in linguistics departments, where the proper analysis of the structures in (1) has remained a lively and ongoing research program for decades. Such analyses begin with the insight that constructions such as (1) involve clauses that take the form of interrogatives – that is, *questions*. For example, the verb "know" in (1b) seems to have as its complement something very similar to the question "Why did Obama win?" Further confirmation that questions are involved in such constructions comes from reflection on their intuitive meaning. A sentence such as (1b) seems true if and only if Hannah knows the answer to the question, "Why did Obama win?" In accordance with this insight, linguists say that constructions of the sort found in (1) involve embedded questions. More specifically, the constructions in (1) involve questions embedded inside the verb "know".

"Know" is not the only verb that can take embedded questions, as the examples in (4) demonstrate:

(4)   a. Bill learned why Obama won.
      b. Bill learned who Obama is.
      c. Bill remembered why Obama won.
      d. Bill told Mary who Obama is.
      e. Bill wondered how to vote.
      f. Bill doubted whether Obama won.

Since "know" is not unusual in taking embedded questions, an analysis of the meanings of the sentences in (1) is presumably one part of a general theory of the meaning of embedded questions as they occur as complements of the sort of verbs in (4).[2]

An account of the meaning of the sentences in (1) presupposes an account of the meaning of questions. But before we turn to such accounts, it is worth dispelling a

---

[2] As we have seen in Chapter 1, embedded questions cannot occur as complements of every kind of propositional attitude verb. It is a cross-linguistic fact that embedded questions cannot occur with words synonymous with the English verb "believe". The oddity of the sentences in (5) shows this phenomenon in English:

(1)   a. *Bill believes why Obama won.
      b. *Bill believes who Obama is.
      c. *Bill believes how Obama plays basketball.

A full theory should explain why embedded questions can occur with verbs such as "know", "learned", "remembered", and "wondered", but not with verbs such as "believe" and "thinks". Unfortunately, there is as yet no clearly persuasive account of these facts.

natural reaction one might have to the project of providing "an account of the meaning of questions". After all, a question is a kind of *speech act*. Speech acts are things people do. It seems *prima facie* odd to speak of the meaning of a speech act such as a question. We should instead seek an account of questions that is located in speech-act theory, which is a branch of pragmatics. This is the *pragmatic* approach to the theory of questions (for discussion, see Groenendijk and Stokhof 1997: 1061–75, and Higginbotham 1993: 213–17).

Just as we can distinguish a sentence in the declarative mood from an assertion, we may distinguish a sentence in interrogative mood from a question. Just as we can ask what kind of thing is expressed, relative to a context, by a sentence in the declarative mood, so we should be able to ask what kind of thing is expressed, relative to a context, by a sentence in the interrogative mood. Furthermore, we are led to this semantic question by the very same sort of considerations that led philosophers to ask the parallel questions about sentences in the declarative mood. For example, obviously a sentence in the declarative mood can occur embedded inside a verb such as "know", as in:

(5)   a. John knows that snow is white.
      b. John learned that snow is white.
      c. John remembered that snow is white.

The embedded sentence "snow is white" is not *asserted* in any of the sentences in (5), just as the embedded question "who Obama is" is not *asked* in an utterance of "Hannah knows who Obama is". Rather, according to standard accounts, it contributes a semantic object, a proposition, to the meaning of the construction in which it occurs. Similar considerations should lead us to seek a semantic object contributed by clauses such as "whether Mary came to the party", "why Obama won", and "who Obama is" to the meanings of more complex sentences in which they occur. In the case of declarative sentences such as "snow is white", the semantic object they contribute to the meaning of more complex sentences in which they occur is what we take assertions of them to express – namely a proposition. Parallel considerations should lead us to the view that there is a semantic object expressed by a sentence that takes the form of a question, and it is both what it contributes to the meaning of larger constructions in which it occurs as a part, as well as its stand-alone semantic content when it is asked.

A further consideration in support of the thesis that questions have a semantic content, one which can be the object of attitudes, is the naturalness of dialogues such as:

(6)   Bill: Who came to the party?
      Sue: I don't know that, but I bet John does.

In the dialogue in (6), Sue asserts that John knows *what Bill asked*. This suggests that there is in fact a semantic object that is the value of the question Bill asked.

These are some of the reasons that have led most semanticists to assume that questions have semantic contents, and that these contents are the objects of ascriptions of the sort found in sentences such as the ones in (1). In what follows, I will explain two classical theories of the meanings of embedded questions, the theory in Karttunen (1977) and the theory in Groenendijk and Stokhof (1982). These theories are representative of the tradition in semantics that analyzes questions in terms of operations on propositions, which includes the classic articles by Hamblin (1973) and Higginbotham and May (1981).

1.

My ultimate goal lies in providing an analysis of the meaning of the constructions in (1). Such constructions involve what linguists call "an embedded question", together with the knowledge verb. In this section, I explain one classic theory of embedded questions, that of Karttunen (1977). Subsequent accounts of the semantics of embedded questions are generally developments of this theory.

There are two "original" semantic theories of questions, from which all contemporary accounts flow. The first is in C.L. Hamblin's 1973 paper, "Questions in Montague English". Hamblin does not discuss embedded questions, but his theory naturally generalizes to them. The second, which we will discuss in some detail in this section, is Lauri Karttunen's theory of questions, presented in his classic 1977 paper, "Syntax and Semantics of Questions".

It is natural to begin discussion of Karttunen's account, as he does, by briefly sketching Hamblin's. According to Hamblin, the semantic content of a question is the set of its possible answers. So, "Who came?" denotes the set of all propositions of the form 'x came'. Similarly, a yes–no question such as "Is it raining?" expresses the set {it is raining, it is not raining}. Following Karttunen's exposition, we can represent these meanings as:

(1) Is it raining? = $\lambda p(p$ = the proposition that it is raining or p = the proposition that it is not the case that it is raining)

(2) Who-came? = $\lambda p(\exists x(p$ = the proposition that x came)

That is, the denotation of a question is the characteristic function of a certain set. "Who came?" denotes a function that takes a proposition to the true if and only if, for some x, that proposition is the singular proposition that x came.

Karttunen gives two arguments against Hamblin's view. The first we can safely ignore for now. The second is more interesting. Karttunen writes:

Another point in favor of letting questions denote a set of true propositions is provided by verbs such as "tell", "indicate", etc... The verb "tell" with a that-complement does not entail that what is told is true; with an indirect question it does. ["John told Mary who passed the test"] definitely says that John told the truth. Letting the embedded question "who passed the test" denote a set of true propositions makes it possible to explicate the meaning of "tell" in [such constructions] in a straightforward way. That is, we can say that "John told Mary who passed the test" is true just in case John told Mary every proposition in the set denoted by the indirect question. Having the denotation of "who passed the test" contain all the false answers as well is of no use to us; on the contrary, it introduces a complication in relating the question-embedding verb "tell" to its that-complement taking counterpart. The same point can be made with regard to other question-embedding verbs such as "be interested in", "investigate", "wonder", etc. In all of these cases, it appears that the meaning of the verb can be satisfactorily explicated on the basis of the more restrictive hypothesis here that indirect questions denote sets that only contain the propositions that jointly constitute a true and complete answer. (1977: 11)

Karttunen here notices that certain question-embedding verbs, such as "tell" (and also "know"), have a certain feature. If you *tell* someone who went to the party, then you know the true answer(s) to the question "who went to the party?", and you communicate to them this knowledge. Similarly, if you know who went to the party, then you know all the *true* answer(s) to that question.

Karttunen correctly recognizes that someone tells someone who went to the party only if they tell them the true answers to the question "Who went to the party?" But verbs such as "wonder" and "investigate" clearly belong in another category. If you *wonder* who went to the party, you certainly don't know who went to the party. Similarly, if you *investigate* who went to the party, you don't know who went to the party. Here, Hamblin's semantics seems more appropriate – the set of all possible answers seems to be a good object to be the object of wondering, certainly better than the set of all *true* answers. Following Groenendijk and Stokhof (1982), let us call verbs such as "know" and "tell", *extensional question-embedding verbs*, and verbs such as "wonder" and "investigate", *intensional question-embedding verbs*. Karttunen claims that one can treat the class of extensional question-embedding verbs via "the more restrictive hypothesis" that embedded questions denote sets that "only contain the propositions that jointly constitute a true and complete answer." But it is not obvious what treatment of intensional question-embedding verbs he has in mind.

Here is one suggestion, due to notes by Kai von Fintel and Irene Heim.[3] Perhaps Karttunen is thinking that each intensional embedding verb is analyzable in terms of notions that take only the "more restrictive" meanings as arguments. So "ask" would be analyzed as *request to be told*, "wonder" would be analyzed as *want to know*, and "investigate" would be analyzed as *trying to come to know*. The verbs "told" and "know" that occur in the lexical entry just take the Karttunen denotation as their argument. Presumably the intensional nature of the whole construction would be located in the intensional verbs "want" and "trying". However, there are worries with the suggestion. Suppose Bill and Sally and Frank committed the robbery. Investigating who committed the robbery does not seem the same as trying to come to know that Sally committed the robbery, Bill committed the robbery, and Frank committed the robbery. After all, I might not even have a *hypothesis* about who committed the robbery.

Karttunen's semantics is, then, a variant of Hamblin's. But it is placed in an attractive compositional setting, one that explains the meanings of a whole host of direct and

---

[3] Thanks to Daniel Rothschild for alerting me to these.

embedded question constructions. To understand the predictions Karttunen's semantics makes, we will now consider what it predicts for a variety of different kinds of
questions.

We begin with Karttunen's account of *alternative questions*, such as "Does John cook
or Mary eat out?" In asking such a question, one is unsure about which of two disjuncts
obtains, and wishes thereby to resolve one's ignorance. Karttunen's semantics predicts
the following semantic value for this question:

["Does John cook or Mary eat out"] = λp (p & [p = the proposition that John cooks]
or [p = the proposition that Mary eats out]).

So "Does John cook or Mary eat out?" denotes that function from propositions to
truth-values, that yields true when given a true proposition that is either the proposition that John cooks or the proposition that Mary eats out.[4] So if John cooks and Mary
does not eat out, then the semantic value of "Does John cook or Mary eat out" yields
true if and only if it is given as argument the proposition that John cooks.

Yes/no questions are questions that one asks when one wants to know whether or
not a particular proposition is true. Karttunen's analysis of yes–no questions – such as
"Does Mary cook?" is as follows:

["Does Mary cook?"] = λp (p & [p = the proposition that Mary cooks] or [p = the
proposition that Mary doesn't cook]).

On this analysis, a yes–no question denotes a function from propositions to truth-
values, that yields true when given either the positive or negative answer to the yes–no
question, depending upon which is true. So if Mary cooks, the denotation of "Mary
cooks" yields the true for the proposition that Mary cooks as an argument, and the false
for every other proposition, and if Mary does not cook, then the denotation of "Mary
cooks" yields the true for the proposition that Mary does not cook as argument, and
the false for every other proposition.

Our central interest is of course *embedded questions*. Karttunen gives an elegant and
straightforward account of embedded questions. The property denoted by "knows
whether John walks" is just:

[knows whether John walks] = λx(knows(x, λp (p & [p = the proposition that John
walks] or [p = the proposition that John doesn't walk]))).

On this account, the denotation of the verb "knows" (or any other question-embedding verb) takes, as a complement, a function from propositions to truth-values (or
alternatively, a set of propositions – that set of propositions relative to which it yields
the true as value).

---

[4] As Karttunen points out, this analysis does not account for the fact that "Does John cook or Mary eat
out?" seems to presuppose that there is one and only one correct answer.

As one can see, on Karttunen's account, question-embedding verbs are a different semantic type than their proposition-taking cousins. So there is an important sense in which on this theory the occurrences of the verb "know" in (1) do not express the same relation as the verb "know" when it occurs in sentences of the form ⌜X knows that p⌝. The occurrence of the verb "know" in an ascription of the latter kind relates persons and propositions, whereas the occurrence of the verb "know" in the sentences in (1) relates persons to *sets* of propositions (or, equivalently, the characteristic functions of such sets). So according to Karttunen, there are two meanings of the verb "know", and two meanings of the verb "remember", and two meanings of the verb "tell", etc. When a verb takes an embedded question as an argument, it takes a function from propositions to truth-values, or alternatively, a set of propositions, as an argument. In contrast, when that self-same verb takes a "that" complement, it takes as arguments propositions, rather than sets of propositions.

The question-embedding verb "know" is of a somewhat different semantic category than the verb "know" that embeds "that" complements. However, they need to be related in a way that validates intuitive inferences such as the one in (3):

(3)   Bill knows whether John walks.
(4)   John walks.
(5)   Bill knows that John walks.

To account for such validities, Karttunen suggests the following meaning postulate (where 'F' is a variable ranging over meanings of embedded questions, and "knows$_q$" is the embedded question taking "know"):

Meaning Postulate Relating embedded question "know" to that-complement taking "know": For all x, for all F, necessarily x knows$_q$ F if and only if for all propositions p, if F(p) = True, then x knows that p, and if there is no proposition q such that F(q) = True, then x knows that there is no proposition q such that F(q) = True.

Note that according to this meaning postulate, if Mary doesn't cook and Bill doesn't eat out, then we can still know whether Mary cooks and Bill doesn't eat out – by knowing that there is *no answer* to the question "Whether Mary cooks or Bill eats out".

Now let us turn to questions headed by so-called "wh-phrases", such as "who", "what", "which N", "when", "why", and "how" (Karttunen only discusses "who", "what", and "which N"). Recall Frege's treatment of the quantifiers, as functions from properties to truth-values. For example, "everything" is defined as a function that takes a property to the true if and only if everything falls under that property (Frege 1966: 12); similarly, "something" is a function that takes a property to the true if and only if at least one thing falls under that property. Karttunen treats wh-phrases as quantificational expressions, where the latter are conceived of according to the Fregean treatment of them, as functions from properties to truth-values. In particular, on Karttunen's treatment, wh-phrases are equivalent to this classic quantificational treatment of existentially quantified noun phrases:

[Which man] = $\lambda P (\exists x [man(x) \& P(x)])$

So "which man" denotes a function from properties to truth-values, one which takes a property to the true if and only if that property is true of at least one man. In short, Karttunen treats the phrases "which man" as having the same semantic content as "some man".

Karttunen treats a question such as "Who dates Mary?" as combining the question word "who" with the question "?he dates Mary". As we have seen, the question "?he dates Mary" has a semantic value, $\lambda p(p \& p = $ the proposition that x dates Mary). The result of combining "who" with the question "?he dates Mary" is to 'bind off' the variable 'x' with the existential quantifier introduced by "who".[5] This results in:

[Who dates Mary] = $\lambda p \; \exists x \; (p \& p = $ the proposition that x dates Mary).

So, "who dates Mary" denotes a function that takes a proposition to the true if and only p is true and there is some object x such that p is the proposition that x dates Mary. So the extension of that function is a set of true singular propositions of the form <x dates Mary>. Karttunen's theory states that x knows who dates Mary if and only if x stands in the $know_q$ relation to this set of singular propositions. Via the meaning postulate relating "$know_q$" to "know", we can conclude that x stands in the $know_q$ relation to this set of singular propositions if and only if x knows each proposition in the set.

Though Karttunen doesn't discuss the matter, the account he gives for "who" and "which" generalizes straightforwardly to "why" and "how". The question word "who" quantifies over *persons*, and is semantically equivalent to the phrase "some man". By analogy, "why" quantifies over *reasons*, and "how" quantifies over *ways of doing things*. The word "why" is semantically equivalent to "some reason", and the word "how" is semantically equivalent to "some way". So, Karttunen's semantics entails that the semantic contents of "How does Bill swim?" and "Why does Bill swim?" are:

[How does Bill swim] = $\lambda p \; \exists w \; (p \& p = $ the proposition that Bill swims in way w).
[Why does Bill swim] = $\lambda p \; \exists r \; (p \& p = $ the proposition that Bill swims for reason r).

Karttunen's account therefore predicts that "John knows how Bill swims" is true if and only if John stands in the $know_q$ relation to $\lambda p \; \exists w \; (p \& p = $ the proposition that Bill swims in way w). By the meaning postulate relating "$know_q$" to that-complement "know", John knows how Bill swims is true if and only if John knows every true singular proposition of the form <Bill swims in way w>.

---

[5] This is accomplished via Karttunen's "WH-Quantification Rule" (1977: 19). This rule is not the paradigm of compositionality.

Karttunen's theory captures the natural reading of most embedded question constructions involving verbs such as "know", "tell", and "recognize". It is natural to think
that one knows how Bill swims only if for each way in which Bill swims, one knows
that Bill swims in that way (and similarly for "tell" and "recognize"). But there are
other readings of embedded questions that Karttunen's theory does not immediately
capture. The discovery of these alternative readings is due to Hintikka. As Karttunen
notes (fn. 4), "Hintikka thinks that . . . wh-questions in general . . . are ambiguous
between a universal and existential reading of the interrogative quantifier." However,
Karttunen is not sympathetic to Hintikka's view, and his semantics does not generate
the existential reading.

However, there is no question that there are at the very least strong *intuitions* of an
existential reading of embedded questions. The examples are simplest to generate with
embedded questions with *infinitive* complements. Three standard examples, due to
Hintikka, are:

(6)   John knows where to buy gas for the car.
(7)   John knows who to look for to collect his passport.
(8)   Mary remembers where to go to get a license.

As Utpahl Lahiri points out:

In order for [6] to be true, John doesn't have to know, of all places that sell gas, that they sell gas:
just one place will do. (2001: 161)

Hintikka seems right, as against Karttunen, that there are genuinely existential readings
of embedded questions. Karttunen's semantics therefore needs to be modified to allow
them. As Stanley and Williamson (2001: 426, fn. 27) note, this can be easily done by
adding an *additional* meaning postulate for question-embedding "know", namely:

Meaning Postulate II Relating embedded question "know" to that- complement taking "know": For all x,
for all F, necessarily x knows$_{q\text{-}\exists x}$ F if and only if for some proposition p, if F(p) = True, then x
knows that p, and if there is no proposition q such that F(q) = True, then x knows that there is no
proposition q such that F(q) = True.[6]

A more significant worry for the actual semantics Karttunen gives comes from
intuitions concerning what has come to be known as *strong exhaustiveness* (Groenendijk
and Stokhof (1982: 180) were the first to raise this problem for Karttunen). According
to the semantics Karttunen gives (9) has the truth-conditions given in (10):

---

[6] It is also worth mentioning that there are readings intermediate between the existential and the universal,
but as Lahiri points out, they are "relatively rare". The examples Lahiri gives (2002: 162) are:

(a) What are the possible structures for the following sentence? (Give at least three.)
(b) I can tell you what the possible structures for the following sentence are.

(9) John knows who dates Mary.

(10) ∀x [x is a person and x dates Mary][John knows that x dates Mary].

But one might think that this is too weak. Suppose (10) is true, but John also has a lot of false beliefs about who dates Mary. Intuitively, is (9) true? Karttunen's theory predicts that it is, but intuitions vary here.

Karttunen argues (1977: 21–2) that the issue is basically whether to think of "John knows who dates Mary" as synonymous with (11):

(11) John knows of every person whether or not she dates Mary.

On p. 22, Karttunen defends his view that (10) is the right truth-condition for (9) in two ways. First, he argues that giving the stronger truth-condition to account for strong exhaustiveness would make "who dates Mary" and "who doesn't date Mary" synonymous, which they don't seem to be.[7] Second, making (9) and (11) synonymous would have the consequence that in order to know who dates Mary, John "must have some knowledge about all the individuals including those he has never heard of and whose very existence is unknown to him."

However, there are definitely examples that go in a different direction. Consider the following example, from James Higginbotham:

(12) John knows which numbers between 10 and 20 are prime.

It seems that if John believes that every number between 10 and 20 is prime, then (12) shouldn't be true. Similarly, here is an example from Barbara Partee (reported by Lahiri on p. 149):

(13) The Maitre d' at Maxim's always knows which customer tips well.

It seems with these latter examples that a representation such as (10) gives a particularly poor account of our intuitions. Something like (14) is much more representative:

(14) The Maitre d' at Maxim's knows, of each customer, whether or not she tips well.

These intuitions are quite strong, and they suggest that having a false belief about who satisfies a property should be incompatible with knowing-who has that property.[8]

There are three worries with Karttunen's semantics for embedded questions which we have discussed in this section. First, Karttunen postulates two meanings for each

---

[7] Note that there is a typo – a crucial missing "not" between "do" and "appear" in the middle of p. 22 in Karttunen's discussion.

[8] The second clause in Karttunen's meaning postulate relating embedded question "know" to the proposition-taking verb "know", which deals with the case in which there is no answer to the question, states that in such a case, bearing the knowing relation to a question requires knowing that there is nothing satisfying the property in question. Irene Heim (1994:132–3) points out that the intuition behind this is basically that "maybe one never really bears the know-relation to a question unless one also knows that the answer to this question is the answer to it." Using this generalization, she shows how to produce a semantics of questions that employs Karttunen denotations for questions, but accounts for strong exhaustiveness.

extensional question-embedding verb, one for embedded questions, and the other for "that" complements. Though Karttunen does relate the two meanings with the use of meaning postulates, a theory that explains the uniformity by appeal to only one meaning assignment is to be preferred. Second, Karttunen's semantics does not give a straightforward account of the crucial distinction between extensional and intensional question-embedding verbs – that is, verbs like "know", "tell", and "remember", on the one hand, and verbs like "wonder" and "investigate", on the other. Finally, Karttunen's theory does not account for the intuitions supporting strong exhaustivity. In the next section, we turn to another theory of questions that was motivated in large part by the desire to provide solutions to these concerns.

2.

The main focus of Groenendijk and Stokhof's 1982 theory of questions (henceforth G&S) is to provide a theory according to which questions, such as "Who went to the party?" denote the same kind of object as "that" complements such as "that Hannah went to the party." Similarly, wh-complements (such as the occurrence of "who went to the party?" in "John knows who went to the party") and "that" complements (such as the occurrence of "that Hannah went to the party" in "John knows that Hannah went to the party") denote the same kind of object. They then hope to use this to solve both the first and second problems for Karttunen's theory. So I begin by explaining it, before turning to their account of strong exhaustiveness.

G&S propose to take the semantic content of both questions and declarative sentences to be functions from what they call *indices* to propositions. We can think of an index, as they do, as a possible world. So, "who came to the party", "whether Mary walks", as well as "Mary came to the party" and "Mary walks" all denote entities of the same semantic type, namely functions from possible worlds to propositions. Let us call entities of this semantic type, *question-meanings*. G&S take questions and declaratives *uniformly* to denote question-meanings. This entails that there is no need for an additional meaning postulate for each extensional question-embedding verb that relates the question-embedding form of a verb to its "that" complement-taking form. For example, the verb "know" as it occurs in a sentence such as "John knows whether Hannah went to the party" and as it occurs in a sentence like "John knows that Hannah went to the party" has the same semantic type. In both cases, it takes as its complement a function from possible worlds (indices) to propositions.

G&S describe their view as one according to which both embedded questions and "that" complements denote propositions. As they write:

there is a relationship between sentences in which a whether-complement occurs embedded under verbs as "know" or "tell" and similar sentences containing a that-complement. The most simple account of this relationship would be to claim that ⌜whether Φ⌝ and ⌜that (not) Φ⌝

denote the same kind of semantic object. Taking 'that (not) Φ' to denote a proposition, this amounts to claiming that 'whether Φ' denotes a proposition too. (1982: 177)

But this is quite misleading. The more accurate description of G&S's theory is that *neither* instances of 'whether Φ' nor instances of 'that (not) Φ' denote propositions. Rather, instances of these schemas uniformly denote functions from indices to propositions, i.e. instances of these schemas uniformly denote question-meanings. In short, the central innovation of G&S's theory is not, as is often said, that they take questions to denote propositions. It is rather that they have found a uniform semantic value for both declaratives and questions that is not a proposition. It is strictly speaking more accurate to say that G&S's innovation is to reject the view that declaratives (and "that"-complements) denote propositions.

So on G&S's theory, both wh-complements and "that"-complements denote functions from indices to propositions, that is, question-meanings. We now need to see what the nature of these functions is, and in particular how G&S recover the felt differences between wh-complements and "that"-complements, given that both denote the same kind of object.[9]

According to G&S, questions (including embedded questions, i.e. wh-complements) denote functions that take an index (possible world) as argument, and yield the true complete answer to that question at that world as a value. So a question such as "Who went to the party?" denotes a function from a possible world, to the true complete answer to that question at that world. If the party at world w was a small dinner party consisting only of Sarah, Hannah, Jonah, and Jacob, then the denotation of "Who went to the party" would yield, for w as an argument, the proposition that Sarah, Hannah, Jonah, and Jacob, and no one else were at the party. Similarly, the denotation of a "whether" question such as "whether Hannah was at the party" would take a possible world w as an argument, and yield the proposition that Hannah was at the party if Hannah was at the party at w, and otherwise would yield the proposition that Hannah was not at the party. So in general, the semantic value of a question will yield different values for different indices (possible worlds) as arguments.

In contrast, though the denotations of "that"-complements are also functions from indices to propositions, i.e. they are also question-meanings, they *never* yield different values for different indices as arguments. That is, "that" complements denote *constant functions* from indices to propositions. Given any world as argument, the semantic value of "that Hannah was at the party" yields the proposition that Hannah was at the party as its value. As G&S write:

---

[9] It is worth mentioning that many of the central ideas of G&S (1982) – that an adequate semantics for questions requires double-indexing, requiring both wh-complements and "that"-complements to be double-indexed, and treating the denotations of the latter as only sensitive to one index, are presented in a few brief pages of Lewis (1982). See his discussion of "Option E". Lewis apparently first presented this material in 1974.

which proposition 'whether Φ' denotes depends on the actual truth-value of Φ. This marks an important difference in meaning between 'that' and 'whether' complements. The denotation of that-complements is *index independent*: at every index 'that Φ' denotes the same proposition. The denotation of a whether-complement may vary from index to index, it is *index dependent*. At an index at which Φ is true it denotes the proposition that Φ; at an index at which Φ is false it denotes the proposition that not Φ. In other words, whereas the propositional concept which is the sense of a that-complement is a constant function from indices to propositions, the propositional concept which is the sense of a whether-concept (in general) is not. So, although at a given index, a whether-complement and a that-complement will have the same denotation, their sense will in general be different. (1982: 177)

While wh-complements and "that"-complements uniformly have as their semantic values (their *sense* in G&S's vocabulary) functions from possible worlds to propositions, the latter have as semantic values constant functions from possible worlds to propositions. For every world as argument, they yield the same proposition as value (as *denotation* in G&S's vocabulary). So the intuition that there are differences between questions and declaratives is preserved. Though both questions and declaratives denote what we have been calling question-meanings, the semantic flexibility allowed by the question-meaning is only exploited by questions.

The index-dependent semantic values G&S introduce serve multiple purposes. First, they account for the fact that verbs such as "know", "tell", and "ask" have a univocal meaning, whether they occur with "that" complements or embedded questions. Second, it yields a straightforward solution to the problem of accounting for the distinction between extensional and intentional question-embedding verbs. As they write:

Verbs such as "know" and "tell" operate on the denotations of their complements, i.e. on propositions, and not on their sense, i.e. propositional concepts. The extensionality of these verbs will be accounted for by a meaning postulate which reduces intensional relations between individual concepts and propositional concepts to corresponding extensional relations between individuals and propositions.

However, there are also complement embedding verbs which do create truly intensional contexts. In terms of Karttunen's classification, inquisitive verbs ("ask", "wonder"), verbs of conjecture ("guess", "estimate"), opinion verbs ("be certain about"), verbs of relevance ("matter", "care") and verbs of dependency ("depend on") count as such. (1982: 178)

G&S's idea is as follows. In the first instance, any question-embedding verb relates a person to a function from indices to propositions. But if the verb is an extensional question-embedding verb, such as "know", then the person stands in that relation at a world to that function from indices to propositions if and only if they stand in that relation to its denotation at that world. It is a fact about extensional question-embedding verbs, accounted for by a meaning postulate, that they ultimately relate persons and the extensions of the arguments of those verbs, rather than the arguments of the verbs themselves.

To understand G&S's treatment of extensional question-embedding verbs, it is useful to recall Montague's treatment of a famous puzzle, due to Barbara Partee. Partee called Montague's attention to sentences like "The temperature rises", and pointed out that one would not want to license the inference from the premises *the temperature is ninety* and *the temperature rises* to the conclusion that *ninety rises*. Montague's solution to the puzzle, discussed in (Montague 1974a, see especially 267–8), is as follows.[10] Montague proposes to treat all predicates as true of *individual concepts* – functions from points of evaluation (such as times and worlds) to objects. So "is 90", "rises", "is warm", etc. are all predicates that are in the first instance true of individual concepts. This treatment of predication allows for predicates such as "rises" to be true of individual concepts – an individual concept (in this case a function from times to temperatures) rises if and only if its extension over time increases – that is, the temperatures it yields as values for times as arguments increase. Montague *generalizes to the worst case* – he treats all predicates as true in the first instance of individual concepts. This yields a smooth account of a predicate such as "rise" – it is true at a point of evaluation of an individual concept in virtue of facts about that individual concept, rather than facts about its extension at that point of evaluation. But then Montague needs something additional to treat predicates that hold of an individual concept at a point of evaluation in virtue of holding of the extension of that individual concept at that point of evaluation. In other words, Montague needs an additional component in his semantic theory to treat *extensional* predicates, which are in fact the majority of predicates.

Most predicates, including "is 90" (and "is warm"), are true relative to a point of evaluation (a time, a world, or a world–time pair) of the *extensions* of individual concepts at those points of evaluation, rather than individual concepts themselves. A sentence such as "The temperature is warm" is true at a world w and a time t in virtue of the warmth of the *extension* of the phrase "the temperature" at w and t – which is a particular temperature – and not the individual concept it denotes (which is a function from world–time pairs to temperatures). To account for extensional predicates, Montague adds a stipulation on interpretations. The stipulation states that, for all extensional predicates P (in short, for all but predicates such as "rise"), P is true of an individual concept at a point of evaluation if and only if P is true of the extension of that individual concept at that point of evaluation (see clause (3) of Montague 1974a: 263). These restrictions on interpretations, following Carnap (1952), are generally called *meaning postulates*.

G&S's method of treating extensional and intensional question-embedding verbs is precisely parallel to Montague's treatment of extensional and intensional predicates. All verbs that take embedded questions as syntactic arguments take as semantic arguments *intensions of sentences*, which are on G&S's framework functions from indices (points of

---

[10] See also Appendix 3 of Dowty et al. (1981) for a helpful discussion of Montague's strategy.

evaluation) to propositions. However, all extensional question-embedding verbs are governed by a single meaning postulate. Just as in the case of Montague's treatment of extensional predicates, the meaning postulate states that an extensional question-embedding verb relates, at a point of evaluation p, a person to a question-meaning if and only if that relation holds between that person and the extension of that question-meaning, relative to the point of evaluation p. So for ⌜knows wh-Φ⌝, the meaning postulate would state that for all worlds w, x knows Φ at w if and only if x knows that p, where p is the value of Φ as applied to the world w. If Φ is an embedded question, like "who was at the dinner party", then p will be the complete true answer to that question at w. If Φ is a that-complement, such as "that Obama is a Democrat", p will be the proposition that is the value of Φ at every world w.[11]

G&S advertise their view as one that overcomes the first problem facing Karttunen, namely that Karttunen is forced to postulate, for each verb that takes both embedded questions and "that" complements, two distinct meanings, related by a meaning postulate. But G&S overstate the differences between their view and Karttunen's. According to G&S, each question-embedding verb takes, as an argument, a question-meaning. They then have a single meaning postulate governing extensional question-embedding verbs (including "know", "tell", and "remember") that gives the conditions under which an agent bears that relation to a question-meaning at a point of evaluation, in terms of relations between agents and the extension of that question-meaning at that point of evaluation (i.e. a proposition). But one might reasonably hold that no single relation can hold between entities of different semantic types. If so, then one would think that no single relation can hold between a question-meaning and the extension of a question-meaning. Then G&S's view does after all entail that there are, for each extensional question-embedding verb V, *two* relations associated with it – one that relates agents to question-meanings, and the second that relates agents to the extensions of those question-meanings. Of course, the obtaining of the former relations is defined in terms of the obtaining of the latter relations. But that does not mean that they are the same relation. If this line of reasoning is correct, then *both* G&S's theory and Karttunen's theory posit two knowledge relations, two telling relations, two remembering relations, etc.

The moral may very well be that there is no way of avoiding postulating two very similar relations to account for embedded questions. But there may still be an overall

---

[11]   To forestall a potential confusion: someone knows whether John went to the party at w in virtue of standing in a relation to the true answer to the question of whether John went to the party at w. But this does not mean that the structured proposition expressed by "x knows whether John went to the party" contains, as a constituent, the true answer to the question of whether John went to the party. The semantic value of "whether John went to the party" is the same in extensional complement-embedding verbs such as "know" as it is in intensional complement-embedding verbs such as "wonder". It is a question-meaning, a function from worlds to propositions. It is just that what it is to bear the knowledge relation to that function at an index (world) is to bear it to its value at that world. Thus, I can say "Bill knows whether John went to the party" without myself knowing the answer to the question of whether John went to the party, because in so saying it I am attributing to Bill a relation to a question-meaning.

theoretical advantage to G&S's theory over Karttunen's theory. G&S's theory involves one meaning postulate that governs all extensional question-embedding verbs, whereas Karttunen's involves one meaning postulate for each verb. But this is a considerably more subtle theoretical issue than G&S make it out to be. It is certainly not obviously the case that G&S successfully evade postulating two different relations for each extensional question-embedding verb (of course, as Montague recognized, the same issue arises in the case of his use of meaning postulates).

As soon as we turn to intensional question-embedding verbs, however, we can see that G&S's theory does yield a quite satisfying explanation of the distinction between extensional and intensional question-embedding verbs. In the case of extensional question-embedding verbs, there is a meaning postulate stating the truth-conditions at a point of evaluation in terms of relations between an agent and extensions at that point of evaluation. One knows who went to the party at a world w in virtue of knowing that the proposition that truly and completely answers that question at world w. But in the case of intensional question-embedding verbs, such as "wonder" and "ask", there is no such meaning postulate. One wonders who went to the party at world w in virtue of standing in the wondering relation to the question-meaning denoted by "who went to the party", full stop. Intuitively, this is the right result. If $X_1 \ldots X_n$ were all and only the partygoers at world w, then question-meaning denoted by "Who went to the party" takes w to the proposition that $X_1 \ldots X_n$ went to the party. When at a point of evaluation one wonders who went to the party, one is wondering what the value of the question-meaning that is the object of the wondering relation is, at that point of evaluation. This is an elegant account of intensional question-embedding relations, and in general, a persuasive account of the difference between verbs like "wonder" and "ask", on the one hand, and verbs like "know" and "tell", on the other.

So far, we have seen the outlines of G&S's account of questions, both free and embedded. G&S take both questions and declarative sentences to have as semantic values question-meanings, functions from points of evaluation to propositions. This explains why one and the same verb can take both "that" complements and embedded questions. As G&S emphasize, it also explains the fact that one can smoothly conjoin embedded questions and "that" complements, as in the examples:

(15)   John knows that Peter has left for Paris, and also whether Mary has followed him.
(16)   Alex told Susan that someone was waiting for her, but not who it was.

Let us now turn to the details of G&S's theory.

We begin with the simplest case, which are "whether" questions such as the embedded question "whether Hannah was at the party" in:

(17)   John knows whether Hannah was at the party.

According to G&S, "whether Hannah was at the party" denotes a function that takes a point of evaluation ("index" in G&S's terms) at which it is true that Mary walks, and yields as value the proposition that Mary walks, and takes a point of evaluation at which it is false that Mary walks and yields the proposition that it is not the case that Mary walks. Here is a slightly more complicated way to state the same semantic value (the additional complexity is necessary to see the generality of G&S's treatment). Let's suppose that our points of evaluation are possible worlds. Another way of saying this is that "whether Mary walks" denotes a function from possible worlds to propositions, such that given a possible world w, the proposition p that is the value of this function at w holds true at an arbitrary possible world w′ iff the truth-value of "Mary walks" at w′ is the same as at w. So suppose that Mary walks at world w. Then the semantic value of "whether Mary walks" will take w as an input, and yield a proposition that is true at a world w′ if and only if the truth-value of "Mary walks" is the same as it is at w, i.e. if and only if Mary walks at w′ (*mutatis mutandis* if Mary doesn't walk at w). More formally, taking sentences to be names of truth-values, the semantic value (G&S's "sense") of "whether Mary walks" is:

[Whether Mary walks] = $\lambda a \lambda i$[walks (a)(Mary) = walks (i)(Mary)]

When you *know* whether John went to the party at a world w, you are in a relation ultimately with the proposition that [whether John went to the party] denotes at w. But when you *wonder* whether John went to the party a world w, you are in a relation ultimately with the 'sense' of 'whether John went to the party', which is a function from worlds to propositions. This is extremely intuitive, because when you wonder whether John went to the party at a world w, what you are wondering is what the answer to the question 'whether John went to the party' is – i.e. you are wondering what the G&S semantic value for 'whether John went to the party' yields at w.

Let us now turn to alternative "whether" complements. (18) is ambiguous, but its natural reading is as an alternative whether-question (a "whether" report, in the vocabulary of David Lewis's prescient 1982 paper).

(18) John knows whether Bill came to the party or Sue came to the party.

According to the natural reading of (18), what is being said is that John knows which of two alternatives obtains: that Bill came to the party, or that Sue came to the party (the less natural reading is that what is being said is that John knows the truth-value of a certain disjunction). According to G&S (1982: 180), "At an index i, *whether Φ or Ψ* denotes that proposition p that holds at an index k iff the truth-values of both Φ and Ψ at k are the same as at i." So suppose that at i, Bill came to the party and Sue did not come to the party. Then (18) is true at i if and only if John knows at i the proposition that is the extension of the sense of "whether Φ or Ψ" at i, namely the proposition that Bill came to the party and Sue did not come to the party. More formally, the semantic content, or sense (in G&S's terms) of "whether Bill came to the party or Sue came to the party" is given in (19):

(19): $\lambda a\lambda i$[Bill came to the party(a) = Bill came to the party(i) & Sue came to the party(a) = Sue came to the party(i)]

(Note that it is a consequence of this definition that if neither Bill nor Sue came to the party at world w, then someone knows whether Bill came to the party or Sue came to party at w if and only if she knows at w that neither Bill nor Sue came to the party.)

Understanding the semantics for wh-complements generally is straightforward, but their compositional derivation is a bit more complex. Consider the question "wh walks". Relative to a point of evaluation i, the sense of "who walks" denotes that proposition p which holds true at a point of evaluation k if and only if the extension of "walk" at k is the same as its extension at i. We may also assume that the distinction between the distinct wh-phrases "who", "what", "where", "how", etc. is that they introduce distinct common noun meanings into the semantics. A word such as "who" introduces the property of being a person; "what" introduces the property of being inanimate, "where" introduces the property of being a place, etc. (equivalently, one can understand each wh-phrase as introducing a lambda-abstract corresponding to distinct ranges of quantification). The semantic content of "who walks" is then given more formally in (20):

(20) $\lambda i\lambda k[\lambda x[person(i)(x) \& walks(i)(x)] = \lambda x[person(k)(x) \& walks(k)(x)]]$

Let us now see how this semantics derives strong exhaustivity. Suppose at world w that John knows, of each person who walks, that she walks, but falsely believes that Susan walks. At world w, does John stand in the knowledge relation to (20)?

Recall the familiar characterization of belief in the possible worlds framework:

A belief state may be represented by a set of possibilities – the possibilities that are not excluded by the agent's conception of the way things are. The set of propositions believed, relative to a belief state, is the set of propositions that are true in all of those possibilities. (Stalnaker 1999: 153)

John believes that Susan walks. Therefore, Susan walks in every world in his belief state, though she is not a walker at w. If John stands in the knowledge relation to (20) at world w, then he believes the proposition $\lambda k[\lambda x[person(w)(x) \& walks(w)(x)] = \lambda x$ $[person(k)(x) \& walks(k)(x)]]$, i.e. a proposition true in a world if and only if the walkers at the world are exactly the walkers in world w. But this proposition is true in none of the worlds in his belief state, since Susan walks in all of the worlds in his belief state, and she does not walk at w. So G&S's semantics entails strong exhaustivity.

G&S's treatment of embedded questions also does not entail that for all x, x knows who walks if and only if x knows who doesn't walk. The denotation of "who walks" is (21), and the denotation of "who doesn't walk" is (22):

(21) $\lambda i\lambda k[\lambda x[person(i)(x) \& walks(i)(x)] = \lambda x[person(k)(x) \& walks(k)(x)]]$

Knowing (21) does not entail that one knows (22):

(22) $\lambda i\lambda k[\lambda x[person(i)(x) \& \sim walks(i)(x)] = \lambda x[person(k)(x) \& \sim walks(k)(x)]]$

Consider a possible world k in which the walkers at i are the same as the walkers at k, but there are more non-walkers at k than there are at i, because the domain of objects at k is larger.[12] In the presence of such a world, knowing (21) does not entail knowing (22).

So, G&S are able to accommodate the intuitions surrounding strong exhaustiveness. G&S also introduce an important distinction between different readings of questions. They point out that a sentence such as (23) is ambiguous:

(23)   John knows which student is late.

On one reading of (23), which they call the *de dicto* reading of (23), it requires John to know, of every individual which is in fact a student and is late, that that individual is a student and is late. It is not enough, on this reading, for John to know of every individual which is in fact a student and is late, that they are late. He must also know that they are students. On another reading of (23), which they call the *de re* reading of (23), it requires John only to know, of every individual which is in fact a student and is late, that that individual is late. John need not know that that individual is a student.

G&S represent the distinction between the *de dicto* and the *de re* reading of "which student is late" as (24) and (25), respectively:

(24) $\lambda i \lambda k[\lambda x[\text{student}(i)(x) \ \& \ \text{late}(i)(x)] = \lambda x[\text{student}(k)(x) \ \& \ \text{late}(k)(x)]]$

(25) $\lambda i \lambda k[\lambda x[\text{student}(i)(x) \ \& \ \text{late}(i)(x)] = \lambda x[\text{student}(i)(x) \ \& \ \text{late}(k)(x)]]$

In order to know (24) at a world w, one needs to know a proposition that is true at a world w′ if and only if the things that are students and late at w are the things that are students and late at w′. Thus, in order to know which students are late, on the *de dicto* reading, one needs to know of every individual who is a student and is late, not only the individual is late, but that the individual is a student. In contrast, knowing (25) at a world w requires less of one. To know (25) at a world w, it suffices to know a proposition true at a world w′ if and only if the late individuals at w′ that are among the students at w are the same as the late things at w that are students at w. Knowing this latter requires only being able to distinguish, among the things that are in fact the late students at w, the ones that are late from the ones that are not late.

A final element to the analysis of questions involves their *context-sensitivity*. Consider a question such as "Who is tired?" Rarely will this question be asked with the desire of finding out a list of all the people in the universe who are tired. Rather, what is sought is a list of people who are tired, in the contextually salient domain. This phenomenon is just like what we encounter with quantificational noun phrases. Rarely is an assertion of "Everyone is tired" made, when what is meant is that everyone in the universe is tired. What is meant rather is that everyone in the contextually salient domain is tired.

---

[12] For ease of exposition, G&S (1982: 181) choose not to consider cases in which the domains vary across worlds, so the relevant inference turns out to be valid because of this formal simplification. But it is not valid *tout court* (see the discussion of exhaustiveness and the inference from "?xPx" to "?x~Px" in Groenendijk and Stokfof (1997: 1109–10)).

The same resources that account for domain restriction with quantificational noun phrases also account for the context-sensitivity of "which" questions, such as "which students are tired?" Stanley and Szabo (2000) argue that context-sensitivity of quantificational noun phrases is due to the fact that each common noun is associated with a quantificational domain. It follows from this hypothesis that the head noun in a question like "Which students are tired?" is also associated with a quantificational domain. In short, the account of quantificational domain restriction in Stanley and Szabo (2000) straightforwardly entails the context-sensitivity we find in "which" questions.

But what about questions that do not appear to contain nouns, such as "Who is tired"? As we have seen, it is natural to construe the semantic content of "who" as expressing the same thing as "which person", and it is natural to construe "what" as semantically expressing the same thing as "which thing", etc. (in subsequent chapters, we will see cross-linguistic evidence for this hypothesis). So, questions such as "Who is tired?" are in fact decomposable into a question word "which" and a common noun meaning, and the latter is associated with a domain property, just as in Stanley and Szabo (2000).

As we have seen, questions are ambiguous between *de re* and *de dicto* readings, depending upon whether the relevant common noun is indexed to the actual world, as in (25), or the world of evaluation, as in (24). We should expect similar ambiguities with the quantifier domain property. Suppose I ask the question, "who walks" where the domain is the students at Edward Smith. Abstracting from the complexities of the structure of the quantificational domain, we may represent the result of intersecting the domain with the common-noun meaning *person* with the single variable, "F". Then the *de re* reading of "Who walks", relative to the envisaged context, is:

(26) $\lambda i \lambda k [\lambda x [\text{Student at Edward Smith (i)(x) & walks(i)(x)}] = \lambda x [\text{Student at Edward Smith(i)(x) & walks(k)(x)}]]$

What I know, when I know (26) at a world w, is a proposition true at a world w′ if and only if, among the actual students at Edward Smith, the walkers are the same in w and w′.[13]

So far, I have explained G&S's view of the semantic content of the question "who walks". That question is particularly simple, but it provides a model for all others, including all the embedded questions in (1). As James Higginbotham writes:

it should be noted that many wh-forms incorporate prepositions or subordinating conjunctions, as "where" incorporates "at", and is effectively equivalent to "at which place", and "why" incorporates either "because" or "in order to". (1993: 201)

So, the G&S denotation for the question that is embedded in (1b) "Why did Obama win?" derives from an underlying representation like "?Obama won for reason x".

---

[13] Giving a *de re* reading of the domain property answers the worry in Higginbotham (1993: 199–200), that we do not ordinarily take "John isn't a student at Edward Smith" to be a partial answer to "Who walks" in the envisaged context. In contexts in which we do take it to be a partial answer to "Who walks", the question is therefore *de dicto*.

More formally, and abstracting from context-dependence, "Why did Obama win?" has as its intension (assuming "because" is a relation between propositions and reasons:

(27) $\lambda i\lambda k[\lambda x[\text{Reason}(x) \,\&\, \text{Because}(i) \,(\text{Obama won }(x)] = \lambda x[\text{Reason}(x) \,\text{Because}(k) (\text{Obama won}, x)]]$

Someone knows why Obama won at a world w if and only if they know a proposition that is true at a world w′ if and only if the reasons Obama won w′ are the same as the reasons that Obama won in w.

The account is the same for a question such as "How is Obama governing?" Just as the question word "why" ranges over reasons, the question word "how" ranges over *ways*. Ways are properties of actions, which are certain kinds of events. Just as "where" means "at which place", "how" means "in what way". In short, the word "how" ranges over the meaning of *adverbs*. Since the work of Donald Davidson, it has been widely thought that a proper treatment of adverbial modification requires event quantification. "Obama governs wisely" would be represented in such a framework as:

(28) $\forall e(\text{Governing}(e) \,\&\, \text{Agent}(\text{Obama}, e) \rightarrow \text{Wisely }(e))$

Let us suppose that such a framework is adequate for the representation of manner adverbials. Where "w" is a variable over ways, the G&S semantic value for "How is Obama governing?" is the (somewhat cumbersome):

(28) $\lambda i\lambda k[\lambda w[\text{Way}(w) \,\&\, \forall e[(\text{Governing}(k)(e) \,\&\, \text{Agent}(k) \,(\text{Obama}, e)) \rightarrow w(k)(e)]]]$
= $\lambda w[\text{Way}(w) \,\&\, \forall e[(\text{Governing}(i)(e) \,\&\, \text{Agent}(i)(\text{Obama}, e)) \rightarrow w(i)(e)]]].$

More understandably – relative to a possible world w (assuming possible worlds as the only points of evaluation), this semantic value yields a proposition that is true at a world w′ if and only if the ways in which Obama governs at w′ are the same as the ways in which Obama governs at w.[14] Someone stands in the knowledge relation to this entity at a world w if and only if they know at w the proposition that is true at a world w′ if and only if the ways in which Obama governs at w′ are the same as the ways in which Obama governs at w.

We have now seen G&S's suggested semantic content for questions. But we have yet to see how they derive the semantic content of a question from the meanings of its parts. It is worthwhile going through this in detail, as I will exploit the discussion in subsequent chapters (I will make minor modifications for the sake of perspicuity, with comment).

Consider again a question, such as "who walks". Prescinding from context-dependence, the semantic content of this question is as in (20):

(20) $\lambda i\lambda k[\lambda x[\text{person}(i)(x) \,\&\, \text{walks}(i)(x)] = \lambda x[\text{person}(k)(x) \,\&\, \text{walks}(k)(x)]]$

---

[14] I am assuming that ways are properties of events that, like other properties, have different extensions relative to different points of evaluation. Nothing hangs on this assumption.

Here is how they derive this semantic content (for the analysis tree, see G&S 1982: 195). First, the open sentence $\ulcorner$x walks$\urcorner$ is taken to contain a world-variable "a", so its semantic content is $walk(a)(x)$. The question word "who" is taken to contribute to the logical form of the sentence a lambda-abstract that binds the variable "x", as well as providing a common noun meaning *person*, resulting in $\lambda x[person(a)(x)\ \&\ walks(a)(x)]$.[15] Then a type-shift occurs – in short, a shift in the semantic type from a *property* to a *proposition* (relative to an assignment of a world to the world-variable "a"). This type-shift turns $\lambda x[person(a)(x)\ \&\ walks(a)(x)]$ into $\lambda k[\lambda x[person(a)(x)\ \&\ walks(a)(x)] = \lambda x[person(k)(x)\ \&\ walks(k)(x)]]$. If one lambda-abstracts over the world-variable "a", the result is (20).

There are two important features of this derivation. The first is that the question word "who" is really on this treatment a lambda-abstract binding an already present variable, and a common noun meaning *person*. Second, the shift from a property semantic value to a proposition-level semantic value is not induced by any expression in the sentence, but by the construction itself.

The theory in G&S (1982) is a theory solely of the so-called "mention-all" readings of questions. Unlike the case of Karttunen's semantics, where there was an obvious modification to represent mention-some readings of questions, there is no obvious way to adjust the semantics I have sketched to allow for mention-some readings, as in the natural reading of Hintikka's examples (6)–(8):

(6)   John knows where to buy gas for the car.
(7)   John knows who to look for to collect his passport.
(8)   Mary remembers where to go in order to get license.

Since the constructions that concern us – attributions of the form "John knows how to swim" – are, like (6)–(8), examples of embedded questions with infinitive complements, they too are most naturally read with the mention-some reading. I will delay introducing until Chapter 5 a semantics that delivers mention-some readings within a framework similar to G&S's framework, where I develop the theory of knowing how to Φ first outlined in Stanley and Williamson (2001).

We have now looked at two of the orthodox theories of embedded questions – Karttunen and Groenendijk and Stokhof. Subsequent work on embedded questions has been mostly devoted to evaluating the relative merits of these two theories, or more specifically, the relative merits of treating questions as denoting sets of propositions, versus functions from possible worlds to complete answers. Thanks to the work of Irene Heim (1994) and Beck and Rullmann (1999), it has emerged that Karttunen denotations are more fine-grained than G&S denotations – one can use Karttunen's denotations to characterize G&S denotations, but not vice-versa (though of course to achieve the same empirical coverage of G&S one must modify Karttunen's original

---

[15]   G&S do not represent the lambda-abstract contributed by the question word in the logical form of the sentence itself, choosing instead to place it in the intermediate translation language. Ignore that.

semantics in the ways proposed in Heim 1994). The debate over the relative merit of the approaches thus concerns whether there are constructions that require the more fine-grained denotations.

For our purposes, however, these debates are not important. Though the jury is still out on which approach is to be preferred (or even whether they are in the end equivalent), nothing I will argue depends upon choosing between these frameworks. I will, for the sake of perspicuity, present my arguments using the framework of Groenendijk and Stokhof. Given that Karttunen denotations can be used to define Groenendijk and Stokhof denotations, I could just as easily have employed Karttunen's question denotations to present my favored view. From the perspective of this book, disputes between advocates of these frameworks are irrelevant. On either account, to know wh is to have propositional knowledge.

However, some have mounted foundational challenges to frameworks such as Hamblin (1973), Karttunen (1977), Higginbotham and May (1981), and Groenendijk and Stokhof (1982). In the rest of this chapter, I turn to two such challenges. The first, less extreme challenge is due to Jonathan Schaffer. Schaffer argues that knowing-wh is in fact a three-place relation, between propositions and *questions under discussion*. Schaffer's important challenge does not threaten the main theses of this book, since Schaffer also holds that ascriptions of the form ⌜X knows that p⌝ also ascribe three-place relations between persons, propositions, and questions under discussion. So Schaffer accepts the view that the verb "know" ascribes the same relation in the sentences in (1), and in ascriptions such as ⌜X knows that p⌝. A more worrisome challenge arises in a series of papers by Jonathan Ginzburg (1995a, b, 1996). In this work, Ginzburg seeks to show that the whole tradition of analyzing the meaning of embedded questions in terms of operations on propositions is mistaken. In Ginzburg (forthcoming), he bases his arguments that knowing how to do something is not a species of propositional knowledge on these arguments. So it is quite important for our purposes to ensure that his challenge to the orthodox frameworks does not succeed.

There is a further reason to discuss Schaffer and Ginzburg's challenges together. Both of them result from a failure to appreciate the ubiquitous effects of quantifier domain restriction on semantic content. Discussing their challenges in detail helps me to extend the argument I have mounted elsewhere that many kinds of apparently disparate forms of context-sensitivity are due to one uniform source, the context-sensitivity associated with nominals (Stanley 2002).

3.

Jonathan Schaffer (2007) has recently inveighed against what he calls the "received view" of knowing-wh, according to which the ascriptions in (1) express relations between persons and propositions. Schaffer argues that certain phenomena drive us towards including a *question* as a third argument of the relation expressed by occurrences of "know" in sentences such as the ones in (1). He then concludes, via the same uniformity considerations that move G&S, that ascriptions of the form ⌜X knows that p⌝ also express three-place relations between a person, a proposition, and a contextually implicit question. Schaffer's goal is to show that there are considerations that derive from giving a satisfactory account of the semantics of ascriptions of knowledge-wh that have consequences for the semantics of ascriptions of the form ⌜X knows that p⌝.

Schaffer's argument against the received view proceeds from what he calls "The Problem of Convergent Knowledge". The problem as he presents it is this. There are certain question pairs that have the same true answer. Yet intuitively standing in the knowledge relation to one question in the pair is a different state than standing in the knowledge relation to another question in the pair. Schaffer's solution to the problem is to include the question as a further argument in the knowledge relation. Then, one can account for the intuitive difference, because the knowledge relation relates persons not just to true answers, but also to the questions that they answer. Via the uniformity of knowledge-wh and knowledge-that, Schaffer concludes that knowledge-that also expresses a relation between a person, a true answer, and a question.

Here is the first of Schaffer's examples of The Problem of Convergent Knowledge. Suppose that George Bush is on television and only George Bush is on television, and Ezra is watching him on television. Consider the following knowledge ascriptions:

(29)   Ezra knows whether George Bush or Janet Jackson is on television.
(30)   Ezra knows whether George Bush or Will Ferrell is on television.

Will Ferrell is a clever George Bush impersonator. Janet Jackson is not. It is easy to imagine us assenting to (29), but not to (30). Certainly, Schaffer is right that they do not intuitively have the same truth-conditions. Yet, according to Schaffer, both the question "whether George Bush or Janet Jackson is on television" and "whether George Bush or Will Ferrell is on television" have the same true answer, namely that that is Bush on television. According to Schaffer, orthodoxy says that both (29) is true at a world w if and only if Ezra knows the true answer to "whether George Bush or Janet Jackson is on television", and (30) is true at a world w if and only if Ezra knows the true answer to "whether George Bush or Will Ferrell on television." Since both of these questions have the same true answer, orthodoxy predicts, contra intuition, that (29) and (30) have the same truth-conditions.

Here is an example of the Problem of Convergent Knowledge with wh-phrases other than "whether". Consider:

(31)   Ezra knows who is on television.

Suppose again that there are two contextually salient situations. In the first, the options are George Bush or Janet Jackson. In the second, the options are George Bush or Will Ferrell. Again, it seems right that whether (31) is true is a context-sensitive matter. Ezra will have a much easier time acquiring the relevant knowledge relative to the first kind of context than the second. The problem of convergent knowledge, if it refutes the orthodoxy on "whether" questions, also refutes orthodoxy for other kinds of questions.

Does the Problem of Convergent Knowledge arise for orthodox theories of embedded questions? Let us begin with the first version of the problem of convergent knowledge, which concerned the questions "Whether George Bush or Janet Jackson is on television?" and "Whether George Bush or Will Ferrell is on television?" The G&S denotation for these questions is (32) and (33), respectively:

(32) $\lambda a\lambda i$[George Bush is on television(a) = George Bush on television (i) & Janet Jackson on television (a) = Janet Jackson on television(i)]

(33) $\lambda a\lambda i$[George Bush is on television(a) = George Bush is on television (i) & Will Ferrell is on television (a) = Will Ferrell is on television(i)]

Suppose that at w George Bush is on television, rather than either Janet Jackson or Will Ferrell. According to G&S's view, Ezra knows at world w whether George Bush is on television or Janet Jackson is on television if and only if he knows at w a proposition that is true at a world w' if and only if George Bush is on television at w' and Janet Jackson is not on television at w'. According to G&S's view, Ezra knows at world w whether George Bush is on television and not Will Ferrell if and only he knows at w a proposition that is true at a world w' if and only if George Bush is on television at w' and Will Ferrell is not on television at w'.

Does G&S's theory face The Problem of Convergent Knowledge? It clearly does not. The proposition *George Bush is on television and Janet Jackson is not* is clearly a different proposition than the proposition *George Bush is on television and Will Ferrell is not*. G&S do not face Schaffer's Problem of Convergent Knowledge.

What about the Problem of Convergent Knowledge for other kinds of knowing-wh? Do they arise for G&S? As we saw in the previous section, straightforward assumptions from the literature on quantifier domain restriction entail that questions too are context-sensitive. I also provided a specific account of how to incorporate context-sensitivity into questions. This account predicts that (31) expresses different propositions, relative to different contexts. Relative to a context in which George Bush and Janet Jackson constitute the domain, the semantic content of "who is on television" is:

(34) $\lambda i\lambda k$[λx[(x = George Bush or x = Janet Jackson) & is on television (i)(x)] = λx [(x = George Bush or x = Janet Jackson) & is on television (k)(x)]]

Relative to a context in which George Bush and Will Ferrell constitute the domain, the semantic content of "who is on television" is:

(35) $\lambda i\lambda k$[λx[(x = George Bush or x = Will Ferrell) & is on television (i)(x)] = λx[(x = George Bush or x = Will Ferrell) & is on television (k)(x)]]

Ezra knows (34) at a world w at which George Bush is the one on television if and only if Ezra knows a proposition that is true at a world w' if and only if among the things that are either George Bush or Janet Jackson, only George Bush is on television at w'. Ezra knows (35) at a world w at which George Bush is the one on television if and only if Ezra knows a proposition that is true at a world w' if and only if among the things that are either George Bush or Will Ferrell, only George Bush is on television w'. These are clearly distinct propositions. The independently motivated account of the context-sensitivity of questions rescues G&S's classic theory of questions from the Problem of Convergent Knowledge.

One might think that one could reconstruct something such as the Problem of Convergent Knowledge for G&S in the following manner (Schaffer 2009: 493–4). According to G&S's account of the semantics of alternative "whether" complements such as (29) and (30), someone knows whether p or q at a world at which p is true and q is false only if that person knows at w that p is true and q is false. Suppose that, as many epistemologists hold, if one knows that $p_1 \ldots p_n$, and performs a competent deduction of q from $p_1 \ldots p_n$ while retaining one's knowledge that $p_1 \ldots p_n$ throughout, one thereby comes to know that q (this is the principle Timothy Williamson (2000: 117 calls "intuitive closure"). Then if one knows that p & ~q, one can thereby come to know p by deduction. If r is a proposition that is obviously incompatible with p, then by one more application of intuitive closure one can thereby come to know that p & ~r. One might worry that this will reinstate the Problem of Convergent Knowledge for G&S's semantics of alternative "whether" complements. Let p be the proposition that is George Bush on television, q be the proposition that is Janet Jackson on television, and r be the proposition that is Will Ferrell on television. The worry is that knowing that that is George Bush on television and that is not Janet Jackson on television entails, via intuitive closure, that one knows that that is George Bush on television and not Will Ferrell.

However, recall that Schaffer's purpose with the Problem of Convergent Knowledge was to show us that there was some *novel* argument for contextualism about ascriptions of knowledge-that that comes from considering knowledge-wh. That is, the Problem of Convergent Knowledge was supposed to be some novel problem that undermined orthodox semantic theories for embedded questions, such as that of G&S, thereby providing us with a *novel* argument for contextualism about ascriptions of knowledge-that. If one wishes to reconstitute the problem of convergent knowledge in this way, one is just the appealing to the *familiar* argument for contextualism via Epistemic Closure principles, which has been employed by all contextualists about knowledge ascriptions, since Gail Stine's classic article (1976). In short, this route to re-establishing the problem of convergent knowledge has nothing to do specifically with knowledge-wh. This is just the age-old problem of simultaneously preserving (a) intuitively compelling epistemic closure principles (b) the judgment that, when we look at George Bush, we know that we are looking at George Bush, and (c) the judgment that we do not know that we are looking at George Bush and not a clever George Bush impersonator (i.e. Will Ferrell). This is the problem of skepticism. Contextualism about ascriptions of knowledge-that is one purported solution, but there are of course many others (including rejecting some of (a)–(c)). Plugging any such solution to the traditional skeptical problem for knowledge into G&S's theory of embedded questions will evade this way of reintroducing the problem of convergent knowledge.

Schaffer is right that ascriptions of knowing-wh involve context-sensitivity. But he is wrong that this context-sensitivity teaches us something novel about knowledge ascriptions. The context-sensitivity associated with knowing-wh is the familiar context-sensitivity associated with quantifier domain restriction generally. Its presence reassures us that standard theories of quantifier domain restriction are on the right track, and not that standard theories of the meanings of questions are not.

4.

In a series of papers and books, Jonathan Ginzburg has argued against approaches such as those of Karttunen and Groenendijk and Stokhof, which he, along with others, calls "alternativist". Ginzburg gives several kinds of arguments against these approaches. One kind of argument appeals to "substitution arguments", of the sort that have also been exploited in the philosophy and semantics literature to show that certain verbs that are usually taken to have propositional complements instead have complements of another kind. A second kind of argument involves putative problems for these approaches arising from a lack of knowledge of the domain of the question. The third kind of argument is based on the context-sensitivity of questions. I will focus on the presentation of these arguments in Ginzburg (1996) and Ginzburg (forthcoming), though they also appear in other work (Ginzburg 1995a, b).

The first set of considerations has to do with what Ginzburg (forthcoming) calls "pure referentiality" tests. Ginzburg argues that "who left yesterday" cannot denote the same thing as "the question who left yesterday", because both substitutivity and existential generalization fail, as exemplified by the pattern below (from Ginzburg forthcoming):

Substitutivity:
  Jean discovered/revealed an interesting question.
  The question was who left yesterday.
  It does not follow that: Jean discovered/revealed who left yesterday.

Existential Generalization:
  Jean discovered/knows who left yesterday.
  It does not follow that: there is a question/issue that Jean discovered/knows.

Ginzburg (forthcoming) concludes that, contra Karttunen, "none of the typically epistemic predicates such as 'know', 'discover', 'forget', 'learn', 'teach' predicate directly of questions."

As Ginzburg recognizes, these kinds of substitution arguments are familiar from the literature on propositional attitude verbs, where they have been employed to argue that "that" clauses do not designate propositions. For many verbs that are widely taken to express relations between persons and propositions, "that" clauses and expressions such as "the proposition that p" also fail both Substitutivity and Existential Generalization:

Substitutivity:
   Jean heard/feared that Bill left his wallet.
   It does not follow that Jean heard/feared the proposition that Bill left his wallet.

Existential Generalization:
   Jean heard/feared that Bill left his wallet.
   It does not follow that there is a proposition that Jean heard/feared.

Some theorists have certainly taken this data to provide evidence against the view that such verbs are best analyzed as relations to propositions (e.g. Bach 1997; Moltmann, 2003).

I believe that there is a correct response to these arguments in the case of "that" complements, which one could use to respond to Ginzburg's use of analogous examples in the case of question-embedding verbs. The response is due to Jeffrey King (2002). Note that a "that" clause like "that p" and its semantically equivalent noun phrase equivalent, "the proposition that p", are expressions of different syntactic categories. In actuality, then, there are two verbs both pronounced "hear", and two verbs both pronounced "fear", one of which sub-categorizes for clauses, and the other of which sub-categorizes for noun phrases. There is no reason to think that the verb "fear" expresses the same relation in (36) as it does in (37):

(36)   I fear Dick Cheney.
(37)   I fear that the Republicans will win the Midterm elections.

King points out that given the natural assumption that verbs like "fear" and "hear" express different relations when noun phrases occur as complements than when clauses occur as complements, one can explain the failure of substitutivity (and existential generalization).

There is an exactly parallel point to be made against Ginzburg's use of the sub-stitutivity argument in this domain. Just as it is natural to take "fear" to express different relations in (36) and (37), it is natural to take "discover" to express different relations in (38) and (39):

(38)   John discovered a new element.
(39)   John discovered who left yesterday.

The point is even *more* obvious in the case of "know", where it is well known that the verb "know", when it takes noun phrases, expresses a different relation than the verb "know", when it takes an embedded question. It is, for example, perfectly obvious that in a sentence such as "John knows an interesting question", the verb "know" expresses a different relation than it does with "John knows who went to the party". The former relation would be expressed in German by "kennen", and the latter by "wissen". King's explanation of the failure of Substitution and Existential Generalization therefore generalizes straightforwardly to Ginzburg's examples. The reason that they fail is because of an equivocation in the relation expressed by the relevant verb.

Ginzburg's second argument is worth quoting in full:

> Consider, for example, the sentence "What is the word for 'relaxation' in Chukotian?" uttered by someone who doesn't know what language family Chukotian belongs to, let alone possible word forms in the language. Clearly, I can ask or understand this question with little or no reference to or acquaintance with *any* singular proposition which instantiates an answer. For such a context, our wonderment about the question does not seem to be plausibly modeled in alternativist terms. In other words, any even *prima facie* psychologically conceivable notion of the update of an epistemic state will not involve the constituents of the Answer-Set. (1996: 400)

According to Karttunen, the semantic value of "What is the word for 'relaxation' in Chukotian" is the set containing the singular proposition <N is the word for 'relaxation' in Chukotian>, where N is the correct word. But Ginzburg's point is that I can grasp the meaning of the question, without having any acquaintance with even a candidate singular proposition of this sort. I can wonder what the word for 'relaxation' in Chukotian is, and thereby stand in a relation to a set containing a singular proposition, without being acquainted with some of the constituents of that singular proposition.

I will not pursue the issue of whether or not this is a cogent objection to Karttunen's theory. It is clearly not a cogent objection to Groenendijk and Stokhof's theory. According to G&S, the intension of the question "What is the word for 'relaxation' in Chukotian" is a function from possible worlds to extensions, which are propositions. Just as I can grasp the intension of "is a citizen of Liechtenstein" without having acquaintance with any members of its extension, so I can grasp the intension of a question without having acquaintance with its extension. On G&S's theory, the fact that I can wonder what the word for "relaxation" is in Chukotian without having acquaintance with any words in Chukotian is no more mysterious than the fact that I can believe that Obama is not a citizen of Liechtenstein without having acquaintance with any citizens of Liechtenstein.

Ginzburg's central argument in all of his work against theories of questions that analyze them in terms of propositions concerns *context-dependence*. This example he uses exemplifies his argument form:

(40)   [Context: Jill about to step off plane in Helsinki]
         Flight attendant: Do you know where you are?
         Jill: Helsinki

(41)   [Context: Jill about to step out of taxi in Helsinki]
         Flight attendant: Do you know where you are?
         Jill: Helsinki

Ginzburg argues that theories such as Karttunen and Groenendijk and Stokhof cannot account for the fact that Jill's answer is acceptable in (40), but not acceptable in (41). In the case of both theories, Jill is in Helsinki, and so both should be acceptable answers. If theories that analyze questions in terms of propositions cannot account for the difference in acceptability between Jill's answer in (40) and Jill's answer in (41), then these theories must be rejected. In their stead, Ginzburg suggests a radically distinct theory, based on resolving goals.

Karttunen and Hamblin treat questions as sets of propositions, and G&S treat questions as functions from worlds to propositions. Is Ginzburg correct that such theories do not have the resources to treat the kind of context-sensitivity exhibited by the difference in acceptability we see in (40) and (41)? He is clearly not correct. As Lahiri writes:

> An alternative to taking such a radical departure from more traditional approaches to the semantics of questions might be to adapt Higginbotham's notion of a 'presentation' of a question. The idea is that the semantic values of questions also have defined on them a kind of object called a presentation of a question where the propositions are constructed in such a way that the restriction of the *wh*-phrase is confined to a certain class of items. The issue of good vs. bad answers relative to Ginzburg's goals is thus put into the restriction of the *wh*-phrase. Thus in Ginzburg's Helsinki example cited earlier, this would mean that we are not dealing with a semantic object that contains all propositions of the type *You are in location l* but rather a set of contextually restricted instances of locations: the context is determined by the goals of the questioner indirectly, and can be seen to be the result of a contextual restriction on the domain of 'where'. Contextual restriction of the domain of phrases (nominal, adverbial, modal, etc.) is after all well-known and is all pervasive in natural language. (2002: 58)

In fact, the solution is even more straightforward than Lahiri suggests. There is no need to appeal to a domain specific to *wh*-phrases.[16]

As we have seen above, wh-phrases like "where" semantically express the same content as "which place". I have defended at length the view in Stanley and Szabo (2000) that each nominal is associated with a domain variable (see the essays in Stanley 2007). Given this independently motivated view, it simply follows that there are domains associated with each wh-phrase, namely the domains associated with the nominals they introduce. This view straightforwardly predicts that any sentence containing a wh-phrase is context-sensitive. In particular, the question "Do you know where you are?" is context-sensitive. Relative to a context in which what is sought are answers involving cities, as in the case of someone exiting a plane, as in (40), the semantic content of this question is a set of propositions of the form $<$I am at x$>$,

---

[16] It seems that those responding to Ginzburg are uniform in the recognition that the phenomena to which he draws our attention are all the result of domain restriction. As Aloni (2002) writes, in response to Ginzburg's argument that the context-sensitivity of embedded question constructions requires one to make the semantics relative to goals and perspectives "Goals and perspectives are not parameters of the answerhood relation, but play a role in selecting a domain of quantification."

where the values of "x" are cities. Relative to a context in which what is sought are answers involving places in a city, as in the case of someone exiting a taxi in Helsinki, as in (41), the semantic content of this question is a set of propositions of the form <I am at y>, where the values of "y" are places within Helsinki. It is not *just* that all the data adduced by Ginzburg is straightforwardly predicted by standard theories of domain restriction that link domain restriction to nominals. The point is rather that if questions were not semantically context-sensitive in this way, these theories of domain restriction would therefore be refuted.[17]

It is worthwhile spelling out this point in detail. Where 'F' marks the domain associated with the common noun meaning *place*, the Groenendijk and Stokhof denotation for "where I am" is:

(42) $\lambda i \lambda k [\lambda x [\text{place} \& F(i)(x) \& \text{I am at } (i)(x)] = \lambda x [\text{place} \& F(k)(x) \& \text{walks}(k)(x)]]$

Relative to a context such as (40), the domain associated with "F" is the property of being a city. Relative to a context like (41), the domain associated with "F" is the property of being a location inside Helsinki. Therefore, the question in (40) has a distinct semantic content than the question in (41), just as "Every student is tired" has one semantic content when uttered at the start of 9 a.m. undergraduate introduction to philosophy, and another semantic content when uttered at the end of my late afternoon graduate seminar.

In Ginzburg (forthcoming), he repeats his arguments against propositional accounts of knowing-wh, and concludes that it follows from these arguments that, *contra* Stanley and Williamson (2001), knowing how to do something is not a kind of propositional knowledge. In short, Ginzburg (like virtually all linguists) accepts the need for a uniform account of knowledge-*wh*, but rejects the view that knowing how is a kind of propositional knowledge, because he rejects orthodox propositional accounts of questions. We have seen that none of Ginzburg's arguments against theories of questions that analyze them in terms of propositions are persuasive. Therefore, he has provided no persuasive argument against the view that knowing how to do something is a kind of propositional knowledge.

5.

I have argued that Schaffer and Ginzburg's challenges to standard accounts of the semantics of questions do not succeed once one incorporates the effects of domain restriction into the semantics of questions. But it is not the case that, at least given the

---

[17] Ginzburg actually considers the response that his arguments against the orthodox views of the semantics of questions are just due to domain restriction, in Ginzburg (1995a). As Lahiri (2002: 59) points out, even accepting Ginzburg's rather recherché intuitions about cases, his response depends upon "the notion that domain-fixing of quantificational elements and the fixing of the value of an implicit argument of a perspectival element are essentially different phenomena: the former semantic, and the latter pragmatic." There is a large body of literature repudiating this view. A good place to start is the essays in Stanley (2007).

resources we have so far employed, domain restriction *exhausts* the context-sensitivity of questions. That a full account of the semantics of questions requires additional resources that we have not yet introduced becomes clear when one considers questions of the form, "John knows who Bill Clinton is". Suppose we assume, *pace* Boer and Lycan (1986), that the "is" in such constructions is the "is" of identity, rather than the "is" of predication. Then the answer to the question "who Bill Clinton is" will be the singleton set containing the singular proposition, Bill Clinton = Bill Clinton. But everyone knows that Bill Clinton is Bill Clinton, whereas not everyone knows who Bill Clinton is. As Aloni (2002) emphasizes, the standard account of questions entails that interrogatives are *trivial*, in the sense that standing in the knowledge relation to them is automatic. Yet obviously, it is not a trivial matter to know who N is, for any given N.

Even if one were to adjust the semantics to overcome the problem of triviality, one must adjust it still further to account for the fact that ascriptions of the form ⌜X knows who N is⌝ are context-sensitive. If I am able to pick out Bill Clinton from a line of people, then in one context, I might be said to know who Bill Clinton is. But if I do not know that Bill Clinton was the 42nd President of the United States, then in another context, despite being able to pick out Bill Clinton from a line-up, I might not be said to know who Bill Clinton is. In subsequent chapters I will introduce the additional elements necessary to solve both of these problems, and will delay the full account of the context-sensitivity of embedded questions until Chapter 4.

3

PRO and the Representation of First-Person Thought

In the previous chapter, we looked in detail at two classical theories of the semantics of embedded questions. We therefore are now in possession of a general account of the meaning of constructions of the form ⌜X knows wh-Φ⌝ and their connection to constructions of the form ⌜X knows wh-Φ⌝. We now know that it is not accidental that so many verbs take as syntactic arguments both embedded questions, such as "who came to the party", and sentential complements, such as "that Bill came to the party". What it is to know wh-Φ at a world is to stand in the propositional knowledge relation to an answer to the relevant question at that world.

In the following chapters, we narrow our focus to a subclass of embedded question constructions in English – those involving *infinitival phrases*, such as "to hit a ball", "to ride a bicycle", "to vote in an election", etc. That is, we narrow our focus to that subclass of embedded question constructions that are exemplified by sentences such as those in (1) (suppose what is under discussion is a game of tennis):

(1) a. John knows whom to hit a ball to.
     b. John knows when to hit a ball hard.
     c. John knows where to hit a ball hard.
     d. John knows why to hit a ball hard.
     e. John knows how to hit a ball hard.

Once we put together our understanding of the structure and meaning of the infinitival phrases that play a role in sentences such as (1) with the general theories of embedded questions we have developed in the previous chapter, we will have an almost complete account of the meaning of sentences that ascribe knowledge how.

What distinguishes the sentences in (1) from other embedded question constructions is that they contain embedded questions with infinitival phrases, such as "to hit a ball hard", rather than finite phrases, such as "hits a ball hard". Such sentences differ in three ways from embedded question constructions containing finite clauses, such as "John knows how Bill hits a ball". First, they contain an unpronounced element that many linguists call "PRO" in the subject positions of the embedded clauses.[1] Second, they contain infinitives, rather than finite clauses. Third, as we have seen in the previous chapter, they are naturally interpreted with "mention-some" rather than "mention-all" readings. That is, it is enough to know where to find a good cup of coffee in New York if one knows *at least one* good coffee place in that city. One does not need to know every good coffee place in New York City. Obtaining a full understanding of what is attributed in sentences such as (1) requires an investigation of the interpretative possibilities for PRO, the interpretive possibilities of the infinitive construction, and finally, a satisfactory account of "mention-some" readings of questions. Two of the next three chapters are devoted to this task.

When reading these chapters, it is important to bear in mind that the commitments about the fine structure of infinitival embedded questions that I here incur are not required in order to defend the thesis that knowing how to do something is a kind of knowing that something is the case. As Pavese and Stanley (2011) remark, to defend the view that knowing how to do something is a kind of knowing that something is the case, it is sufficient to defend the validity of the following schema:

For every s and F, s knows how to F iff for some way w of F-ing, s knows that w is a way to F.

If this schema is valid, then knowing how to do something is a species of knowing that something is the case. No commitments about the meaning of infinitivals are needed to defend the view that knowing how to do something is a species of propositional knowledge. The commitments I adopt in this chapter and the subsequent one therefore go well beyond what is needed to defend the intellectualist thesis.

Nevertheless, my goal is not just to defend the view that knowing how to do something is a kind of propositional knowledge. It is to advance a very specific analysis of knowing how to do something. I want to argue that the analysis of knowing how to do something I develop is what is expressed by ordinary English ascriptions of knowing how. One can easily agree with the view that knowing how to do something is a kind of propositional knowledge, without agreeing with the specific account I advocate of the syntax and semantics of infinitives, or the specific account I advocate of mention-some readings of questions. One way to do so is to have different views about the interpretation of PRO and the *de se* more generally. Another way is to have another view of the proper interpretation of infinitives as they occur in embedded questions than the one I defend in this chapter. In that case, one might very well agree with the view that knowing how to do something is a species of propositional knowledge, but reject the specific analysis of

[1] Hornstein (1999) is a radical attack on the whole notion of PRO. Hornstein argues that PRO is instead the trace of Noun Phrase movement, construed in the terms of Minimalist syntactic theory. On Hornstein's view, the occurrences of PRO in (2) should be replaced by copies of the name "John" (at least on the non-PRO$_{arb}$ reading). Adoption of Hornstein's view would actually not make any difference to our purposes, since the end semantic result would be the same (that is, Hornstein's view is fully compatible with my analysis of knowing how to F). I have chosen the orthodox theory over Hornstein's because I find the criticisms of Hornstein's view in Landau (2003) to be particularly compelling.

knowing how to do something I develop. Similarly, one might adopt a different analysis of mention-some readings of questions, yet still agree with the view that knowing how to do something is a species of propositional knowledge.

This chapter is, in the first instance, an analysis of the semantic contribution of PRO, which is the unpronounced pronoun in the subject position of infinitival embedded questions. But I accept the wide-spread consensus that infinitival constructions like this are expressions of *de se* attitudes, attitudes towards oneself; this consensus is even broader than the consensus surrounding the existence of PRO. So, for the most part, this chapter is really a contribution to the literature on the nature of *de se* attitudes. Of course, a full account of the nature of *de se* attitudes would include an account of how we manage to think of ourselves, which is a topic that would require a distinct book. My purpose is the more restricted one of showing how, assuming such a full theory, one can provide a Fregean, or quasi-Fregean, analysis of the content of *de se* thought, and to show that such an account is preferable to alternative analyses of the content of first-person attitudes.

1.

Though they differ on details, a large class of linguists holds that the subject-positions in embedded clauses of the sentences in (1) contain an empty pronoun PRO. So, the standard representation of these sentences is as in (2):

(2) a. John knows who PRO to hit a ball to.
     b. John knows when PRO to hit a ball hard.
     c. John knows where PRO to hit a ball hard.
     d. John knows why PRO to hit a ball hard.
     e. John knows how PRO to hit a ball hard.

The unpronounced element PRO is assumed to be the subject of infinitival clauses generally. So PRO occurs not just as the subject position of embedded infinitival interrogatives, as in (1), but also in non-interrogative infinitives, as in (3):

(3) a. John wants PRO to win the race.
     b. John tried PRO to win the race.
     c. John expects Hannah PRO to win the race.

In (3a) and (3b), PRO must be interpreted as co-referential with "John". In (3c), PRO must be interpreted as co-referential with "Hannah". The relation between the unpronounced element PRO and its antecedent ("John" in (3a) and (3b), "Hannah" in (3c)) is called, in syntax, *Control* – which is the theory of the understood subject of the different occurrences of the verb "win" in (3), and the different occurrences of the verb "hit" in (2).

The theory of Control has been a central part of Syntax since Chomsky (1981), and the view that there is "a distinct control module in the theory of grammar" (Chomsky 1995: 110) has been a governing hypothesis of much subsequent work in syntax. In his 1981 *Lectures on Government and Binding*, Chomsky postulated two kinds of what he called "empty categories": trace of movement and PRO (an *empty category* is a type of syntactic position that contains no lexically overt material). By a *trace of movement*, Chomsky meant an unpronounced element in the syntactic structure that is left as the result of a "moved" element, such as a noun phrase that has "moved" from that position to a higher position before the sentence is uttered, as in a passive transformation, or the trace of movement of a question word such as "who" or "what" in a question such as "Who did John meet?"[2] By *PRO*, Chomsky meant an unpronounced element in the syntactic structure that is the subject of infinitival phrases, as we see in (2) and (3).[3]

Idan Landau (2000: 2) helpfully describes the questions that the theory of control must ultimately answer as follows:

(a) What elements/positions can control?
(b) What elements/positions can be controlled?
(c) What is the typology of control? (How many different types are there?)
(d) Can the typology be deduced from principles of Universal Grammar?
(e) How is the controlled position (PRO) interpreted?
(f) How is a controller picked up in a given structure?

Only some of these questions are relevant to us here. Question (b) is certainly relevant, and, as we have seen, the answer to it is typically taken to be *the subject position of non-finite (infinitival) clauses*.[4] The other two questions that are of relevance for us in interpreting the occurrences of PRO in structures such as (2) are (c) and (d).

The answer to Landau's question (c) is that there are two types of control structures – contexts of *Obligatory Control*, and contexts of *Non-Obligatory Control*. A context of Obligatory Control is one in which PRO must be linked to a grammatical antecedent within its clause, which gives PRO its interpretation (Landau 2000). So the examples in (3) are ones in which PRO is taken to be in a context of Obligatory Control. In (3a) and (3b), PRO receives its interpretation from the matrix subject "John", and in (3c), PRO receives its interpretation from the matrix object, "Hannah". A context of Non-

---

[2] In the Minimalist Program of Chomsky (1995), the earlier theory of movement was replaced by a "copy theory of movement", where what formerly were considered to be variable-like elements left by movement were instead taken to be unpronounced copies of the "moved" element.

[3] In Chomsky (1981), he recognized a third kind of empty category, "*pro*", which is the unpronounced subject of finite verbs in languages such as Italian and Spanish, which differs from PRO in that it can be used to refer demonstratively to a salient object.

[4] In recent years, there has been a good deal of attention focused on the possibility of *finite control* – that is a PRO-like element occurring in the subject position of finite clauses in some languages (such as the Balkan languages, and Hebrew). The element is taken to be PRO rather than pro, because it must have a controller. For a summary of some of the literature, see Landau (2004).

Obligatory Control is one in which PRO has an available interpretation in which it is not linked to a grammatical antecedent within its clause.

There are several diagnostics to distinguish between contexts of Obligatory Control, and contexts of Non-Obligatory Control (Landau 2000: 31ff.). The most widely used diagnostic is the availability of the so-called *arbitrary* reading of PRO, where it is synonymous with "one", as in the examples in (4):

(4)   a. PRO to drive fast is to risk oneself needlessly.
      b. It is obligatory PRO to behave oneself in front of the Queen.

The expression "oneself", like "himself" or "herself", is an anaphoric expression that requires an explicit linguistic antecedent in its own clause. The argument that PRO in these constructions is interpreted as "one" is that this assumption is required in order to explain the fact that "oneself" can grammatically occur (is "licensed") in (4a) and (4b). It is this so-called "PRO_{arb}" interpretation of PRO that licenses the anaphoric expression "oneself". These are instances in which PRO is not controlled by a prior linguistic antecedent, and therefore are contexts of Non-Obligatory Control. In contrast, in contexts of Obligatory Control, PRO must have an antecedent within its clause. The occurrence of PRO in (5) cannot be interpreted as PRO_{arb}:

(5)   *John expects to behave oneself at his parties.

Since at least Chomsky (1981), it has been widely assumed that infinitival embedded questions are contexts of Non-Obligatory Control. Chomsky (1981: 75) gives the first three examples, and (6d) is added for illustration:

(6)   a. It is unclear how PRO to feed oneself.
      b. John asked Bill how PRO to behave oneself under such circumstances.
      c. John was asked what PRO to do.
      d. John knows what PRO to do in emergency situations.

In such examples, PRO must be interpreted as PRO_{arb}. Therefore, the occurrences of PRO in (2) are Non-Obligatory Control occurrences. They can either be understood as being controlled by the subject of the main verb, "John", or as PRO_{arb}.[5]

When PRO is interpreted as PRO_{arb}, the embedded infinitival question is a *generic* construction. We can assume with much of the literature that generic constructions involve a generic operator GEN, which quantifies over individuals (for an introduction to the semantics of GEN see, Krifka et al. 1995). PRO_{arb} is obligatorily bound by a sentential generic operator (Moltmann 2006: 262). What is unclear in (6a) is

---

[5] As I have noted, Idan Landau (2000: 38ff.) argues that it is a mistake to take PRO to be PRO_{arb} in infinitival questions, even when it licenses "oneself". Instead, Landau argues that what has traditionally been taken to be an arbitrary PRO interpretation is instead an instance of Partial Control, where PRO is interpreted as denoting some group that contains the matrix subject. Landau's arguments are persuasive. But whether PRO is interpreted as PRO_{arb} or as denoting some group that includes the matrix subject is not relevant for our discussion. So I will adopt the traditional view in what follows.

how generally one should feed oneself; what John asked Bill in (6b) was how generally one should behave oneself under such circumstances, what John was asked in (6c) was what generally one ought to do, and what John knows in (6d) is what one ought to do in emergency situations. In short, PRO$_{arb}$ seems to be synonymous with the English generic "one". As Moltmann (2006: 260) notes, "Arbitrary PRO in fact appears to be the manifestation of generic 'one' when an overt NP, for syntactic reasons (such as Case assignment) is not possible."[6]

The more controversial case is when PRO appears to receive its entire interpretation from a previous linguistic antecedent, when PRO is *controlled*. So in infinitival embedded questions, PRO can either be interpreted as controlled PRO – that is, PRO with a linguistic antecedent, usually the subject of the matrix verb – or as PRO$_{arb}$. There are two general theories in the literature about the interpretation of controlled PRO. The first theory is the *predicational* theory. According to this account of the interpretation of controlled PRO, PRO is not in fact a pronoun at all, but is rather a λ-abstract. Infinitival phrases containing PRO denote *properties*. The second theory is the *propositional* theory. According to this account, controlled PRO is a pronoun, which inherits its reference from its antecedent. Infinitival phrases containing PRO denote *propositions*.

When PRO is controlled, it can either be controlled by the subject of the matrix verb, as in (7a), or its object, as in (7b):

(7)   a. Bekele$_i$ expects PRO$_i$ to win the race.
      b. Mottram expects Bekele$_i$ PRO$_i$ to win the race.

Cases in which PRO is controlled by the subject of the matrix verb, as in (7a), are cases of *subject control*, and cases in which PRO is controlled by the object of the matrix verb, as in (7b), are cases of *object control*. Here is how the predicational theory accounts for the natural interpretation of subject and object controlled occurrences of PRO. The predicational theory treats the sentences in (7) as equivalent to the ones in (8):

(8)   a. Bekele expects λx(x to win the race)
      b. Mottram expects Bekele λx(x to win the race)

The predicational theory treats certain attitudes as essentially relations to properties, rather than propositions. (7a) is true if and only if Bekele stands in the expectation relation to the property of winning the race. Bekele stands in this relation to the property of winning the race if and only if Bekele has an expectation of having that property. When "expect" takes both an object and a property, as in (7b), the semantic clause for "expect" is of course different. The verb "expect" in (7b) holds of x, y, and a property F if and only if x expects y to have the property F. So, in particular (7b) is true

---

[6]   If Landau is right that these are cases in which PRO denotes a group containing the matrix subject, the semantics does not significantly differ. They are still generic constructions; the group denoted by PRO serves as the restriction for the generic operator.

according to the predicational theory if and only Mottram expects Bekele to have the property of winning the race.

The propositional theory treats all occurrences of controlled PRO as a pronoun with a prior antecedent; the occurrences of PRO in (7a) and (7b) are just like occurrences of pronouns like "he" in sentences such as "Bekele$_i$ believes that he$_i$ is a runner". The advocate of the propositional theory treats the verb "expects" in (7a) as a relation between a person and a proposition. (7a) is true, on the propositional theory, if and only if Bekele stands in the expectation relation to the proposition that Bekele will win the race (assuming that the meaning of the infinitive "to win" in (7a) is equivalent to the modal "will"). The verb "expect" in (7b) is taken to be a relation between a person, an object, and a proposition; it holds between x, y, and the proposition that F(y) if and only if x has the expectation of y that F(y). So, in particular (7b) is true according to the propositional theory if and only Mottram has the expectation of Bekele that Bekele will win the race.

The predication and propositional approaches to PRO mark the major division in views about its proper interpretation. We turn now to an evaluation of the two views.

2.

The predicational and propositional approaches yield the same truth conditions in basic cases. But advocates of the predicational approach claim that it explains various features of PRO that are left unexplained on the propositional theory.[7] One early linguistic argument in favor of the predicational approach was given in Gennaro Chierchia (1984).[8] It involves appeal to inferences such as:

(9) (P1) John tried PRO to win the race.
     (P2) Everything John tried, Sue tried.
     (C) Sue tried PRO to win the race.

This inference is intuitively valid. The predicational theory easily explains its intuitive validity. According to the predicational theory, the first premise (P1) states that John stands in the trying relation to the property $\lambda x(x$ wins the race). The occurrence of "everything" in (P2) quantifies over properties – (P2) states that every property that John stands in the trying relation to, Sue also stands in the trying relation to. The conclusion simply follows from (P1) (P2), and universal instantiation.

In contrast, one might think that the propositional theory cannot capture the intuitive validity of this inference. According to the propositional theory, the first premise (P1) states that John stands in the trying relation to a proposition about John. The second premise seems to state that every proposition that John stands in the trying

---

[7] Landau (2004: 812–4) provides arguments against the predicational view of controlled PRO, from considerations about finite control. I will not discuss these arguments in this chapter.

[8] See also Chierchia and McConnell-Ginet (2000: 317).

relation to, Susan stands in the trying relation to as well (since only propositions are the objects of tryings). What follows is that Sue stands in the trying relation to the proposition about John – and hence that Sue tries to make it the case that John wins the race. Not only do (P1) and (P2) not intuitively entail that Sue tries to make it the case that John wins the race, but the propositional theory does not appear to capture the validity of the inference in (9).

This argument against the propositional theory is too quick. Consider the following argument:

(9*) (P1) John's mother wants everything John wants.
     (P2) John wants to become a doctor.
     (C) John's mother wants to become a doctor.

The predicational view predicts that (9) is valid. But for the same reason, it falsely predicts the validity of (9*). Every theory will need resources to distinguish valid arguments of this form from invalid arguments of this form.[9]

The propositional theory successfully predicts the invalidity of (9*). Does the propositional theory have the resources to predict the validity of (9)? The issue turns on the proper interpretation of premise (P2). Intuitively, the occurrence of "everything" in (P2) of (9) quantifies over *properties*, not propositions. The advocate of the propositional theory can account for this, if we assume that (P2) contains an elided "to do", as in:

(P2*) Everything John tried PRO to do, Sue tried PRO to do.

If (P2) is really (P2*), then the propositional theorist can easily account for the validity of the inference in (9). Admittedly, this amounts to a small dose of special pleading for these sorts of inferences – we must read (P2) as containing a suppressed "to do". But, as we shall soon see, the advocate of the predicational view also needs exactly parallel doses of special pleading to account for certain invariant interpretations. The story the advocate of the predicational view will have to provide about invariant readings of PRO under various anaphoric processes is more *ad hoc* than the not implausible claim that (P2) and similar examples contain an elided "to do".[10]

The phenomenon of the *de se* is one motivating source for advocates of predicational accounts. As Stanley and Williamson (2001: 436) note, "uses of 'PRO' where they are controlled by the subject in the main clause invariably give rise to *de se* readings, that is, readings involving a first-person way of thinking." Here is the example they give (ibid.: fn. 41):

---

[9] Thanks to Carlotta Pavese here.

[10] Alternatively, "everything" in (P2) is some kind of substitutional quantifier. Its instances are of the form "PRO to F". A co-variant reading of PRO would be predicted, and hence the intuitive validity of the inference in (20). So there are multiple ways for the advocate of the propositional theory to account for the intuitive validity of inferences such as (9).

suppose Hannah sees a picture of a woman in the newspaper who appears to be buying a lottery ticket, and furthermore appears greatly burdened by poverty. On this basis, she forms the desire that the woman in the newspaper win the lottery. Hannah herself is quite happy with her middle-class salary, and rightly suspects that the accumulation of more money would make her into an unpleasant person. Unbeknownst to Hannah, however, the woman in the newspaper is Hannah herself, who was buying a pack of cigarettes, rather than buying a lottery ticket. With respect to this context:

(a) Hannah wants to win the lottery.

has only a false interpretation. Two facts explain the lack of a true interpretation. First, the structure of (a) is:

(b) Hannah$_i$ wants [PRO$_i$ to win the lottery].

Second, "PRO", when controlled by the subject in the main clause, permits only *de se* readings.

Similarly, suppose that Timothy Williamson suffers from amnesia, and forgets that he is Timothy Williamson. Reading *Knowledge and Its Limits*, he forms the desire for Williamson to write another book. But it does not follow that he wants to write another book. Perhaps he thinks he won't write a good one (after all, he has forgotten that he is a professional philosopher). There is a difference in meaning between (10a) and (10b), and that difference is explicable by the fact that (10a) contains an occurrence of PRO controlled by the matrix subject, and (10b) does not contain an occurrence of PRO controlled by the matrix subject:

(10) a. Tim wants Tim$_i$ PRO$_i$ to write another book.
      b. Tim$_i$ wants PRO$_i$ to write another book.

One might think these facts support the predicational theory. One might, for example, think that the predicational theory provides an explanation of the obligatory nature of the *de se* reading in these constructions. For example, one might think that the *de se* nature of a construction like (10b) simply *falls out* of the fact that there is no subject position for the embedded predicate "to write another book". In a structure like (10b), "want" simply expresses a relation between a person and a property — (10b) is true if and only if Tim wants to have the property of writing another book.[11] Second, one might make the obvious *negative* point that the propositional theory cannot provide an explanation of the obligatory nature of the *de se* reading in these constructions. After all, it appears that on the propositional theory the complement of (10b) is just the singular proposition, about Timothy Williamson, that he writes another book. But as long as Tim does not realize that he is Timothy

---

[11] Roberts (2009) argues that the obligatory *de se* nature of PRO favors a predicational account. But she does not make the error of assuming that the *de se* nature of PRO is straightforwardly explained on such an account. She argues that the predicational theory, plus the assumption that verbs like "try" and "want" are "epistemically reflective" explains this fact. See Pavese and Stanley (2010) for discussion and critique of Roberts' position.

Williamson, Tim might want this singular proposition to be true, without wanting to write another book.

It should be clear that there is a challenge to the propositional theorist that is considerably broader simply than debates about the semantics of PRO. The challenge is to explain how any obligatory *de se* construction could be taken to express a proposition. Even more generally, the challenge is to explain how the content of any *de se attitude* could be a proposition. The defender of the propositional view of PRO must meet this broader challenge from the philosophy of mind, by defending an account of propositions that can answer the negative point that propositional theories cannot provide explanations of obligatory *de se* readings.

A second argument in favor of the predicational account comes from consideration of *Verb Phrase Ellipsis* – cases in which the verb phrase is elided in a second conjunct, as in (11):

(11)   John loves his mother, and Bill does too.

Note that (11), with the overt pronoun "his", has two readings:

(12)   a. John loves John's mother, and Bill loves Bill's mother.
        b. John loves John's mother, and Bill loves John's mother.

The first reading (12a), is called the *sloppy* (or *co-variant*) reading, because the elided pronoun "his" switches its referent between the clauses. The second reading (12b), is called the *strict* (or *invariant*) reading, because the elided pronoun "his" has the same reference in both clauses. The standard theoretical account of the distinction between the two readings is that they are due to distinct syntactic structures:

(13)   a. John λx(x loves x's mother), and Bill λx(x loves x's mother).
        b. John$_i$ loves his$_i$ mother, and Bill loves his$_i$ mother too.

The sloppy (or co-variant) reading, represented in (13a), is due to the fact that a λ-abstract binds the pronoun "his". The strict reading is due to the fact that "his" is unbound, but receives its interpretation from "John".

The relevant point for our purposes is that controlled PRO only gives rise to sloppy (co-variant) readings in Verb Phrase Ellipsis. For example (14a) can only mean (14b) – it cannot mean (14c):

(14)   a. John wants PRO to run, and Bill does too.
        b. John$_i$ wants PRO$_i$ to run, and Bill$_j$ wants PRO$_j$ to run too.
        c. * John$_i$ wants PRO$_i$ to run, and Bill$_j$ wants PRO$_i$ to run too.

If we assume that the sloppy reading is due to a λ-abstract, that is some evidence for the predicational view that PRO introduces a λ-abstract rather than functions as an independent pronoun.

How strong are these motivations for the predicational view? One problem for the advocate of the predicational theory is that, as Higginbotham (1992: 85) points out, "PRO may be invariant with respect to certain anaphoric processes". Higginbotham's example, due to Tanya Reinhart, is:

(15)   John wants [PRO to become a doctor], but his mother doesn't want that.

On one natural reading of (15), what John's mother doesn't want is *that John becomes a doctor*. On this reading, the use of "that" clearly denotes a proposition about John. This is evidence for the propositional theory, over the predicational theory, since the propositional theory has no problem accounting for this reading. It is quite unclear how the predicational theory can account for such readings. The advocate of the predicational view will need to resort to special pleading about this kind of anaphora.

Here is another worry for predicational theories. The two motivations – the desire to explain *de se* readings, and the desire to account for the fact that a *de se* pronoun like PRO only gives rise to sloppy readings in Verb Phrase ellipsis – come apart. A pronoun with a *de se* reading can easily give rise to strict (invariant) readings in Verb Phrase ellipsis, as in (16):

(16)   I believe I am a philosopher, and you do too.

The pronoun "I" can give rise to *de re* readings.[12] But it is natural to take the belief-ascription in (16) as a *de se* belief ascription. If, to account for the *de se* reading of (16), we treat (16) as having the structure as in (17), then we predict that (16) *only* has the interpretation (18b), and not the interpretation (18a):

(17)   I believe λx(x is a philosopher), and you do too.

(18)   a. I believe I am a philosopher, and you believe I am a philosopher.
       b. I believe I am a philosopher, and you believe you are a philosopher.

Yet (16) can clearly have both the readings in (18). Furthermore (18a) is in fact the more preferred reading. To capture reading (18a), we must treat the *de se* pronoun "I" in (16) as an expression that refers to the speaker. Therefore, the property of being a *de se* pronoun, and the property of contributing a λ-abstract are distinct. It is hard to see how any theory that treats "I" as anything but a referring expression in (16) can account for these facts. It therefore is simply not the case that *de se* readings of pronouns are *explained* by treating those pronouns as lacking reference. Sentence (16)

---

[12] Here is a nice example, from Moss (forthcoming): "Looking at the mirror, Kaplan sees that his pants are on fire, without realizing that his own pants are on fire. In recounting his experience, suppose Kaplan utters the sentence 'I expected that I would be rescued.' Kaplan can truly utter this, even though he was not aware of being in danger when he looked at the mirror." This is an example in which "I" is used to report a *de re* belief report, rather than a *de se* belief report.

involves a pronoun with a *de se* reading, which we must nevertheless take as a referring expression.[13]

The fact that there are *de se* readings that are not explained by the predicational account shows that one needs an *independent* account of *de se* readings – independent, that is, of the distinction between a propositional reading of a complement clause and a predicational reading. Even the predicational theorist should agree that (16) reports a relation between a person and a proposition. So everyone needs an account of when a sentence that expresses a proposition expresses a *de se* proposition. But once this account is in place, the presence of an obligatory *de se* reading is no longer any evidence for a predicational account.[14]

Why have so many theorists have taken *de se* readings of pronouns to pose a problem for the view that such pronouns are referring expressions? It is because they have suffered under the grip of a false theory of propositions. The *locus classicus* of this reasoning is Lewis (1979). According to Lewis (1979: 521), "Some beliefs and some knowledge cannot be understood as propositional, but can be understood as self-ascription of properties." Lewis's famous example to make this point involves his "case of the two gods":

Consider the case of the two gods. They inhabit a certain possible world, and they know exactly which world it is. Therefore they know every proposition that is true at their world. Insofar as knowledge is a propositional attitude, they are omniscient. Still I can imagine them to suffer ignorance: neither one knows which of the two he is. They are not exactly alike. One lives on top of the tallest mountain and throws down manna; the other lives on top of the coldest mountain and throws down thunderbolts. Neither one knows whether he lives on the tallest mountain or on the coldest mountain; nor whether he throws down manna or thunderbolts.

Surely their predicament is possible . . . But if it is possible to lack knowledge and not lack any propositional knowledge, then the lacked knowledge must not be propositional. (Ibid.: 520–1)

Here is a straightforward argument to show that that both gods lack propositional knowledge about their worlds. Suppose that one god is named "Manna" and the other god is named "Thunderbolt". Both gods know the propositions expressed by the sentences in (19):

(19)   a. Manna throws down manna.
       b. Thunderbolt throws down thunderbolts.

---

[13] Egan (2009) argues that while genuine *de se* thought contents are not fully propositional, we should take sentences containing the first-person pronoun to express genuine propositions. Obviously, these examples are not a problem for Egan's view.

[14] One might however respond to this particular argument against the predicational view by arguing that PRO involves a *stricter de se* reading than use of the first-person pronoun. Perhaps use of PRO gives rise to one kind of *de se* thought, and explicit uses of the first-person pronoun give rise to another (cf. the distinction in Recanati 2007: ch. 26, between "explicit" and "implicit" *de se* thoughts).

However, Manna does not know that he is Manna, and Thunderbolt does not know that he is Thunderbolt. That is, Manna does not know the proposition that he would express to himself by uttering (20a), and Thunderbolt does not know the proposition that he would express to himself by uttering (20b):

(20)   a. I throw down manna.
       b. I throw down thunderbolts.

What Manna would express by (20a) is a proposition that is true at the envisaged world. What Thunderbolt would express by (20b) is a proposition that is true at the envisaged world. Neither god knows the relevant proposition. Therefore, neither god knows every proposition that is true at their world.

Why does Lewis so confidently assert that the two gods know every proposition that is true at their world? Suppose Manna's utterance of (20a) expresses a proposition, and Thunderbolt's utterance of (20b) expresses a proposition. Lewis is assuming a model of semantic content according to which, if the sentences in (20) express propositions, then (19a) expresses the same proposition that would be expressed by an utterance of (20a) by Manna, and (19b) expresses the same proposition that would be expressed by an utterance of (20b) by Thunderbolt. Given this view, and given that both gods know the propositions expressed by the sentences in (19), it would follow that both gods know the propositions they would express, respectively, towards (20a) and (20b), and that therefore their ignorance cannot be modeled as ignorance of the propositions they would express to themselves by utterances of (20a) and (20b).

I have given an argument that, in Lewis's envisaged case, Manna and Thunderbolt do not know every proposition true in their world. Lewis's reaction is to deny that (20a) and (20b) express the propositions they intuitively seem to express (since he takes Manna and Thunderbolt's utterances of them to express the same thing as the propositions expressed by utterances of the sentences in (19)). But another reaction is to reject the model of semantic content with which Lewis operates. Lewis writes (ibid.: 521), about the case he describes, "The trouble might perhaps be that they have an equally perfect view of their world, and hence cannot identify the perspectives from which they view it". Lewis assumes a model of propositional content according to which propositions cannot be perspective dependent. But intuitively, Manna's utterance of (20a) expresses a proposition, grasp of which *does* require identifying a certain perspective on the world. There are some propositions, such as those expressed by utterances of sentences containing pronouns such as "I", "here", and "now", grasp of which requires thinking of a world from a particular perspective. One might think that if a view of propositional content cannot accommodate this, it is that view of propositional content that should be jettisoned.

Lewis thinks of propositions as sets of possible worlds. It is indeed difficult to square such a view of propositional content with the observation that some contents are perspective-dependent (though see Stalnaker 2008 for one attempt). The set of possible worlds in which I am running is the same set of possible worlds as those in which Jason Stanley is running, given the necessary truth that I am Jason Stanley. But that is a problem with views of propositions that take them to be sets of possible worlds. To paraphrase Anscombe (1981: 27), the sense of the lie "I am not Jason Stanley" is hardly retained in "Jason Stanley is not Jason Stanley." The thought that I am Jason Stanley is a distinct thought from the thought that Jason Stanley is Jason Stanley, because, under the grips of amnesia, I might believe one without believing the other. If a model of propositional content cannot account for this fact, we should conclude that it is the wrong model of propositional content – rather than conclude that some apparently propositional attitudes are in fact attitudes towards properties.[15]

3.

Suppose we accept that the thought that I am Jason Stanley is distinct from the thought that Jason Stanley is Jason Stanley. If so, we must also accept that "I", as used by Jason Stanley, contributes something different to the thought expressed by an utterance of "I am Jason Stanley" than "Jason Stanley" contributes to the thought expressed by "Jason Stanley is Jason Stanley". Saying what this propositional contribution is has proved to be difficult. Is it Frege's "special and original way in which each of us is presented to himself, and not to any other"?[16] Or is it a way of thinking of Jason Stanley that is publically accessible? This is clearly a hard question, and there are multiple distinct attempts to answer it. No wonder a framework that appears to reject it has proved so popular.

There are several ways of implementing the view that "PRO" contributes a distinctive first-person way of thinking to the propositions expressed by clauses containing it. One influential recent suggestion is due to James Higginbotham (2003). According to Higginbotham, the occurrence of "PRO" makes the proposition thereby expressed *reflexive*, in the sense that it is about a state of the speaker. Indexical thought is distinctive because it is thought about occurrent states of the speaker. As Higginbotham writes:

Following the analogy of reflexive thoughts with respect to time, suppose that we identify as the peculiar semantic contribution of PRO that it presents the subject as *the subject (or experiencer) of the event or state e* as given in the higher clause, or σ(e) for short. (2003: 514)

Higginbotham also holds that "it is a primitive property of PRO" that it requires the subject to think of herself as the agent of the predicate of which it is the subject:

I suggest that the "internal" aspect of PRO results from that element's being considered, either exclusively or in conjunction with its value as given by its antecedent, as the bearer of some

---

[15] Of course, Anscombe (1981) wishes ultimately to argue that some uses of "I" are not referring. I criticize Anscombe's view that "I" is ambiguous between referring and non-referring uses in Stanley (1998).
[16] From Frege (1918: 66); my translation.

thematic role that its syntactic position selects for the bare predicate with which it is in construction. On this hypothesis, for example, the interpretation of the subject in:

PRO falling downstairs

is as in:

falling downstairs $(\theta(e),e)$

where $\theta(e)$ expresses the relation, something like *undergoer*, that a thing falling downstairs bears to an event of so falling . . . it will be a primitive property of PRO that it is construed as the bearer of one or another relation to events as classified by the predicate it appears with. (Ibid.: 517)

So there are two aspects of the propositional contribution of PRO, in a construction like "X Vs PRO to F", such as "Bekele expects to win the race", or "John wants to cook dinner". First, PRO contributes the mixed descriptive/demonstrative content, *being the subject of that very act of V-ing*. Second, PRO contributes the mixed descriptive/demonstrative content, *being the agent of an act of F-ing*. In sum, the propositional contribution of such an occurrence of PRO is the conjunctive description, *the thing that is the subject of that very act of V-ing and the agent of the act of F-ing*. This is not a description in "purely general terms", because there is demonstrative reference to an act or state.

According to this suggestion, the propositional content of "Bekele expects PRO to win the race" is that *Bekele has the expectation that there will be race-winning event and that the subject of that very expectation will be the subject of that race-winning event*. Where e is the state of having the expectation, the propositional contribution of "PRO" is *the subject of e who is the subject of w*, which is a descriptive content containing a demonstrative reference to e, a presently occurring event or state, and a variable "w", which is bound by a quantifier over events. This thought is distinct from the *de re* thought expressed by "Bekele expects that he will win the race", which has the content that *Bekele has the expectation that Bekele will be the subject of the race-winning*. The latter expectation, but not the former, is one that Bekele could come to form by seeing a graceful, fluid, fast runner through what he thinks to be a window, but is in fact a mirror.[17]

Higginbotham's theory captures the intuition that *de se* thoughts have different propositional contents than *de re* thoughts about oneself. But it does so by a route that is not traditionally Fregean. The distinctive first-person way of thinking on Higginbotham's view turns out to be a thought about one's own occurrent experiences. A perhaps more direct way of implementing a Fregean view is developed in Evans's classic paper, "Understanding Demonstratives" (1985). For the Fregean (ibid.: 315), "A way of thinking about an object is given by an account of what makes some thinking about that object." Accordingly, Evans proposes that the identity conditions

---

[17] As Higginbotham recognizes, this view entails that what Bekele expects, when Bekele expects to win the race, can only occur in possible worlds in which he has that expectation. Given that propositions are the objects of expectations, Higginbotham is therefore led to deny that modal operators are predicates of propositions.

for first-person ways of thinking are given by a statement of the conditions under which one thinks of oneself in the right way:

In the case of a particular "I"-thought, for example, I envisage statements of the form
(11) S is thinking of S' at t because $R_1(S,S',t)$
where R1 is an as yet unspecified relation which can only be satisfied by a triple of S, S', and t if S = S'. (Ibid.)

Evans's "as yet unspecified relation" is a placeholder for an account of first-person thought (the kind of account he attempts to provide in Evans 1982: ch. 7). Evans then suggests (1985: 316) that when N entertains the thought N would express by "I am hot", N entertains the content $<N, \lambda x\lambda y(R_1(x,y))$, sense of "x is hot">. When Bekele expects to win the race, the content of Bekele's expectation will be $<Bekele, \lambda x\lambda y (R_1(x,y))$, sense of "will win the race">. When Bekele merely has the *de re* expectation that he will win the race (formed by e.g. seeing himself in a mirror, and mistaking the mirror for a window), the content of his expectation will not contain $\lambda x\lambda y(R_1(x,y))$ as a constituent.

On both of these accounts, the propositional contents of genuinely *de se* thoughts are distinct from the propositional contents of non-*de se* thoughts. There are objections to both accounts Recanati (2007: ch. 25) has summarized a series of worries against Higginbotham's account. A potential worry with Evans's theory in "Understanding Demonstratives" is as follows. Evans's relation R_1 is supposed to be that relation that one bears to an object if and only if one thinks of that object as oneself. Since Evans holds that this relation is itself in the content of any first-person thought, he thereby attributes to any person having a first-person thought a thought whose content contains the relation determined by the account of what it is to have a first-person thought about an object. And one might worry that this is too sophisticated. On one way of viewing it, even trained philosophers do not have beliefs containing Evans's relation R_1. If so, then having a thought with this relation as its content is not a precondition for having a first-person thought.

However, given a successful account of the relation one has to stand in to an object in order to think of that object as oneself, one can give an account of first-person thoughts that does not face this potential objection to Evans's account in "Understanding Demonstratives". We can use Evans's relation R_1 to provide a contextual definition of first-person ways of thinking. Take two cognitive relations, R_i and R_j, between persons, objects, and times – intuitively such a relation states the conditions under which one is thinking of that object in a certain way at that time. R_i and R_j determine the same way of thinking of a given object o at a time t if and only if $\forall x (R_i(x,o,t) \leftrightarrow R_j(x,o,t))$. If we replace "$R_i$" and "$R_j$" by Evans's R_1, we obtain a contextual definition of certain entities, first-person ways of thinking. It follows from the nature of R_1 that one can only stand in that relation to that object at a time if that object is oneself, i.e. $\forall x\forall y(R_1(x,y,t) \rightarrow x = y)$. The fact that certain thoughts contain these first-person ways of thinking as constituents is what makes them first-person thoughts.

The framework I have described yields a fully satisfactory account of Lewis's two gods. On a Fregean account of propositions, Lewis's two gods do not know every proposition true at their world. Manna does not know the proposition he may express to himself by "I throw down manna", and Thunderbolt does not know the proposition he may express to himself by "I throw down thunderbolts". The true proposition Manna does not know involves a first-person way of thinking of Manna, and the true proposition that Thunderbolt does not know involves a first-person way of thinking of Thunderbolt. But the fact that these propositions contain first-person ways of thinking of Manna and Thunderbolt does not preclude them from being propositions true at their world.

Though the Fregean view of first-person ways of thinking I have described gives an elegant account of Lewis's two gods case, it faces a familiar problem. First-person ways of thinking are not publically accessible. I cannot grasp someone else's first-person way of thinking. Given this fact, I cannot report the first-person mental states of others with the use of sentences that express propositions that contain those ways of thinking (assuming that I am generally capable of grasping the propositions expressed by the reports I issue). How, then, is the advocate of the Fregean framework I have described to explain third-person reports involving PRO, such as (7a), and all the examples in (1)? Such reports cannot contain first-person ways of thinking, since, on the Fregean view I advocate, these are not publically accessible. The worry is ably stated by Christopher Peacocke, who uses it to motivate the distinction between *employing* a way of thinking and *referring* to a way of thinking:

Unlike Evans, however, I hold that this apparatus is only defensible if we distinguish between *employing* a [way of thinking] and *referring* to a way of thinking. '[self$_{john}$]' cannot have as its *sense* that distinctive token way of thinking under which only John and no one else can think of himself: if it were to have such a sense, sentences containing it could only be understood by John. '[self$_{john}$]' rather *refers* to that [way of thinking] which can be a constituent only of John's, and no one else's, thoughts. From the fact that only John can think thoughts containing this m.p., it does not follow that we cannot know which thoughts he thinks, or that we cannot think about the constituent m.p.s of his thoughts. (1981: 191)

On Peacocke's view, when we employ a way of thinking to (say) express our own first-person thoughts, we use an expression the propositional contribution of which is the non-publically accessible first-person way of thinking. However, when we describe the first-person mental states of others, the relevant expressions occur within *opaque contexts*, in this case, *propositional attitude contexts*. It is part of the Fregean view that the propositional contribution of expressions occurring under the scope of attitude verbs is their sense and not their reference. Peacocke's point is that, in ascribing first-person mental states to others, the propositional contribution of the relevant expressions will be the *sense* of the non-publically accessible first-person ways of thinking, rather than those non-accessible first-person ways of thinking themselves. In saying "Bekele expects to win the race", the proposition I express does not contain as a constituent Bekele's first-person way of thinking of himself. It only contains a way of referring to that first-person way of thinking, which way I can grasp, without being able to entertain Bekele's first-person way of thinking of himself.

Peacocke's solution is elegant, since it straightforwardly follows from independent principles associated with a Fregean semantics for propositional attitude contexts. However, it is also possible to employ first-person ways of thinking without adopting a fully Fregean framework. Let us use "self" to denote a function from persons to their first-person ways of thinking. When PRO is used in first-person ascriptions of mental states, it denotes the personal way of thinking. But when PRO is used in third-person ascriptions of mental states, its propositional contribution of PRO is the complex $self_i$, where "i" is a variable over persons. So, a sentence like "Bekele expects PRO to win the race" expresses the proposition that $Bekele_i$ expects $self_i$ to win the race. The propositional content of "Bekele expects PRO to win the race" therefore does not contain Bekele's first-person way of thinking. Rather, it contains a functional expression, whose value is Bekele's first-person way of thinking. Just as one can entertain the content of the definite description "the first person born in the seventh century A.D." without knowing who that person is, so one can entertain the content of this functional expression, without grasping Bekele's first-person way of thinking.

Of course, when I ascribe to Bekele the expectation of winning the race, I am not ascribing to him a *descriptive thought*, one containing descriptive reference to his first-person way of thinking. Rather, I am ascribing to him an attitude towards a proposition containing his first-person way of thinking as a constituent. So unlike Peacocke's suggestion, this suggestion involves appeal to a scope-like mechanism to allow the definite description that appears to be in the scope of an attitude verb nevertheless to ascribe a singular thought.

The issue is a familiar one. Suppose that John has a brother named Bill. John and Bill were separated at birth, and John believes that he is an only child. He meets Bill, and becomes friends with him, and over time forms the belief that Bill is kind. He also regularly beats Bill at chess. Here is the epistemic situation of the rest of us. We are not acquainted with Bill. We know that John has a brother, who he has met and thinks is kind, and regularly beats him in chess. We also know that John thinks he is an only child. In such a situation we can truly say, "John thinks his brother is kind" and "John knows how to beat his brother at chess." In so doing, we are not ascribing to John a descriptive thought containing the possessive description "his brother". After all, we are perfectly aware that John believes he is an only child. We intend to ascribe to John the *de re* belief about that person that he is kind. However, we are forced to use the definite description "his brother", since we lack the resources to ascribe to him belief in the relevant singular proposition.

The standard way to treat definite descriptions that superficially appear to be in the scope of attitude verbs in *de re* attitude ascriptions is by a mechanism of scope. In the above cases, "his brother" contains a pronoun that receives its reference from "John". So, in "John thinks his brother is kind" and "John knows how to beat his brother in chess" the possessive description "his brother" must take scope between "John" and the attitude verbs "thinks" and "knows".

The suggested treatment is the same in third-person ascriptions of first-person mental states, such as "Bekele expects to win", or "John knows how to swim". In such an ascription, the functional expression contributed by PRO takes scope between the subject of the matrix clause and the attitude verb. The logical form of a sentence like "Bekele expects to win" is:

(21)   Bekele$_i$ is such that (the x: self$_i$ x) expects x to win.

The functional expression "self$_i$" is a descriptive quantifier ranging over ways of thinking.[18] This representation successfully ascribes to Bekele an expectation the content of which contains his non-publically accessible first-person way of thinking. It exploits only syntactic mechanisms that are independently needed to treat perfectly ordinary cases of *de re* readings of possessive descriptions that superficially appear in the scope of attitude verbs.

Let us now turn to a brief comparison between the Evansian/Fregean view I have sketched of genuine *de se* thought, and the Lewisian account of *de se* thought, according to which it involves relations to properties, rather than propositions. A full account of the contents of first-person ways of thinking requires one ultimately to give an account of the nature of the R$_1$ relation, i.e. an account of what it is to think of oneself as oneself. As Evans writes:

such an account must presuppose some of the profoundest philosophy. In the case of 'I' for example, one might think that an account of the relation R$_1$ which explicates 'self-identification' must incorporate the insights, as well as illuminate the struggles, of Descartes, Kant, and Wittgenstein, and many others. (1985: 318)

A principal attraction of a view that treats first-person thought as self-ascriptions of properties is the sense that it appears to allow us to evade the extraordinarily difficult task of explaining what it is to take a first-person perspective on the world.

However, it is simply an error to think that the Lewisian view of first-person thought evades the hard philosophical task of giving an account of something like Evans's R$_1$ relation. The sense that the self-ascription framework provides an explanation of the *de se* is due merely to the fact that it uses the *de se* vocabulary in the metalanguage. What was to be explained is the fact that "John wants to win" only has a *de se* reading, and cannot be true if John merely wants someone to win who in fact

---

[18]   If one thought that Bekele himself should also be part of the content of his *de se* expectations, one could alternatively take "self$_i$", when "i" receives its value from "Bekele", to yield an ordered pair of Bekele and his third-person way of thinking. In this case, "x" in a sentence like (21) would range over ordered pairs of persons and first-person ways of thinking. I discuss more about these different construals of "self$_i$" in section 2 of Chapter 4.

unbeknownst to John turns out to be John himself. The self-ascription framework claims to explain this fact, by appeal to the fact that John wants to self-ascribe a property. But this is not an explanation. What we desired was an explanation of *what it means to self-ascribe*, not just using that vocabulary in the metalanguage.

Once one tries to provide an explanation of what it is to self-ascribe a property, the problem of explaining first-person thought reemerges. Ascribing a property to myself is not simply ascribing a property to a thing that happens to be myself. After all, I might ascribe a property to Jason Stanley under the grip of amnesia, and thereby fail to ascribe it to *myself*. So what is it to ascribe a property to *myself*, rather than ascribe it to something which in fact merely happens to be myself? The explanation will take the form of an account of what it is to ascribe a property to a thing one regards as oneself – in other words, it will include an account of what it is to think of something as *oneself*, an account, that is, of Evans's R_1 relation. In short, an explanation of the framework of self-ascriptive content will include an account of the first-person way of thinking. One ascribes something to *oneself*, rather than something one does not conceive of as oneself, if and only if one thinks of that thing in the first-person way. But once one has an account of the R_1 relation, there is no longer any need for the framework. We can return to traditional talk of propositions, albeit propositions that contain first-person ways of thinking as constituents.

Consider again a sentence such as "John expects PRO to win". Advocates of the predicational view maintain that the predicational view explains the *de se* character of PRO. As we have seen, this is not the case. To explain how the *de se* character of PRO follows from the predicational view, its advocates must explain how self-ascription differs from ascription of a property to something that is in fact oneself. In short, they must explain what it is to think of a property as being ascribed to oneself. This is precisely what the advocate of the propositional view must explain, in explaining the first-person way of thinking conventionally associated with PRO.

The self-ascription framework does not free us from the task of explaining the nature of the first-person perspective. This is not an advantage it has over approaches that try to reflect the first-person perspective in the content itself.

4.

There is another motivation for the view that there are uses of apparently first-person pronouns that do not refer. This motivation has a distinguished history, dating back to a much-cited passage in Wittgenstein:

There are two different cases in the use of the word "I" (or "my") which I might call "the use as object" and "the use as subject". Examples of the first kind of use are these: "My arm is broken", "I have grown six inches", "I have a bump on my forehead", "The wind blows my hair about". Examples of the second kind are: "I see so-and-so", "I hear so-and-so", "I try to lift my arm", "I think it will rain", "I have toothache". One can point to the difference between these two categories by saying: The cases of the first category involve the recognition of a particular person, and there is in these cases the possibility of an error, or as I should rather put it: The possibility of an error has been provided for . . . It is possible that, say in an accident, I should feel a pain in my arm, see a broken arm at my side, and think it is mine, when really it is my neighbor's. And I could, looking into a mirror, mistake a bump on his forehead for one on mine. On the other hand, there is no question of recognizing a person when I say I have toothache. To ask "are you sure it's *you* who have pains?" would be nonsensical. (1958: 66–7)

In this passage, Wittgenstein makes a distinction between "uses of 'I' as object", and "uses of 'I' as subject". A number of philosophers have been tempted to take uses of "I" as subject as cases in which "I" does not refer. Since PRO invariably gives rise to uses of "I" as subject, this motivation carries over to a motivation for the predicational view of controlled PRO, where it is not a referring expression.

What is meant by a "use of 'I' as subject"? Suppose that I judge that I see a canary. In an ordinary case, my judgment that I see a canary is not based on the judgment that x sees a canary, and the subsequent judgment that I am x. If it were based on these two judgments, then it would be possible to discover that it was false that I am seeing a canary, but have my justification still survive as a justification for the belief that someone is seeing a canary. But in an ordinary case (i.e. one not involving mirrors, special glasses, etc.) in which I judge that I am seeing a canary, if I find out that it is false that I am seeing a canary, I cannot subsequently judge that someone is seeing a canary, and I have just misidentified that something as myself. In the vocabulary of Shoemaker (1968), my judgment that I am seeing a canary is, under ordinary circumstance, *Immune to Error through Misidentification* (or *IEM*, for short).

A judgment Fa is immune to error through misidentification if and only if, when it is defeated, its grounds cannot survive as the sole grounds for the existential generalization that something is F. Here is a judgment which does not meet this criterion, and is hence not IEM. Suppose I hear someone walking down the stairs, and, thinking it is Sally, judge that Sally is walking down the stairs. Then, I turn around, and bump into Sally, who all the while was standing behind me. My judgment that Sally is walking down the stairs has been defeated, but my grounds survive as grounds for the judgment that someone is walking down the stairs. Thus the judgment that Sally is walking down the stairs is not IEM.

The reason why my judgment that Sally is walking down the stairs is not IEM is because it was "based on an identification". I identified Sally as the person who was walking down the stairs, and the judgment's defeat was due to the failure of this identification. Judgments which cannot be defeated in this matter are those which are IEM.[19]

---

[19] Evans (1982: 180) writes that when a judgment is *identification-dependent*, it is based on "knowledge of the truth of a pair of propositions, 'b is F' (for some distinct Idea, b) and 'a=b' ". Evans intends IEM judgments to be ones that are not identification-dependent. However, Evans's description is not quite correct (see Pryor 1999, for discussion). My judgment that Sally is walking down the stairs is not identification-dependent in

Immunity to error though misidentification is the best way of explicating the idea of a predicate's being directly ascribed to the subject of a judgment. The predicate in a non-IEM judgment is not directly ascribed to the subject of a judgment; it is rather first ascribed to the reference of some other singular concept, which is then identified with the subject of the judgment.[20] In a judgment which is IEM, on the other hand, the predicate is directly ascribed to the subject of the judgment. Judgments in which "I" is used as subject, in Wittgenstein's sense, are IEM. They are cases in which the predicate is directly ascribed to the subject.

Sentences containing controlled uses of PRO also seem to be direct self-ascriptions, i.e. "uses of 'I' as subject". As Recanati (2007: ch. 26) writes, "Reports using the PRO construction, such as ["He remembers PRO delivering a speech to the salesmen"], can only be reports of basic *de se* thoughts." Since Recanati holds that basic *de se* thoughts are IEM, he also holds that reports using the PRO construction are invariably IEM. And he seems right. Suppose I am watching a video of someone in the distant past giving a speech to a group of salesmen. The person looks exactly like me. On this basis, I form the belief that I gave a speech in the past to a group of salesmen. I cannot on *this* basis assert "I remember delivering a speech to the salesmen". In order to use the construction involving controlled PRO, my memory of the speech cannot be based on an identification. Reports using the PRO construction have to be direct self-ascriptions of properties.

Recanati takes this fact about reports using controlled PRO to be evidence for the predicational view. That is, Recanati takes it to be strong evidence for the view that controlled PRO is not a referring expression that it cannot be used on the basis of an identification. But this is a weak argument for the predicational view. It has been known since Shoemaker (1968) that expressions other than the first-person pronoun can be used to express judgments that are IEM. Shoemaker considers a case in which a customer wants a red necktie. Seeing a red necktie, I point to it and say "This is red." As Shoemaker writes, there is, in this case, "no identification and hence no possibility of misidentification." But it would of course be incorrect to conclude that my use of "this" does not refer in my utterance of "this is red".

More generally, the correct explanation of why judgments involving a term are immune to error through misidentification, far from providing evidence that the term does not refer, *presupposes* that the relevant term refers. In my view, the most successful explanation of the nature of judgments that are IEM is due to Gareth Evans (1982). Evans argues that our ability to refer to an object with the use of a referring term "a" is due to an information link between us and the referent of "a". When the information

---

Evans's sense, as it is based upon my judgment *that someone is walking down the stairs*, and *that the person walking down the stairs = Sally*. The first of these judgments does not take the form 'b is F'. Nevertheless, the judgment is identification dependent, because it depends upon a judgment of the form a=b, i.e. the judgment that the person walking down the stairs = Sally.

[20] The three previous paragraphs overlap with Stanley (1998: 169–70).

that a certain property F is instantiated is delivered to us by the very information link that enables us to use "a" to refer, then the judgment that a is F is immune to error through misidentification. As Evans writes:

No one can be regarded as thinking of an object demonstratively, or of a place as "here", if his thinking is not controlled, or disposed to be controlled, by the deliverances of certain ways of gaining knowledge of the object of his thought. Where 'a' is schematic for an Idea-of-an-object of this kind, there is a way of gaining information of the condition of objects such that for a subject to have information that the property of being F_i is instantiated in this way (for some one of the relevant properties $F_1 \ldots F_n$) just is for the subject to have information that 'a is F_i' is true . . . The Idea tolerates no gap between the deliverances of the relevant information channel, and thoughts employing the Idea. Consequently, if a subject judges, upon the basis of the information received, that 'a is F_i' is true, it will not be possible to regard the belief that he expresses as the result of two distinguishable beliefs: the belief that 'b is F_i' is true, for some distinct Idea b, and the identity belief that 'a=b' is true. (1982: 180)

So, a judgment expressed by an utterance "a is F" is IEM if and only if the information channel that secures the reference of "a" is how we discover that the property F is instantiated. In Shoemaker's example of the necktie, the envisaged utterance of "This is red" is IEM, because what secures my ability to refer to the necktie with the word "this" is the very same information link that informs me that there is something red at that location.

Demonstrative thought about objects is secured by information links that are actively delivering information that properties are instantiated. "I" and "here" thoughts about people and places do not need to be based on information links that are currently providing information; as Evans argues, it is enough that we are *disposed* to take information from those people and those places via those information links for reference to be secured. But "I" thoughts are nevertheless information based thoughts. My judgment that I am seeing a canary is, in the normal case, IEM because the information that someone is seeing a canary is delivered by the same information link that allows for thought about me in the first instance.

Evans of course recognized that his theoretical explanation of immunity to error through misidentification precluded explaining immunity to error by the hypothesis that the implicated terms are non-referring expressions:

It is worth briefly observing, first, that where this is immunity to error through misidentification, Wittgenstein draws the conclusion that 'I' is not being used to refer to (talk about) a particular object (a person). This seems to be just a mistake. For we have seen . . . that immunity to error through misidentification is a straightforward consequence of demonstrative identification; it will exist whenever a subject's Idea of an object depends upon his ways of gaining knowledge about it. And demonstrative identification is, precisely, a way in which a thought can concern (be about) an object. (1982: 217)

However, even if Evans's theoretical explanation of IEM is incorrect, the very fact that all sorts of judgments involving obviously referring terms are IEM shows that the presence of immunity to error through misidentification is not explained by lack of reference. So the fact that reports using controlled uses of PRO are IEM provides no evidence whatsoever for the predicational theory.

Accounting for the fact that controlled uses of PRO give rise to judgments that are IEM is also a principle feature of the account of the *de se* given in Higginbotham (2003). Recall that, for Higginbotham, the content of the sentence "Bekele expects PRO to win the race" is that *Bekele has the expectation that there will be race-winning event and that the subject of that very expectation will be the subject of that race-winning event.* This entails that Bekele's expectation of winning the race cannot be based on Bekele's belief that he is the F, and his expectation that the F will win the race. For the content of Bekele's expectation is that the subject of that very expectation will be the subject of the race-winning event. It is not that the subject of that very expectation is identical to some other thing x, and x will be the subject of the race-winning event.

However, there is a worry with Higginbotham's account that parallels the concern I have raised for accounts of IEM that try to account for it by non-referentiality. The account is insufficiently general. It is an account of the phenomenon of immunity to error through misidentification that applies only to *embedded* first-person pronouns. An embedded use of PRO, as it occurs in a sentence like "Bekele expects PRO to win the race", has a content that links the subject of "expects" and subject of "win the race". The semantic contribution of PRO includes the information *the subject of the expectation*. But suppose Bekele just asserts, "I am tired". In the normal case, Bekele's judgment is immune to error through misidentification. In the normal case at least, Bekele has not arrived at his judgment by identifying himself with someone who appears to be tired, and on that basis concluded that he is tired. Most of the stock examples of judgments that are IEM involve cases in which there is a non-embedded first-person pronoun, that is, a first person pronoun that does not occur within the scope of a psychological verb. However, Higginbotham's account crucially relies upon the embedding, as it exploits the fact that the embedded occurrence of the first-person pronoun makes reference to the subject of the embedding verb. This cannot serve as a general account of immunity to error through misidentification.[21]

So what accounts for the fact that an embedded occurrence of PRO can only report a state that is IEM? I do not see the need to account for this fact as part of the propositional contribution of PRO. There are some features of me in virtue of which I think of a certain object as myself. If Evans is right, one of those features involves the possession of a certain kind of information link to that object – to take information from that object as relevant to my actions in certain distinctive ways. This information link grounds our

---

[21] In forthcoming work (Folescu and Higginbotham), Higginbotham has taken up this challenge. Like Anscombe (1981: 32–3), he links his account of a use of "I" to the embedded case, by appeal to the reflexive reference rule for the first person pronoun "I". On this account, an utterance u of a sentence of the form "I am F" will express the proposition *that the agent of u is the subject of the property of F.* Higginbotham clearly advances this as the reference rule governing all uses of "I". But then the reference rule cannot be the source of the explanation of judgments that are IEM, since "I" can occur in all sorts of judgments that are *not* IEM.

ability to think about ourselves as ourselves. A first-person judgment that I am F is IEM if and only if the information that F is instantiated comes from that very information link. It is a fact about PRO that one can only use it in the subject position of an embedded verb, when the information that the verb is instantiated has been delivered to that subject via the same information link that gives rise to her own self-concept. This is a fact about PRO, but not a fact about its propositional contribution.

5.

I have proposed a Fregean framework for the treatment of *de se* readings of PRO (and the *de se* generally). In this section, I show how it accounts for the range of classic *de se* cases that have been discussed in the literature. In the next, I defend the approach against more general criticisms of the Fregean framework.

The first case is John Perry's famous case of Heimson and Hume:

> Now suppose Heimson is a bit crazy and thinks himself to be David Hume. Alone in his study, he says to himself, "I wrote the Treatise." However much his inner life may, at the moment, resemble Hume's on that afternoon in 1775, the fact remains: Hume was right, Heimson is wrong. Heimson cannot think the very thought to himself that Hume thought to himself, by using the same sentence. (1977: 487)

According to Perry, the right account of this example requires drawing a distinction between *the sense under which a thought is entertained*, and the thought itself. When Heimson thinks the thought that he is Hume, he believes something different than what Hume believes when he thinks that he is Hume. Heimson's thought is false, and Hume's thought is true. But both entertain the distinct thoughts under the same way of thinking.

David Lewis has quite a different reaction. According to Lewis, the right response is that Heimson and Hume believe the same thing. Here is Lewis's first argument for this conclusion:

> Doubtless it is true in some sense that Heimson does not believe what Hume did. But there had better also be a central and important sense in which Heimson and Hume believe alike. For one thing, the predicate "believes he is Hume" applies alike to both: Heimson believes he is Hume and Hume believes he is Hume. Do not say that I equivocate, and that what is true is only that Heimson believes that he (Heimson) is Hume and Hume believes that he (Hume) is Hume. Everyone believes that Hume is Hume, but not everyone believes that he – he himself – is Hume. There is a general, univocal predicate, which appears for instance in "Not everyone believes that he is Hume," and that is the predicate that applies alike to Heimson and Hume. (1979: 525)

Lewis is right that there is a general, univocal predicate that applies to both Heimson and Hume. It is the predicate 'λx(believes x is Hume)'. From the fact that this predicate applies to both Heimson and Hume, it does not follow that Heimson and Hume have the same belief. The latter would only follow if the result of applying the univocal predicate to Heimson and to Hume yields the same belief content for both. And it clearly does not. Applying "λx(believes x is Hume)" to Hume yields a different content for the object of "believes" than applying "λx(believes x is Hume)" to Heimson.

Lewis's passage contains a riposte to this response. Lewis writes "Do not say . . . that what is true is only that Heimson believes that he (Heimson) is Hume and Hume believes that he (Hume) is Hume. Everyone believes that Hume is Hume, but not everyone believes that he – himself – is Hume." However, this riposte is irrelevant to the Fregean view currently under consideration. On the Fregean view, the result of applying the predicate "λx(believes x is Hume)" to Hume is not the proposition that Hume believes Hume is Hume. This is not a Fregean view. On the view described in the previous section, the univocal predicate that applies to both Heimson and Hume is:

λx((the x: self$_i$ x) believes <x, sense of 'is Hume'>)

Applying this univocal predicate to Hume yields the proposition: *that Hume is such that the x, x = self$_{Hume}$, is such that Hume believes <x, sense of 'is Hume'>*. Hume's belief is not one that everyone believes. In fact, given the Fregean assumption that only Hume is capable of grasping his first-person way of thinking, Hume's belief is one that *only* Hume believes. Lewis's entire line of argument here is completely irrelevant to the Evansian/Fregean theory I have proposed.

Lewis's second argument has to do with the functional role of belief:

What is more important, Heimson may have got his head into perfect match with Hume's in every way that is at all relevant to what he believes. If nevertheless Heimson and Hume do not believe alike, then *beliefs ain't in the head*! They depend partly on something else, so that if your head is in a certain state and you're Heimson you believe something else. Not good. The main purpose of assigning objects of attitudes is, I take it, to characterize states of the head; to specify their causal roles with respect to behavior, stimuli, and one another. If the assignment of objects depends partly on something besides the head, it will not serve this purpose. The states it characterizes will not be the occupants of the causal roles. (525–6)

This argument is just as plausible as the internalist conception of belief states it presupposes. But even the internalist presupposition is not sufficient to support the conclusion. Even those who agree with Lewis that there is a psychologically important level of content that does not depend upon relations to the environment have come to think that belief states do not individuate on that level (e.g. Fodor 1987). It is a standard internalist view that the internal psychological states are not belief states, but rather something like properties that determine belief states, given a context. If one is inclined to think that psychology requires an important level of internalist content, the Fregean framework I have described can offer one – namely the univocal property that Heimson and Hume share, the one expressed by "λx((the x: self$_i$ x) believes <x, sense of 'is Hume'>)".[22]

---

[22] Of course, the sense of "is Hume" (like its reference) is object-dependent. A thoroughgoing defense of an internalist view requires characterizing this psychologically important level of content with the use only of terms that have their content independently of their users' relations to the environment. Little wonder then

A more difficult class of cases involves Bernard Williams's well-known discussion of imagination, in "Imagination and the Self". Williams calls our attention to the example of *imagining being Napoleon*. As Williams notes (1973: 44) describing this as "imagining *myself* being Napoleon" is "possibly misleading". I cannot imagine myself being Napoleon, where "myself" is "the ordinary empirical one" (ibid.), for then "what I imagine seems to be straightforwardly self-contradictory, which stops me in my tracks; and this will not do, for I know that, in imagining being Napoleon, I am not stopped in my tracks" (ibid.). Imagining being Napoleon and imagining that I am Napoleon are both possible exercises of the imagination. But they cannot be conceived of as imaginings whose contents concern my own empirical self-concept.

This is a difficult case for any Fregean view of the content of PRO, of the sort I have described. But the reason it is difficult has to do with the nature of imagining, and not the proposed semantics for PRO. Let us make a distinction, familiar from David Kaplan's classic paper "Demonstratives", between the *character* of a sentence and its *content* relative to a context. The character of a sentence is its context-independent meaning; the content of a sentence relative to a context of use is the proposition that sentence expresses, relative to that context. The character of a sentence such as "I am a philosopher" can be thought of as a function from contexts of use to propositions. Relative to a context in which Saul Kripke is the agent, the sentence "I am a philosopher" expresses the true proposition that Saul Kripke is a philosopher. Relative to a context in which Tom Brady, the quarterback for the New England Patriots, is the agent, it expresses the false proposition that Tom Brady is a philosopher.

The moral of Williams's example is that the verb "imagine" can take the character of a sentence as its object. In imagining that I am Napoleon, the object of my imagining *does* contain the self concept. However, the first-person index associated with the self concept "the x: self$_i$ x" is left unsaturated. What I am doing in having an imagining with this as its object is imagining this object being evaluated relative to a context in which Napoleon is the agent. As David Velleman writes:

In "Smith believes he is Napoleon," the quasi-indicator "he" marks the place of the first-person pronoun in "I am Napoleon" as it might actually be said by Smith. The quasi-indicator thus stands in for a pronoun referring to Smith. But in "Smith imagines that he is Napoleon," the quasi-indicator marks the place of the first-person pronoun in "I am Napoleon" as it might be imagined by Smith but as said in this imagining by Napoleon.

Thus, the "he" in "Smith imagines that he is Napoleon" echoes an imagined use of "I" that would refer to Napoleon and not to Smith. So it does not pick out Smith as the object of Smith's imaginings; it merely introduces the self-concept, or "I," under which Smith imagines Napoleon, as he would express by going on to imagine saying, "I am Napoleon." The same goes for the second occurrence of "I" in "I'm imagining that I am Napoleon." This "I" isn't a reference to me, David Velleman. It simply marks the place of the first-person pronoun in the

---

that Lewis (1979: 526) is led to the view that the proper moral of the externalist turn in semantics is "that beliefs are ill-characterized by the meanings of the sentences that express them."

utterance-image "I am Napoleon," which would demonstrate the orientation of my imagining from within. (1996: 56–7)

As Velleman says, in imagining that I am Napoleon, the function of the pronoun "I" is to *introduce the self-concept*. The verb "imagine" takes, not the content of "I am Napoleon" as its object, but something like its character, in Kaplan's sense.[23] The object of our imagining is something like $<$(the x: self$_i$ x), sense of 'is Napoleon'$>$. What it is to imagine this object is to imagine it as evaluated in a context in which Napoleon is the agent; *mutatis mutandis* for *imagining PRO being Napoleon*. But if so, we need exactly the account of PRO I have given above.

---

[23] Like Evans (1985), I do not imagine that the nature of the self-concept is exhausted by any of the simple formulas mentioned in Kaplan (1989a).

4

Ways of Thinking

Knowing how to do something is first-person knowledge. It is knowledge about oneself, or knowledge *de se*. My favored account of the *de se* appeals centrally to *ways of thinking* of things. But many find appeal to ways of thinking of things of any kind objectionable, preferring an ontology of the mental that consists simply of the things themselves. The bias is understandable. Cloaking its constituents in various garments seems to obscure rather than illuminate the task of explaining how we manage to have thoughts about the world.

I have two central aims in this chapter. The first aim is to demystify ways of thinking of things (i.e. modes of presentation) and motivate their inclusion in an account of the contents of thought. The second is to show that the view that the contents of thought include ways of thinking, conceived of as I describe in this chapter, entails that propositional knowledge is not behaviorally inert – indeed even *entertaining* certain thoughts is not behaviorally inert, but entails the possession of dispositions.

I begin in the first section by explaining and responding to the overarching worries with accounts of the nature of thought that appeal to an ontology of ways of thinking. In the second section, I describe different ways in which an account of the nature of thoughts can incorporate ways of thinking. In the third section, I show how the recognition that propositions contain ways of thinking is precisely the missing ingredient that allows one to account for the remaining unresolved problems in the semantics of questions from Chapter 2. Finally, in the fourth section, I show that the view of ways of thinking I have sketched allows us to see the error in the thought that propositional knowledge is behaviorally inert, a thought that provides much of the intuitive motivation to postulate a non-propositional epistemic state.

1.

There are three reasons accounts of the ontology of the mental that appeal to ways of thinking have been thought to be problematic. First, they are ontologically mysterious entities. Second, ways of thinking are "conceived in sin" – the sin of confusing semantic questions with metasemantic questions. Third, ways of thinking are widely associated with controversial claims in the philosophy of psychology.

On the Fregean framework I have sketched, ways of thinking are abstract entities that are constituents of our thoughts. But as such, they are often held to be mysterious.

Alternative frameworks seem not to require such mysterious entities. For example, the Lewisian framework appeals only to properties and objects, and does not need ways of thinking as semantic contents. It is a view common among advocates of the Lewisian account of the *de se* that that this is an advantage it possesses over the sort of framework I have described.

Recall the discussion of the R_1 relation, which, following Evans, we have been calling that relation that holds between x and y in virtue of which x thinks about y as *self*. Giving an account of the R_1 relation is a philosophical project that we certainly cannot undertake here. But obviously, there is such a relation, because there is something in virtue of which I think of the object that is in fact myself *as* myself. That is, when x thinks that x is F, in the first-person way, there is some account of what it is for x to think of x in the first personal way, rather than simply thinking of x in a (say) third-person way. But given the existence of such a relation, we can simply define ways of thinking into existence, via the sort of contextual definition described in section 3. Ways of thinking are not ontologically problematic.

Furthermore, advocates of the Lewisan framework are committed to accepting the existence of ways of thinking. For the Lewisian, for x to think a *de se* thought to the effect that x himself is λyFy is for x to self-ascribe the property λyFy. As we have seen, this presupposes an account of self-ascription. There is a distinction between x ascribing a property to a thing x regards as itself, and x ascribing a property to a thing that happens in fact to be identical to x. Like the Fregean account, the Lewisian account too presupposes a philosophical account of what it is for x to think of y as *self*. The Lewisian framework too is committed to the existence of R_1. But, as we have seen, given R_1, the existence of first-person ways of thinking follows immediately. There is no ontological worry with ways of thinking not equally shared by alternative frameworks.

Some object to ways of thinking because they are *conceived in sin*, the sin of confusing semantic questions with metasemantic ones. Here is Kaplan on the distinction:

> The fact that a word or phrase *has* a certain meaning clearly belongs to semantics. On the other hand, a claim about the *basis* for ascribing a certain meaning to a word or phrase does not belong to semantics. "Ohsnay" means *snow* in Pig-Latin. That's a semantic fact about Pig-Latin. The reason why "ohsnay" means *snow* is not a semantic fact; it is some kind of historical or sociological fact about Pig-Latin . . . because it is a fact *about* semantics, as part of the *Metasemantics* of Pig-Latin . . . Again, the fact that "nauseous" used to mean *nauseating* but is coming to mean *nauseated* is a historical, semantic fact about contemporary American English. But neither the reason why the change in semantic value has taken place nor the theory that gives the basis for claiming that there has been a change in meaning belongs to semantics. For present purposes let us settle on *metasemantics*. (1989b: 573–4)

A *semantic* thesis is a thesis of the form: "water" refers to the substance water. A *metasemantic* (or *foundational semantic*) thesis is a thesis of the form: "water" refers to the substance water, because there is some kind of law-like causal co-variation between our uses of "water" and instances of the substance water.

A number of authors have accused Fregeans of conflating two distinct questions – the question of what makes it the case that a term has the semantic content it does, and the question of what that term's semantic content is. As Kripke writes:

> Frege should be criticized for using the term "sense" in two senses. For he takes the sense of a designator to be its meaning; and he also takes it to be the way its reference is determined. (1972: 59)

The worry with conflating the foundational semantic question of what makes it the case that a designator has the reference it does, and the semantic question of what the meaning of that designator is, is that it will result in a false sense that one has answered the former foundational semantic question by providing an answer to the latter, semantic one:

> the conflation of the two questions masks the fact that the sense theory, interpreted as an answer to the question of descriptive semantics, is also a non-answer to the foundational question. Suppose we were to accept the Fregean thesis that names have the referent that they have because they have a sense that determines a function whose value (at the actual world) is that referent. This simply raises the question: what is it about the capacities, behavior, or mental state of the users of the name that makes it the case that the name has the sense that it in fact has? (Stalnaker: 1997: 543)

The charge of conflating semantic questions with metasemantic ones is an especially natural one to raise given the way I have introduced first-person ways of thinking. Giving an account of the relation of R_1 that holds between a person and themselves in virtue of which that person thinks of an object as herself is clearly some kind of foundational, metasemantic task. Yet I have claimed that this metasemantic account delivers a semantic value, viz. the propositional contribution of a first-person pronoun such as a controlled use of PRO. Have I therefore failed to give an account of the metasemantics of first-person pronouns?

The answer is: yes, but so what? These questions are, in the first instance, about language. It must be granted that an account of the R_1 relation does not tell us what it is for a first-pronoun to be semantically associated with the way of thinking that is its propositional contribution. Some other foundational story has to be told about how (e.g.) PRO is conventionally associated with the R_1 relation. But this fact is no objection at all against the proposal that the denotation of an occurrence of PRO_i is the $self_i$ concept, where this semantic object is determined by some foundational account of what it is to take an object in the world as oneself. It just shows that some additional account is needed of the relation between the linguistic item that is the first person pronoun and the meaning it expresses. Taking PRO_i to express $self_i$ makes this story no easier, but also no harder.

There is a deeper semantics/metasemantics concern about the Fregean approach to the *de se* I have described. The Fregean first-person way of thinking is determined by a foundational account of what makes it the case that a certain thought I have is about myself, conceived of in the right way. But this looks like an account of *the facts that make it the case that my thought is about a particular object* – not an account of *the contents of my thought*. It may seem like a kind of conceptual error to conclude, from the cognitive relevance of the facts that make it the case that my thought is about a particular object, that there is a thought with a special kind of content, containing a way of thinking that is determined in this metasemantic way.

It is odd that those who advance this kind of criticism of the Fregean approach themselves advocate treatments of Frege's puzzle according to which informativity is explained by metasemantic facts. Indeed, virtually *everyone* agrees with the fundamental Fregean insight that something like metasemantic facts are cognitively relevant. As Robert Stalnaker writes, in a work that is harshly critical of the notion of Fregean sense:

> As is emphasized in both Perry's discussions of reflexive content, and in my uses of the diagonalization strategy, to explain cases of ignorance of the truth of identity statements involving proper names, we need to bring in information, not just about the referent of the names, but also about the facts that connect those names to their referent. (2008: 59)

For example, as Stalnaker here notes, his well-known treatment of the informativity of utterances of identity statements such as "Hesperus is Phosphorus" involves taking what is informative about such utterances to be the fact that they convey meta-semantic information, "about the facts that connect those names to their referent." That is, according to Stalnaker (1978), what is informative about an utterance of "Hesperus is Phosphorus" is that it communicates the proposition that the name "Hesperus" co-refers with the name "Phosphorus". Furthermore, Stalnaker's diagonal proposition ultimately does enter the semantics as a semantic value, for example in belief ascriptions.

As Stalnaker notes, John Perry's notion of reflexive content, designed primarily to deal with the cognitive significance of utterances containing indexicals (2001: 74), is explicitly metasemantic. The reflexive content of an utterance contains information about the "conditions of designation" of the terms in the sentence uttered. In other words, what terms contribute to the reflexive content of utterances of sentences containing them is straightforwardly metalinguistic information. For example, the reflexive content of an informative utterance of "Paderewski is Paderewski" is the proposition *that the person associated with 'Paderewski' by the conventions exploited by the first use of that name in that utterance is the person associated with 'Paderewski' by the conventions exploited in the second use of the name in that utterance* (ibid.: 114).

In short, even those theorists who press most vigorously an important distinction between semantics and metasemantics recognize that the cognitive puzzles to which Frege drew our attention lead inexorably to the conclusion that informational contents themselves must possess something like a metasemantic character. The debate is not then over this widely accepted point. It is rather about the nature of the metasemantic like information that is the content of our cognitive states. Is it, as Stalnaker advocates, *metalinguistic* in character? Or does it involve something like a way of thinking, in Frege's sense?[1]

There are powerful reasons that mitigate in favor of Frege's approach, rather than the even more explicitly metasemantic approach to informational content advocated by anti-Fregeans such as Stalnaker. Suppose I want to attribute to the ancient Babylonians the belief that Hesperus is not Phosphorus. Suppose further I have no idea what language the ancient Babylonians used. The Babylonians certainly didn't believe the diagonal proposition that would be conveyed in English by an utterance of "Hesperus is Phosphorus", since they had no beliefs about English. On Stalnaker's account, I lack the resources to ascribe to them they belief they had. In contrast, the Fregean view has no problem with belief ascriptions to monolingual speakers of languages that we ourselves do not know and with which we lack connections. The ways of thinking of Venus associated with "Hesperus" and "Phosphorus" are, for the Fregean, themselves not explicitly metasemantic. In short, the Fregean view is *less* metasemantic than the views advanced by many of its detractors, and therefore more plausible as a general account of belief ascription.[2]

Fregean ways of thinking are, in a sense, ways of hypostasizing our relations to objects in virtue of which we can think about them. But this does not prevent our thoughts from being genuinely about the world. As Stalnaker (2008: 137) writes, "In the end, we must recognize that even our most stable and robust representations have the content that they have in virtue of our relations to what we represent." It is all of our tasks to explain why, again in Stalnaker's words (ibid.), "[t]his does not prevent us, even in the most local context, from thinking about the world as it is in itself."[3]

There is a third concern about ways of thinking, which is that they over-psychologize our practice of attitude ascription. Frege called our attention to the fact that our ordinary practice of attitude ascriptions would lead us to distinguish the beliefs states of two people with beliefs about the same object, who are thinking of that object in very different ways. Frege himself thought of ways of thinking as abstract objects. But in recent decades many of those who have wished to give theories of attitudes that stay true to the ordinary practice of attitude ascription have been less Platonist than Frege about the contents of these attitudes. Many theories have identified ways of thinking with token representations in something like Fodor's Language of Thought (1975). One might therefore think that the only naturalistically acceptable way to individuate contents finely, with the use of Fregean ways of thinking, involves commitment to something like a Language of Thought. Even if one does accept the

---

[1] Stalnaker's (2008) account of indexical thought is not metalinguistic in character. But he still retains his account of Frege cases like "Hesperus is Phosphorus", in terms of the metalinguistic apparatus introduced by diagonal propositions.

[2] For a full evaluation of Stalnaker's account of non-indexical instances of Frege's puzzle, see Stanley (2010).

[3] It is an interesting question, worthy of further discussion, whether the Fregean approach allows one to evade some of the more untoward consequences of the picture developed in Stalnaker (2008).

Language of Thought hypothesis as an explanation of how propositional attitudes are implemented, it may seem a bit much to think that ordinary attitude ascription by its very nature involves a commitment to it.

This objection is mistaken. It is fully consistent with the Fregean picture of content to concur with Stalnaker (2008: 110) that "[p]ropositions, whether they are Fregean thoughts, Russellian complexes, or sets of possible states of the world, are abstract objects that we use to represent certain capacities and dispositions of people, and certain kinds of social relations between them." For example, Evans's explanation (1982: ch. 7) of the R_1 relation makes no appeal to representations in a language of thought. According to him, I am thinking of an object in the world as myself mainly in virtue of having a stable disposition to take my thoughts and actions to be controlled by information from that object received via first-person ways of gaining information. For example, if I gain the information via proprioception that that object's legs are crossed, I should be led to uncross them when I stand up. If R_1 is explained solely in terms of dispositions and capacities of the speaker, and without appeal to the language of thought, then the first-person way of thinking it determines does not implicate the existence of a language of thought. There is no connection whatsoever between the fineness of grain of propositional contents and issues about how the possession of propositional attitudes is implemented in the mind/brain.

2.

In the previous chapter, I advanced a semantic theory of PRO, as it occurs as the subject of infinitives, in contexts such as "Bekele expects to win the race" or "John knows how to field a ball". However, my account appealed crucially to first-person ways of thinking. Therefore, I needed to show that the notion of a way of thinking of an object is both metaphysically and conceptually sound. But there are different ways of employing ways of thinking in the individuation of the contents of thought. Since it is possible that someone may confuse an objection to one of these ways with an objection to appeals to ways of thinking generally in the individuation of thought content, it is important to be clear about the options.

Frege used the notion of a way of thinking to give an account of the meaning of propositional attitude ascriptions, which are sentences involving propositional attitude verbs such as "believes", "doubts", and "knows". A propositional attitude ascription, such as "John believes that Hesperus is a planet", appears to relate an agent to a thought (or proposition); in the case of this sentence, it appears to relate John to the thought that Hesperus is a planet. According to Frege, while the *referent* of a sentence is a truth-value, the *sense* of a sentence – the way it presents its referent – is a thought. Within the scope of a propositional attitude verb, an expression denotes, not its ordinary referent, but rather its ordinary sense. So propositional attitude verbs (such as "believes") create what are called *opaque contexts*, linguistic contexts in which substitution of co-referring expressions fails. The claim that propositional attitude verbs create opaque contexts accords with our intuition that "John believes that Hesperus is a planet" may be true, whereas "John believes that Phosphorus is a planet" is false, even though "Hesperus" and "Phosphorus" refer to the same object, viz. the planet Venus. "Hesperus" and "Phosphorus" cannot be substituted for one another in the scope of a propositional attitude verb, despite the fact that they have the same referent. Frege's account of the meaning of propositional attitude constructions explains this, because according to this account, "Hesperus" and "Phosphorus", within the scope of a propositional attitude verb, refer to their ordinary senses, rather than the object Venus. Therefore, within the scope of a propositional attitude verb, "Hesperus" and "Phosphorus" do not after all have the same referent.

I have argued that the proposition that I am tired and the proposition that Jason Stanley is tired are distinct propositions, despite the fact that I am Jason Stanley. The former proposition contains a first-person way of thinking of Jason Stanley, and the latter proposition does not contain a first-person way of thinking of Jason Stanley. My use of the first-person pronoun has a distinct propositional contribution from my use of the name "Jason Stanley" – the former expresses a first-person way of thinking, and the latter does not. But the fact that "I" and "Jason Stanley" have distinct propositional contributions, on my view, does not require us to follow Frege to the letter.

Let us say that an occurrence of an expression e is within an *extensional context* in a sentence S if and only if one can substitute for that occurrence of e any expression with the same extension as e, without changing the truth-value of S. So "I", as it occurs in "I am tired", as used by Jason Stanley, can be substituted for "Jason Stanley" without changing the truth-value of S at the time of utterance. Similarly, "Hesperus", in "Hesperus is a planet", can be substituted for "Phosphorus", without changing the truth-value of the sentence "Hesperus is a planet". So these occurrences of "I" and "Hesperus" are in extensional contexts.

Expressions that occur inside the scope of propositional attitude verbs, such as "know" or "believes", are intuitively not in extensional contexts – intuitively, it is not possible to substitute co-referring terms inside the scope of "knows" or "believes" while invariably preserving the truth of the whole sentence. For example, "John believes that Hesperus is a planet" intuitively does not entail "John believes that Phosphorus is a planet", and vice versa. In the classical construal of a Fregean semantic theory, due to Church (1951), one accounts for this fact by shifting the semantic value of an expression. In extensional contexts, expressions denote entities that are typically not ways of thinking. However, inside the scope of a propositional attitude verb, such as "know" or "believes", expressions denote ways of thinking, or senses. On this strict Fregean view, the objects of propositional attitudes (i.e. propositions) consist solely of ways of thinking. If we were to employ this kind of semantic theory, the way to understand the descriptive quantifier "self$_i$", introduced in section 3, is as ranging solely over ways of thinking.

But there is another way of exploiting ways of thinking to give fine-grained accounts of propositions, which is one that Rudolf Carnap (1958) exploited in the analysis of *de re* modality. A *de re* modal sentence is a sentence that contains a free variable in the scope of a modal operator, such as "∃x□Fx", or in English, a sentence like "There is something such that necessarily it is rational" (a *de dicto* modal sentence is a sentence that contains a modal operator with no free variables in its scope). In *de re* modal sentences, a quantifier such as "something" or "everything" binds a variable within the scope of a modal operator, such as "necessarily" or "possibly". But terms occurring within the scope of a modal operator are not in extensional contexts. Even if the winner of the Boston Marathon is the same as the winner of the New York City Marathon, "the winner of the Boston Marathon" cannot be substituted for "the winner of the New York City Marathon" inside modal contexts without potentially altering the truth of the original sentence. After all, it is not necessary that the winner of the New York City Marathon is the winner of the Boston Marathon.

The way that Carnap dealt with the problem raised by *de re* modal contexts involved his "method of extension and intension", which involved simultaneously assigning to each expression, including variables, both an intension and an extension (ibid.: 42–6). When a variable occurs within the scope of a modal operator, the value that is relevant is the intension, rather than the extension. But nevertheless, even when the relevant value of an occurrence of an expression is its intension, that occurrence still has an extension as one of its semantic values. Carnap contrasted his "method of extension and intension" with what he called *the method of the name relation* (ibid.: ch. 3). According to the method of the name relation, each occurrence of an expression has only one semantic value. The strict Fregean method is a special case of the method of the name relation. Frege took each occurrence of an expression in a sentence to have only one semantic value. If the occurrence is within a non-extensional context, then the occurrence has as its semantic value something other than its ordinary reference; if the occurrence is embedded under only one non-extensional operator, then it has its ordinary sense as its referent.

From one contemporary perspective both the Frege/Church method and Carnap's method of treating the problem of *de re* modality are species of the same genus. Both treat variables occurring in modal contexts as special in some way, as not *simply* contributing ordinary referents, relative to an assignment function, to the semantic value of the sentence in which they occur. For both Church and Carnap, the semantically relevant value of an occurrence of a variable in a non-extensional context, relative to an assignment function, is not an extension of a singular term, but something like a sense. Because this contemporary perspective is dominant in current philosophy of language, it is easy to forget that there are distinct ways to individuate content with the use of ways of thinking.

On a strict Fregean view, propositions contain *only* ways of thinking – this is the method of the name relation. On such a view, the object of Bekele's expectation to win the race would be a pure Fregean proposition, one that contained only ways of thinking as constituents. Therefore, on such a view, "self$_i$" would quantify only over first person ways of thinking. If, on the other hand, we thought in terms of the method of intension and extension, propositions would contain both ways of thinking and objects. An occurrence of the first-person pronoun "I" would contribute both its sense and its referent to the proposition expressed by the sentence containing it. On this Carnapian way of thinking, one would take the propositional contribution of "I" to be an ordered pair of a first-person way of thinking and the referent of "I" on that occasion of use, i.e. the person who employs it. If we were to employ this way of thinking of propositions, "self$_i$" would quantify over ordered pairs of first-person ways of thinking and persons.

On the strict Fregean view, first-person thoughts do not contain objects as constituents, but only ways of thinking. On the Carnapian variant, first-person thoughts contain ordered pairs of objects and ways of thinking (and similarly, ordered pairs of properties and ways of thinking). There is a sophisticated contemporary defense of fine-grained propositions in the Carnapian tradition, and it is due to David Chalmers (forthcoming). Chalmers takes the *enriched intension* of a term to be an ordered pair of its "primary intension" and its extension. The objects of propositional attitudes are *enriched propositions*, by which he means structured entities composed out of enriched intensions. The propositional contribution of a use of "I" will be an ordered pair of the first-person "primary intension" and its referent on that occasion. If we replace Chalmers's primary intensions with ways of thinking, this is precisely the Carnapian alternative to the strict Fregean view.

I have argued that there are first-person ways of thinking, and I have argued that they are constituents of propositions that we know. However, I have not taken a stand on whether the advocate of fine-grained propositions should prefer the strict Fregean view, where propositions contain only ways of thinking, or the Carnap/Chalmers variant, where thoughts contain both ways of thinking and objects ("intensions" and "extensions"). Furthermore, both Carnap and Chalmers think of senses as modal intensions of various kinds – functions from state descriptions, or possible worlds, to extensions. I do not think of ways of thinking in this way, but rather as abstract objects determined by functional roles. Nevertheless, for my purposes in this book, nothing hangs on what we take the nature of these abstract objects to be.

3.

If thoughts are, as Frege and Evans supposed, structured entities containing ways of thinking of objects, then we should expect that theoretical employment of less-fine-grained views of thoughts raises intractable problems. An obvious example here is the problem facing any account of propositional attitudes that does not appeal to such a view of propositions. A less obvious example occurs with the two problems for standard accounts of the nature of questions with which we concluded Chapter 2. Both problems involved ascriptions of knowing-who, as in "Hannah knows who Sarah is". The first, following Maria Aloni, we called the problem of triviality. The second was the distinctive additional kind of context-sensitivity present in such ascriptions, which was not obviously captured by the standard mechanisms for domain restriction. Like Frege's puzzle, both of these problems turn out to be consequences of the failure to recognize that thoughts are structured entities composed at least in part of ways of thinking.

Here is the problem of triviality again. A complete answer to "who is Bill Clinton" is a proposition of the form "N is Bill Clinton". But then knowing that Bill Clinton is Bill Clinton is sufficient for knowing-who Bill Clinton is. If so, then everyone knows who Bill Clinton is. But clearly, there are some people who do not know who Bill Clinton is.

Here is the problem of context-sensitivity again. Suppose that Hannah can pick Bill Clinton out of a line-up of people, but Hannah has no idea that he was the 42nd President of the United States. Relative to some contexts, the sentence "Hannah knows who Bill Clinton is" is true, but relative to other contexts it is false. Any account of the context-sensitivity of questions should account for this kind of context-sensitivity. But Hannah knows that Bill Clinton is Bill Clinton. So it seems that "Hannah knows who Bill Clinton is" is true in every context.

The problems are obviously related. Suppose we assume a coarse-grained account of propositions, where propositions are either sets of possible worlds or structured combinations of objects and properties. Suppose we also assume a view of names and demonstrative pronouns according to which they are directly referential expressions, and hence contribute only the objects they denote to the propositions expressed by sentences containing them. Then it follows that Hannah knows who Bill Clinton is, provided that she knows that Bill Clinton is Bill Clinton.

However, this is a problem created by the failure to recognize that ways of thinking are semantically relevant. Let us adopt a view of the semantics of names that is akin to Carnap's method of intension and extension discussed in the previous section – perhaps they denote "enriched intensions" in the sense of Chalmers (forthcoming). On this sort of view, an occurrence of a name contributes an ordered pair of its referent and a way of thinking.[4] Given that the domain of individual-level semantic values consists now of ordered pairs of objects and ways of thinking, we must adjust our conception of domains of quantification similarly. The things in the first-order domain of quantification are no longer objects. Rather, they are ordered pairs of objects and ways of thinking.

As we saw in Chapter 2, the proposition expressed by "Hannah knows who Bill Clinton is" is the same as that expressed by "Hannah knows which person Bill Clinton is". There is a domain of quantification associated with the common noun "person". The things in the domain of quantification are ordered pairs of objects and ways of

---

[4] Chalmers (forthcoming) would describe the ordered pair of an object and a primary intension itself as the way of thinking. This is just a terminological distinction, brought on by the fact that Chalmers operates with an ontology of modal intensions instead of Fregean senses, in the way that I am conceiving of them here.

thinking.[5] Let us see how this view accounts for the context-sensitivity of ascriptions of knowing-who, and the problem of triviality.

Suppose Hannah knows what Bill Clinton looks like, but does not know that he is a politician. In a context where picking Bill Clinton out of a line-up of men is at issue, I utter "Hannah knows who Bill Clinton is". The occurrence of "Bill Clinton" denotes an ordered pair of an object and a way of thinking. We can suppose that the way of thinking associated with this occurrence of "Bill Clinton" is informationally equivalent to the metalinguistic description "the famous person named 'Bill Clinton'". So "Bill Clinton" denotes <Bill Clinton, ml-w>, where ml-w is the abstract object determined by the metalinguistic description ML. The domain associated with the occurrence of "who" consists of ordered pairs of objects and ways of thinking. Intuitively, the domain consists of ordered pairs of people in the line-up, and a visual way of thinking of them. Since Bill Clinton is in the lineup, one element in the domain is <Bill Clinton, v-w>, where v-w is a visual way of thinking of Bill Clinton.

Relative to the envisaged context c, the semantic value of "who Bill Clinton is" is:

[who Bill Clinton is]$_c$ = $\lambda i\lambda k[\lambda x[$In the line-up (x)(i) & x = Bill Clinton (i)] = $\lambda x[$In the line-up(x)(i) & x = Bill Clinton(k)]]

Assuming that identity and distinctness are both necessary, this reduces to:

$\lambda i\lambda k[\lambda x[$In the line-up (x)(i) & x = Bill Clinton (i)]]

Variables range over ordered pairs of objects and ways of thinkings of those objects. A sentence of the form "x=y" is true if and only if the first members of the ordered pairs are the same. So, a sentence like "Hesperus is Phosphorus" is true, because the first member of the ordered pair <Venus, Hesperus-mode-of-presentation> is identical with the first member of the ordered pair <Venus, Phosphorus-mode-of-presentation>. So, Hannah stands in the knowledge relation at world w to $\lambda i\lambda k[\lambda x[$In the line-up (x)(i) & x = Bill Clinton (i)]] if and only if Hannah knows that $\lambda k[\lambda x[$In the line-up (x)(w) & x = Bill Clinton (w)]]. Since we are operating with a Fregean framework, we also adopt the Fregean view that propositions are structured. For Hannah to know that $\lambda k[\lambda x[$In the line-up (x)(w) & x = Bill Clinton (w)]] is for her to stand in the knowledge relation to the proposition that has the structure like "$\lambda k[\lambda x$ [In the line-up (x)(w) & x = Bill Clinton (w)]]."

Suppose that Bill Clinton is in the line-up. The sentence "Hannah knows who Bill Clinton is" will be true relative to this context at a world w if and only if Hannah knows that <Bill Clinton, v-w> is in the line-up and that <Bill Clinton, ML-w> is <Bill Clinton, v-w>. This is a different structured proposition than the proposition that <Bill Clinton, ML-w> is in the line-up and <Bill Clinton, ML-w> is <Bill Clinton, ML-w>. Knowing the latter proposition does not entail knowing the former

---

[5] Actually, the domain of quantification is a property, the extension of which is a set of ordered pairs of objects and ways of thinking (Stanley and Szabo 2000: 252). The simplification does not affect the discussion.

proposition (I might know the latter proposition on the basis of testimony, but this does not give me knowledge of the former proposition). More generally, knowing that <Bill Clinton, ML-w> is <Bill Clinton, v-w> is non-trivial, whereas knowing that <Bill Clinton, ML-w> is <Bill Clinton, ML-w> is trivial. Only the proposition that <Bill Clinton, ML-w> is <Bill Clinton, v-w> occurs as a constituent in an answer to the question "Who Bill Clinton is" in the envisaged context of the line-up. Knowing that <Bill Clinton, ML-w> is <Bill Clinton, ML-w> does not help at all in knowing the answer to the question in this context.

Once one recognizes that ways of thinking are semantically relevant, the problem of triviality no longer arises. Furthermore, the context-sensitivity of ascriptions of knowing-who follows straightforwardly from the account of domain restriction defended in Stanley and Szabo (2000), the so-called nominal restriction theory. Relative to a context in which a line-up is at issue, the domain of quantification consists of ordered pairs of persons in the line-up and visual ways of thinking of those people. Relative to a context in which the issue is which president Bill Clinton was, the domain of quantification consists of ordered pairs of presidents of the United States, and descriptive ways of thinking of the kind *the nth president of the United States*. Relative to the latter context, "Hannah knows who Bill Clinton is" is not true, despite the fact that she knows that <Bill Clinton, ML-w> is <Bill Clinton, v-w>. In order for "Hannah knows who Bill Clinton is" to be true relative to this context, she must know that <Bill Clinton, ML-w> is <Bill Clinton, the-42nd-president-w>.

Both the problem of triviality and the problem of accounting for the full range of context-sensitivity associated with ascriptions of knowing-who are artifacts of a failed theory of propositions. Recognizing that the Fregean view of propositions is correct – that thoughts are structured entities composed at least in part of ways of thinking of objects – dissolves these otherwise intractable puzzles.

4.

Following Evans, I have argued that first-person ways of thinking can be obtained from an account of what makes it the case that I am thinking of the object that is myself at a given time. One can assume that such an account will take the form of a characterization of the *functional role* of the self-concept. To think of an object in the world as myself is to possess certain dispositions involving that object in the world. If that object in the world is cold, I will clothe it; if it is wet I will dry it, etc. In general, I think of an object in the world as me if and only if I treat it in a first-person way. The difficulty in giving an account of the first-person lies in specifying in non-circular terms what a first-person way is. I have certainly not attempted that difficult task here. My aim has only been to sketch the general form of such an account.

Given what I have said about the first-person way of thinking, one can see the form in which one might explain ways of thinking of other kinds. For example, a demonstrative way of thinking of an object will be given by an account of what it is to think of a perceptually presented object in a demonstrative way. Here too one would expect such an account to involve the attribution to the thinker of dispositions involving the demonstratively presented object. If a belief of mine is a demonstrative belief about a perceptually presented object, then I will be disposed to have changes in that object affect my belief. For example, perceptible color changes in that object will cause me to give up the belief that that object is red. A change in that object's location will cause my beliefs about its location relative to me to change accordingly. In many cases, a way of thinking of an object is given in large part by an account of the dispositions I have towards that object, dispositions both regarding the beliefs I have and the actions I may undertake. Given such a functional role account of a singular concept, one can use it to characterize the abstract object that is a way of thinking about the object in question.

I am now ready to fulfill a promissory note made in section 3 of the first chapter. The thought that propositional knowledge is inert provides a natural motivation for philosophers to distinguish between knowing how to do something and propositional knowledge. Ryle's conception of propositional knowledge did not entail possession of dispositions. Yet it is impossible to deny that agents do possess dispositions to behave in various ways, and that they have these dispositions in virtue of the attitudes they possess. Since there is pressure to recognize epistemic states of the speaker that *do* entail the possession of dispositions, and on this model of propositional attitudes their possession does *not* entail the possession of dispositions, the pressure takes the form of an argument for the existence of epistemic states that consist merely of dispositions or abilities.

Once one recognizes that thoughts contain ways of thinking, the pressure is relieved. Ways of thinking are characterized in terms of dispositions speakers have both to form beliefs about objects and to engage in various actions with respect to those objects. What one contemplates when one entertains a proposition is often something that requires one to have certain kinds of dispositions towards objects. As we have seen, this is particularly obvious in the case of first-person thought. When it comes to thoughts about oneself, there is simply no possibility of contemplation without the disposition to execute.

5

Knowledge How

Knowing how to do something is a kind of knowledge-wh, a relation to a question. It is also a first-person mental state. We have looked at a general account of knowing-wh, and also an account of first-person mental states. It is time to add the remaining elements of the analysis of the practical knowledge. These two remaining elements are the *modality* associated with infinitival embedded questions, and the distinctive *mention-some* reading of infinitival questions.

As Rajesh Bhatt (2006: 117) notes in a major study of modality in infinitive constructions in natural language, "All infinitival questions involve modality". The problem lies in delineating the various types of modality that appear in such constructions – in other words, we have to decide how the modality associated with infinitival questions can be interpreted. Before I address this question, it is useful briefly to lay down some very basic points about modality that have been widely assumed in the literature since Kratzer (1977). This is the task of the first section. I conclude the section with a brief discussion of the modalities associated with infinitival embedded questions. In section 2, I give a semantic account of the distinction between mention-some and mention-all readings of questions within a Groenendijk and Stokhof framework. In section 3, I introduce and defend the final part of the analysis, practical ways of thinking, and bring the full account to bear on an explanation of the relation between knowing how to do something, ability, and skilled action.

1.

Explicit modals, such as "must" and "can", as one can see from the examples in (1), appear to have distinct readings:

(1) a. I can smoke in this restaurant.
    b. I must pay my taxes.
    c. I can lift 200 pounds.
    d. I must sneeze.
    e. I can treat students however I want.
    f. I must treat students more kindly.
    g. I might have been born in the United States.
    h. I must have been born in the United States.

In (1a), "can" naturally means "permitted by laws"; in (1b) "must" means "obligated by laws". In (1c), "can" means something like "being able"; in (1d) "must" means something like "necessitated by my current dispositions". In (1e), "can" means "morally permitted"; in (1f), "must" means "morally obligated". In (1g), "might" means "consistent with my evidence"; in (1h), "must" means "entailed by my evidence".

One way to treat all of these distinct readings of "must" and "can" is to suppose that modals are systematically ambiguous. Both "must" and "can" permit widely different readings – minimally a *legal* reading, as in (1a, b), an *ability/dispositional* reading, as in (1c, d), a *deontic* reading, as in (1e, f), and an *epistemic* reading, as in (1g, h). But this obviously misses a generalization. It is no accident that modals have all of these different readings. What is needed is an account that preserves a unified meaning of "must" and "can", yet predicts that the unified meaning, together with context, can yield all the diverse contents we see in (1). This is the contribution of Angelika Kratzer's seminal work on modality (1977). The essential idea is that modal statements make claims about a contextually supplied set of possibilities. The differences between various "flavors" of modalities are due to variations in this contextually supplied set.

We only need to sketch the very basics of Kratzer's analysis; we may abstract away from features of the analysis that are irrelevant for our purposes. According to her account, which we shall adopt, the context of use fixes a single modal parameter, which determines the content of modal terms that are used in that context. The modal parameter is a function f that yields, for each possible world w, *a set of propositions*. If we treat propositions as sets of possible worlds, the modal parameter yields, given a world, a set of sets of possible worlds. Let us call the intersection of all of these propositions that are the value of the modal parameter, given a possible world, *the modal base* for the relevant modal. The modal base will be a set of worlds – intuitively, the set of worlds in which all of the propositions that are the value of the modal parameter are true. "It must be the case that p" is true relative to a world w and a modal parameter f if and only if p is true in all of the worlds in the modal base determined by f relative to w. "It can be the case that p" is true relative to a world w and a modal parameter f if and only if p is true in at least one world w' in the modal base determined by f relative to w. Different modal parameters yield potentially different sets of propositions, given a possible world, and hence potentially different modal bases. What appear to be different kinds of modality are just different values for the modal parameter, and even the same kind of modal "force" can be evaluated with respect to distinct modal parameters, and hence distinct modal bases.[1]

In the case of legal necessity, as in (1a, b), f(w) yields the set of propositions that are the legislative laws in w. (1a) is true if and only there is at least one possible world w' in which I smoke, and all the legislative laws are followed; (1b) is true if and only if in every world in which all the legislative laws are followed, I pay my taxes. (1c, d)

---

[1] For our purposes, we will not need to make reference to an ordering within the modal base (an "ordering source").

involve a modal parameter that is determined by my physical dispositions and capacities. (1c) is true at w if and only if there is some possible world in which I have all the physical capacities and dispositions I have at w, and no others, and I lift 200 pounds. (1d) is true at w if and only if I sneeze at all the worlds in which I have the physical capacities and dispositions I do at w and no others. (1e, f) involve a modal parameter that determines the set of worlds at which everyone obeys all the moral laws at the original world of evaluation. (1g, h) involve a modal parameter that determines the set of worlds in which my evidence is the same as it is in the world of evaluation. This is how Kratzer's basic semantics preserves a uniform meaning for all modals, yet captures the distinct contents we see in the examples in (1).

Let us now return to infinitival embedded questions. We need to decide what modal readings are permitted by such constructions. It will help to look at some examples:

(2) a. John knows who to call in case of an emergency.
     b. John knows where to buy an Italian newspaper.
     c. John knows when to call a doctor.
     d. John knows whether to call a doctor.
     e. John knows how to solve the problem.
     f. John knows what to do.

Natural paraphrases of the sentences in (2) are:

(3) a. John knows who he ought to call in case of an emergency.
     b. John knows where he could buy an Italian newspaper.
     c. John knows when he ought to call a doctor.
     d. John knows whether he ought to call a doctor.
     e. John knows how he could solve the problem.
     f. John knows what he ought to do.

Note that it is not possible to read the modality associated with infinitival embedded questions as *epistemic* modality. Such constructions seem only to allow either deontic necessity readings (such as those associated with "ought") or possibility modals involving abilities. As Stanley and Williamson write, summarizing this data:

So, infinitives appear to have at least two different kinds of readings. On the first reading, they express deontic modality. In this case, a use of "to F" expresses something like "ought to F". On the second reading, they express some kind of possibility. On this reading, a use of "to F" expresses something like "can F". These are the two readings which seem available for infinitives in embedded questions. (2001: 424)

However, it seems something more specific can be said about the interpretive possibilities for infinitival embedded questions. Whether a deontic necessity reading is most natural (that is, something like "ought") or some kind of "ability" or dispositional possibility modal (like "could" or "can") seems to depend on the question word used. As Bhatt (2006: 122) notes, "A paraphrase with 'can/could' seems appropriate when the extracted element is 'where' or 'how'". In all other infinitival embedded questions – those formed with "who", "what", and "whether", a paraphrase with "ought" seems most natural. However, with enough context, it is certainly possible to elicit deontic readings even with embedded questions involving "how" and "where" – and the naturalness of a deontic reading seems also to depend on the choice of the predicate (as in "John knows how to behave at a party"). Bhatt (122) nicely summarizes the data as follows:

If we try to paraphrase an infinitival question with a finite question, we find that the paraphrase involves a modal word. The quantificational force of the modal word that we choose seems to vary depending upon a variety of factors such as the embedding predicate, the extracted element [the question word], the predicate in the infinitival question, and the context. The modal that we choose can be "could", "should", or "would".[2]

The kind of construction that chiefly concerns us is exemplified by the sentences in (4):

(4)   a. Hannah knows how to solve the problem.
       b. Hannah knows how to swim.
       c. Hannah knows how to ride a bicycle.

As we have seen, the most natural interpretation of the modal force associated with the infinitives in these constructions is what we might call an *ability* or *dispositional* modal – one would paraphrase (4a), for example, as "Hannah knows how she could solve the problem", and (4b) as "Hannah knows how she could swim". The fact that these are natural paraphrases of the constructions in (4) is due to the fact that the infinitival embedded questions contain an occurrence of PRO that is controlled by "Hannah", the matrix subject, and the fact that infinitival "how" questions, like infinitival "where" questions, are most naturally (but not invariably) associated with a dispositional modal reading.

As we shall see in detail below, the fact that the modal force associated with infinitives in constructions such as (4) is what we have called an "ability" or "dispositional" modal does not entail that it is governed by the exact same modal parameter that governs explicit ability modals, like "is able to", or explicit ability modal readings of "could". The reason that I have called it an ability modal is that the modal parameter, like the modal parameter associated with "is able to" and "could", involve capacities of the agent. But, as I will show below, there are clear differences between the range of worlds relevant for determining the modal base of an explicit use of "is able to", and the range of worlds relevant for the modalities associated with infinitives.

We have thus addressed two pieces of the puzzle – the interpretation of PRO, and the natural interpretation of the modality associated with embedded infinitival ques-

---

[2] As Bhatt points out, the modality depends upon the embedding predicate as well – so "John knows where to get gas" seems to have a "could" paraphrase, but "John and Mary agreed where to get gas" seems to have an "ought" paraphrase (2006: 123).

tions. I now turn to the next piece of the puzzle – the interpretation of "mention-some" readings of questions.

2.

As we have seen in the previous chapter, the natural interpretation of most finite embedded questions is in fact the mention-all reading. To know who went to the party seems to require knowing, of each person who went to the party, that they went to the party (and, if "strong exhaustivity" is correct, of each person in the domain who did not go to the party, that she did not go to the party). However, embedded questions with infinitival complements do not naturally give rise to mention-all readings:

(5)   a. Hannah knows where to find an Italian newspaper in New York.
      b. Hannah knows how to ride a bicycle.

The natural reading of the examples in (5) is not a mention-all reading. Example (5a) means that Hannah knows, of some place, that it is a place where she could find an Italian newspaper in New York. Example (5b) means that Hannah knows, of some way of riding a bicycle, that it is a way in which she could ride a bicycle. It is not necessary for the truth of (5a) and (5b) that Hannah know of *every* place that is a place she could buy an Italian newspaper in New York, that it is so, or that Hannah know of every way that is a way in which she could ride a bicycle, that it is so. All that is required for the truth of (5a) is that Hannah knows, of *some* place, that it is a place where she could find an Italian newspaper in New York. Similarly, all that is required for the truth of (5b) is that Hannah knows, of *some* way of riding a bicycle, that it is a way in which she could ride a bicycle. But the Groenendijk and Stokhof semantics for questions we discussed in the previous chapter was designed to deal with only the so-called "mention-all" readings of embedded questions, and so cannot explain the natural readings of embedded infinitival questions.

Unfortunately, there is no commonly accepted proposal for treating mention-some readings of questions in the literature. Each proposal faces obstacles. For example, suppose that we adopted Kartunnen's semantics, where a question denotes the set of its true answers. Then, as we saw in the last chapter, one could easily capture the mention-some reading of embedded questions by a special meaning postulate for question-embedding verbs. Each extensional question-embedding verb V would then have three distinct meanings. The first meaning V_1 would relate persons to propositions, and the second two would relate persons to sets of propositions. The second meaning V_2 would relate a person to a set of propositions if and only if that person stood in the V_1 relation to all the propositions in the set (this would be the mention-all reading). The third meaning V_3 would relate a person to a set of propositions if and only if that person stood in the V_1 relation to at least one proposition in that set (see the discussion of Meaning Postulate II in Chapter 4, section 1).

This is a simple emendation to the Kartunnen semantics for questions. However, it faces empirical problems. Consider the following example, due to Will Starr (p.c.):

(6)   John knows which Beatles albums are good and where to find them.

In this example, there are conjoined embedded questions. The first of the questions is "which Beatles albums are good". Intuitively, for John to know which Beatles albums are good he needs to know, for every good Beatles album, that it is a good Beatles album. The second of the questions is "where to find them". Intuitively, for John to know where to find the good Beatles albums he only needs to know, for *some* place that is a place at which one can find all the good Beatles albums, that it is such a place. The problem with treating the distinction between mention-some and mention-all readings of questions as a distinction in the meaning of the question-embedding verb, is that there is only one question-embedding verb in (6). Neither assigning it the meaning knows$_2$ (the mention-all meaning) or knows$_3$ (the mention-some) will capture the fact that the first conjunct is mention-all, and the second conjunct is mention-some. The moral is that the distinction between a mention-some reading and a mention-all reading, if it is semantic, has to do with the meanings of the embedded questions themselves, and not the question-embedding verb. The difficulty in accounting for mention-some meanings lies in explaining the meaning difference between a question that we hear as a mention-some question and a question that we hear as a mention-all question.

One proposal, due to unpublished work by Craige Roberts, involves taking mention-some readings to have the exact same semantics as mention-all readings. The difference between mention-some and mention-all readings is due to *quantifier domain restriction*. The idea is that the impression of an existential reading is due to the fact that the extension of the quantifier domain property for the relevant question just contains one thing satisfying the relevant property. So when I utter (5a), the domain for the question just contains one place where one can buy Italian newspapers in New York City. The semantics is the same – what is said is that Hannah needs to know of all places in the domain that are places to buy Italian newspapers in New York City, that they are such places. What gives rise to the impression of a distinct mention-some reading is that there is only one place in the extension of the domain property that is a place to buy Italian newspapers in New York City.

This proposal deals elegantly with the fact that one can conjoin mention-some and mention-all readings of questions. However, there are some concerns with it. The mention-all reading requires that the agent know the complete answer, which is either all the answers in the question set, or the conjunction of all the answers. The function of the domain is to narrow down the question set, or shorten the conjunction, to make it plausible that the agent knows all the answers, or the entire conjunction. But there are difficulties in formulating the domain restriction to arrive at truth conditions that are not too demanding. Suppose, for example, that the domain restriction in (7) consists of the stores with which John is acquainted:

(7)   John knows where to buy an Italian newspaper.

Suppose John is acquainted with ten stores. One of them sells Italian newspapers, and John knows this. So, intuitively (7) is true. But another store to which he regularly goes also sells Italian newspapers, though John isn't aware of this. In this situation, we predict incorrectly that (7) is false, since John doesn't know of all the stores with which he is acquainted, which ones are one at which he could buy an Italian newspaper.

A second more theoretical worry is that the proposal does not capture the fact that mention-some readings seem to be *systematically* associated with certain kinds of embedded questions – in particular, infinitival embedded questions, and in particular, infinitival embedded questions in which the modal has an existential "could" like reading. If the distinction had simply to do with pragmatics (the choice of the quantifier domain), then we would not expect the mention-all/mention-some distinction to correlate so strongly with the particular linguistic construction chosen.

It is not clear to me how significant these worries are. But just in case there is in the end no plausible way to motivate the required domain restrictions to preserve a uniform mention-all reading of questions, it is worthwhile having in place an alternative account. Here is one such natural alternative treatment of mention-some readings of questions, one that respects the fact that they seem conventionally associated with certain constructions. Suppose we took the semantic content of a mention-some reading of "where to buy a newspaper" to be as follows (supposing x to be the value of PRO in the subject position of "to buy an Italian newspaper"):

[where to buy an Italian newspaper] = $\lambda j \lambda i (\exists p [(x$ can buy an Italian newspaper at p, j) & (x can buy an Italian newspaper at p, i)])

Like Groenendijk and Stokhof's treatment of mention-all readings, the denotation of a mention-some reading is a function from worlds to propositions. The meaning we have given for "where to buy an Italian newspaper" is such that, given a world w as input, it yields a proposition true at a world w' if and only there is a place at which x can buy an Italian newspaper at w' that is also a place at which x can buy an Italian newspaper at w. More generally, the denotation of a mention-some reading of "wh-to-Φ", where x is the value of PRO, is:

[wh-to-Φ] = $\lambda j \lambda i (\exists p [(x$ can Φ (p, j) & (x can Φ (p, i)])^3

---

^{3} There is a difficulty with this treatment, which I owe to Josh Dever. Suppose that I am facing two stores. I know that one of them sells Italian newspapers, but I do not know which one. I do not know where to buy an Italian newspaper. But I do know that there exists a place with which I am acquainted at which I could buy an Italian newspaper. The solution to this problem for my analysis of mention-some readings of questions is to make the domain property more complicated – in this case, the property of being known to me as a place to buy Italian newspapers. The problem could also be solved by giving the existential quantifier wide-scope with respect to the embedding verb, but it is difficult to accomplish this compositionally.

If the question word is "where", then the existential quantifier ranges over places. If the question word is "how", then the existential quantifier ranges over ways.

Given this denotation for mention-some readings of questions, we can employ the normal Groenendijk and Stokhof denotation for extensional question-embedding verbs. Recall the meaning postulate for "knows wh" in the previous chapter (where x is a person and w is a possible world):

(Knows-wh) Knows (x, Φ, w) if and only x knows that Φ(w).

We can apply this meaning postulate straightforwardly to the meaning of "how to F" or "where to F", etc., given [wh-to-Φ]. On this account, mention-some readings have entirely to do with the meaning of the complement, and not the meaning of the embedding verb. One can therefore easily account for examples such as Starr's (6), where a question with a mention-all reading and a question with a mention-some reading are conjoined.

Let us see how the semantics works with example (7), "John knows how to solve the problem". Abstracting from the inner complexities of the clause, the denotation for "how to solve the problem" is:

$\lambda j \lambda i (\exists m[(x$ can solve the problem (m, j) & (x can solve the problem $(m, i)]$)

Relative to a world w, John stands in the (knows-wh) relation to this semantic value (a function from worlds to propositions) if and only if John knows that $\lambda i (\exists m[($John can solve the problem (m, w) & (John can solve the problem $(m, i)])$, i.e. John knows at w a proposition that is true at a world w′ if and only if there is a way John can solve the problem in w′ that is also a way in which John can solve the problem at w.

As we have seen, because question words introduce properties associated with domains, questions are context-sensitive constructions for the same reason that quantified noun phrases are context-sensitive constructions. We have seen in detail in Chapter 2 how to treat this kind of context-sensitivity. Recall that a question word like "who" introduces the property of being a person, which is associated with a domain. Let us represent the property of being a person in this domain with the predicate "F". So we can represent the context-sensitivity of a question like "who walks?" as:

[who walks] = $\lambda i \lambda k [\lambda x [F(i)(x)$ & walks$(i)(x)] = \lambda x [F(i)(x)$ & walks$(k)(x)]]$

The context of use assigns a domain property to the domain variable "F", say in this case the property of being F. Someone knows who walks at a world w relative to a context c if and only if they know a proposition true at a world w′ if and only if the set of things that are F at w and walkers at w are the same as the set of things that are F at w and walkers at w′. The proposition known is a function of the domain assigned by the context of use. Questions with mention-some readings are similarly context-sensitive − they depend on a salient domain, associated with the relevant noun meaning. Uniformity demands a similar treatment.

Context-sensitivity arises from the same source in both mention-some and mention-all readings of questions, which, as we have seen, is the same source as with quantified noun phrases. So we should also treat the context-sensitivity of mention-some questions as deriving from a contextually provided property in a similar manner:

$$[\text{wh-to-}\Phi] = \lambda j \lambda i (\exists p[(F(p, j) \; \& \; x \text{ can } \Phi \, (p, j) \; \& \; (F(p, i) \; \& \; x \text{ can } \Phi \, (p, i)])$$

Suppose I utter "Hannah knows where to find an Italian newspaper in New York City". I am most probably excluding places at which they cost over $100 — what I mean is that Hannah knows where to find a *reasonably priced* Italian newspaper. In this case, context restricts the locations to ones in which the newspapers sold at that location are reasonably priced (this is the property context assigns to the variable "F" in the above representation of the meaning of instances of the schema "wh-to-Φ"). According to the semantics we have given, relative to a context in which this is the domain, "Hannah knows where to find an Italian newspaper" is predicted to be true at a world w if and only if at w, Hannah knows a proposition that is true in a world w′ if and only if there is a place Hannah can buy reasonably priced Italian newspapers at w′, which is also a place Hannah can buy reasonably priced Italian newspapers at w.

Ascriptions of knowing how of course behave like ascriptions of knowing where with respect to domain-sensitivity. Here is how to use the domain sensitivity of knowing-wh to account for some subtle data, due to Katherine Hawley (2003). Hawley writes, "in a UK context, it would be reasonable to infer from Sarah's knowing how to drive that she knows how to drive a manual, stick-shift car. In most US contexts, however, this would not be a reasonable inference". We can account for this data with two assumptions. The first assumption is that the domain of this question in the UK is the singleton set containing *via manual stick-shift* and the domain of this question in the US is the set containing both *via manual stick-shift* and *via automatic*. The second assumption is that virtually everyone who can drive a car via manual stick shift can drive that car via automatic. Then, one can account for Hawley's judgment.

The fact that ascriptions of knowing how, like all ascriptions of knowing-wh, involve sensitivity to a domain also explains a number of other cases Hawley discusses. For example, "a child might be said to know how to cook if she knows how to use the stove safely, whilst we would set standards higher (have a different task in mind) for an ordinary adult's 'knowing how to cook', and set them higher still when discussing a chef in training." The presence of this kind of context-sensitivity is straightforwardly predicted from the independently motivated account of domain restriction I have provided. If ascriptions of knowing how were not context-sensitive in the way Hawley describes, then the theory of domain restriction in Stanley and Szabo (2000) would be false.

Mention-some readings of questions semantically presuppose that there is at least one thing of the relevant sort that satisfies the description. "John knows why to vote for Obama" could not seriously be asserted by someone who believed that there was no reason to vote for Obama, and "John knows why to square the circle" cannot be seriously asserted by anyone who is aware of the fact that the task is impossible. Similarly, "John knows how to square the circle" could only be seriously asserted by someone who believed that there is a way to square the circle. In short, mention-some readings of questions semantically presuppose that, given any world w as input, the semantic value of a mention-some reading of a question yields a non-empty set as output. If the semantic value of a mention-some reading does not yield a non-empty set as an output, given a world, then it is not knowable at that world.[4]

Sometimes, in order to know where to F or how to F, it is enough to know that there is some place or other at which one can F, or some way or other in which one could F. Dialogues like the following are quite natural:

(8) I know where to get a good Italian meal in this neighborhood. Steve told me that there was some really good place on Second Avenue. We will walk up and down until we find it.

(9) I know how to open this door. Hannah told me that there was some way of doing it that involves using a credit card. We will figure it out.

The semantic clauses I have given for mention-some readings easily capture these readings. But it is typically the case that, when one knows where to Φ or knows how to Φ, one has *de re* knowledge of a place to Φ or a way to Φ – when one knows where to get a good Italian meal, one knows *of* someplace that it is a good place to get an Italian meal. This additional requirement comes from the *domain* associated with mention-some questions.

In those cases in which acquaintance is required for knowing where to Φ or how to Φ the context sets additional demands on the domain for the embedded question. In order for a place to Φ or a way to Φ to be sufficient for knowing where to Φ or how to Φ, the agent must be *acquainted* with that place or that way. So, in a case in which I utter, "Hannah knows where to find an Italian newspaper in New York City", where I mean Hannah knows of a *specific* place to find an Italian newspaper in New York City, I intend a domain F such that a place satisfies F only if Hannah has *de re* acquaintance with it; and *mutatis mutandis* for knowing how.

Examples of knowing where to Φ and knowing how to Φ where the subject is a *quantified* expression raise complexities familiar from the study of quantifier domain restriction. Just as one can "bind" into quantifier domains (von Fintel 1994; Stanley and Szabo 2000), so one can bind into question domains. An example of this sort is as in (10):

(10) a. Every philosopher knows where to find a good coffee.

b. Everyone knows how to swim.

---

[4] Daniele Sgaravatti and Elia Zardini (2008) claim that ascriptions of knowing how differ from other kinds of ascriptions of knowing-wh in that so-called "negative answers" are not permitted. As we have seen, this is clearly true for ascriptions of knowing why to do something as well.

In these cases, the domain varies with the different values of the variable introduced by the quantified expression in subject position ("every philosopher" in (10a), "everyone" in (10b)). Example (10a) is true in a world w if and only if every philosopher x knows at w a proposition that is true in a world w′ if and only if there is some place at which x could find good coffee at w′ that x is acquainted with at w′, that is also a place at which x could find good coffee at w that x is acquainted with at w. Example (10b) is true at a world w if and only if everyone x knows at w a proposition that is true at a world w′ if and only if there is a way of swimming x is acquainted with at w′ that is a way in which x could swim at w′ that is also a way of swimming x is acquainted with at w via which x could swim at w.

To arrive at the right truth-conditions for the examples in (10), we need to incorporate more detail from the standard literature on quantifier domains. As I have noted in previous chapters, Stanley and Szabo (2000) argue that quantifier domains have the structure "f(x)", where "x" is an object variable, and "f" is a variable over functions of type $<e, <e,t>>$, i.e. a function from objects to properties, which are the quantifier domains. Following von Fintel (1994), they do so to account for examples such as (11):

(11)   Everyone answered every question.

Example (11) can naturally express the proposition that everyone x answered every question on x's exam. The quantifier domain associated with "every question" is "bound" by the quantifier "everyone". Stanley and Szabo suggest that the structure of (11) is really as in (12):

(12)   Everyone$_i$ answered every question f(i).

Relative to a context in which (12) expresses the proposition that everyone x answered every question on x's exam, the variable "i" is bound by "everyone", and the variable "f" takes as a value a function from persons to the property of being a thing on that person's exam.

Given that question domains just are the familiar quantifier domains, one can straightforwardly account for the natural readings of the examples in (10). Each question domain is of the form "f(x)", where the value of "f" is a function that takes objects to properties, intuitively the domain. In the case of (10a), the question domain takes a person and yields the property of being something with which that person is acquainted, and similarly for (10b). This yields the desired interpretation of the examples in (10).

Now that we have settled on the semantic contents of these constructions, let us turn to their compositional derivation from the subparts of the sentence. Our discussion will for the most part mirror the derivation of mention-all readings of questions discussed in the previous chapter. Consider an infinitival question like "how PRO to swim". The question word "how" has been extracted from an adjunct position next to the verb "swim", so the full syntactic representation is "how$_i$ PRO to swim w$_i$". The semantic content of "PRO to swim w$_i$", where x is the value of PRO, is *x could swim(w,a)*, which is a function taking a way in which x could swim to the true if x could swim in that way in world a, and to the false otherwise. The question word "how" adds a λ-abstract over ways (or methods), yielding the semantic value *λm(x could swim(m,a))*. So far, everything is exactly as in the derivation of mention-all readings of questions. The distinction between mention-some and mention-all readings of questions arises at this stage of the semantic derivation. Where 'F' represents the domain, the question is a mention-all reading, then the type-shift is to the meaning in (13); if it is a mention-some reading, then the type-shift is to the meaning in (14):[5]

(13) $\lambda i \lambda k[\lambda m(F(i)(m)$ & x could swim in way m at world i$) = \lambda m(F(i)(m)$ & x could swim in way m at world k$)]$.

(14) $\lambda i \lambda k(\exists m[(F(m, i)$ & x could swim in way m at world i & $F(m, k)$ & x could swim in way w at world k])$.

The rest of the semantic derivation of the truth-conditions of a sentence like "x knows how to swim" proceeds as above.

3.

We have now looked in detail at each element of the interpretation of attributions of knowing how – the account of PRO, the account of the meanings of the infinitival construction in infinitival embedded questions, and the account of mention-some readings of questions within the more general framework of the semantics for embedded questions we discussed in the previous chapter. Putting all of these elements together yields a full interpretation of ascriptions of knowing how. Relative to a context in which the domain is the set of normal ways of doing things with which John is acquainted, a sentence like "John knows how to swim" is true at a world w if and only if John knows at w a proposition true in a world w′ if and only if there is some way in which John could swim in w′ with which John is acquainted, and that way is also a way John is acquainted with by means of which John could swim in w.

I have said that this is a full account of knowing how to do something. But there are *prima facie* counterexamples. As Stanley and Williamson (2001: 428–9) write:

Suppose that Hannah does not know how to ride a bicycle. Susan points to John, who is riding a bicycle, and says, "That is a way for you to ride a bicycle". Suppose that the way in which John is riding his bicycle is in fact a way for Hannah to ride a bicycle. So, where the demonstrative "that way" denotes John's way of riding a bicycle (28) seems true:

---

[5] In these representations, I have represented the domain with a property variable "F" – in actuality, the proper representation would be "f(x)", as in the discussion above. The proper representation for e.g. (13) would then be: $\lambda i \lambda k[\lambda m(f(y)((i)(m))$ & x could swim in way m at world i$) = \lambda m(f(y)((i)(m))$ & x could swim in way m at world k)]. The domain "f(y)" would have as a value a property of ways.

(28)   Hannah knows that that way is a way for her to ride a bicycle.

Relative to this context, however:

(29)   Hannah$_i$ knows [how PRO$_i$ to ride a bicycle].

seems false.

Stanley and Williamson's solution to this problem is to invoke *practical ways of thinking*. They argue that in the case of their example (28), the way of riding a bicycle demonstrated by Susan is thought of under a demonstrative way of thinking. But attributions of knowing how to do something are conventionally associated with practical ways of thinking, rather than demonstrative ways of thinking. So their examples (28) and (29) involve the same proposition known, but entertained under distinct ways of thinking.

Some philosophers are concerned with Stanley and Williamson's account of knowledge how because it appeals to practical ways of thinking. The general charge is that practical ways of thinking are mysterious or *ad hoc*. But this is simply not true. *Anyone who accepts that cognitive states involve ways of thinking will have to accept practical ways of thinking.*

Suppose that we accept what Gareth Evans calls "Frege's intuitive criterion of difference":

the thought associated with one sentence S as its sense must be different from the thought associated with another sentence S' as its sense, if it is possible for someone to understand both sentences at a given time while coherently taking different attitudes towards them, i.e. accepting (rejecting) one while rejecting (accepting) the other. (1982: 18–19)

As Evans (ibid. pp. 19–20) points out, "if the notion of 'a way of thinking about something' is to be elucidatory of Frege's notion of sense, ways of thinking about things must be identified and distinguished in harmony with the Intuitive Criterion of Difference." If so, we will *have* to accept practical ways of thinking. It is simple to imagine cases in which one thinks of a way of acting (say, a way of playing a piano) in such a manner as to be surprised by the discovery that a given demonstratively presented (or explicitly described) way of thinking of that method of playing a piano is a way of thinking of the same method of playing.

The point that any Fregean must accept practical ways of thinking is not novel. It has been widely accepted and acknowledged for decades by advocates of Fregean accounts of content:

some thoughts have an essential connection with action: for there are action-based ways of thinking of things. A particular type of gesture, which a subject is able to make on demand, even when the limb with which he makes it is anaesthetized, may be thought by the agent in such a way; when thought of in such a way, it may come as a surprise to him to see precisely what shape his limb traces when he makes the gesture thought of in that way. Equally, a pianist is capable of thinking of a chord in an action-based way, one whose employment is compatible with his not knowing which notes compose it or even, without further reflection, exactly which fingers he is pressing on the keyboard when he sounds it. What seems to be constitutive of these ways of thinking is that when a thinker acts on an intention to perform an action thought of in one of these ways, he tries to act in a certain way (and does so in favourable circumstances). We cannot make sense of the possibility that someone is employing just these ways of thinking of a movement in the content of his intentions without such connections obtaining. (Peacocke 1986: 49–50)

Peacocke here describes a case of the envisaged sort, where a perfectly rational person is surprised to learn that a limb he thinks of in one way, a *practical* way, is the same limb as the limb thought of in another way. The existence of practical ways of thinking is a straightforward consequence of the Fregean framework of individuating ways of thinking of things, one that has nothing directly to do with knowing how.

One might think that practical ways of thinking are problematic, because in thinking of a way of doing something in what Peacocke calls "an action-based way", one's thinking does not seem to be mediated by a representation. But this is simply a straightforward confusion about ways of thinking:

we can appreciate how wrong-headed it is to consider a Fregean sense as necessarily *intermediary* between thinker and referent, as something which must, from a certain point of view, *get in the way*, or anyway render indirect what might be direct. A way of thinking of an object is no more obliged to get in the way of thinking of an object, or to render thinking of an object indirect, than is a way of dancing liable to get in the way of dancing, or to render dancing somehow indirect. (Evans 1985: 302–3)

Evans's discussion here concerns not action-based ways of thinking, but rather demonstrative ways of thinking. However, it applies *mutatis mutandis* – neither demonstrative nor action-based ways of thinking *intervene* between thinking and the world.

We have seen in detail why it is wrong to think of first-person ways of thinking as somehow intervening between subject and object. To think of an object in a first-person way is for that object to occupy a certain functional role – to be something towards which first-person dispositions are directed. Similarly, explaining what it is to think of a way of doing something in a practical way is, as Peacocke makes vivid, a matter of spelling out the distinctive practical functional role that way occupies in the mental life of the speaker.

The need for practical ways of thinking in explaining intentional states is widely recognized:

Equipment can genuinely show itself only in dealings cut to its own measure (hammering with a hammer, for example); but in such dealings an entity of this kind is not grasped thematically as an occurring Thing, nor is the equipment-structure known as such even in the using. The hammering does not simply have knowledge about the hammer's character as equipment, but it has appropriated this equipment in a way which could not possibly be more suitable. In dealings such as this, where something is put to use, our concern subordinates itself to the "in-order-to" which is constitutive for the equipment we are employing at the time; the less we just stare at the hammer-Thing, and the more we seize hold of it and use it, the more primordial

does our relationship to it become, and the more unveiledly is it encountered as that which I'' is –
as equipment. The hammering itself uncovers the specific "manipulability" of the hammer.
(Heidegger 1962: 98)

Heidegger here draws our attention to the fact that there is a practical way of thinking
about a thing, one that is revealed paradigmatically in operating with a tool. Such a way
of thinking about a thing is distinct from the way of thinking about a thing that is
revealed by "just staring" at it. In the vernacular of the Fregean, a visual way of
thinking of a hammer is distinct from a practical way of thinking of a hammer.

So there is no specific objection to the practical ways of thinking invoked by Stanley
and Williamson (2001). The need for practical ways of thinking of things, and their
distinctness from (e.g.) visual ways of thinking of things, must be acknowledged by any
Fregean about content. There are only general concerns about the ontology of Fregean
accounts of content, of the sort we dispensed with in the previous chapter.

Nevertheless, it is possible to distinguish between Stanley and Williamson's examples
(28) and (29) without the use of practical ways of thinking. Susan's utterance of "Hannah
knows that that way is a way in which she could ride a bicycle," and an utterance of
"Hannah knows how to ride a bicycle" simply have different propositions as their
contents, even when we think of propositions in non-Fregean terms. The difference is
due to the distinct modal parameters associated with explicit modals, on the one hand,
and the modal associated with infinitival embedded questions, on the other.

Recall that on Kratzer's treatment of modals, they are highly context-sensitive.
A use of a modal is evaluated with respect to a contextually salient modal parameter.
Given a world of evaluation, the modal parameter yields a set of propositions, i.e. a set
of sets of possible worlds. Even uses of modals with the same "flavor" (e.g. ability
modals, deontic modals) may be evaluated with respect to distinct modal parameters.
For example, suppose I successfully bench-press 200 pounds at the gym, and my trainer
says to me – "You can lift 200 pounds!" It is natural to interpret the modal parameter in
this context as one that takes the actual world and yields a set of propositions,
intuitively the set of propositions that characterize my actual, current physical state.
"I can lift 200 pounds" is true relative to this context, because there is at least one
possible world in which all of these propositions are true, and I lift 200 pounds (in fact,
it is the actual world). Suppose in contrast that I go to the trainer, having not worked
out in several years. I am completely out of shape, and could certainly not at that
moment bench-press 200 pounds. But the trainer, eyeing my impressive yet out of
shape physique, remarks "You can lift 200 pounds." The contextually salient modal
parameter for her remark is one that takes the world of evaluation, and yields a set of
propositions that characterize my physical state after months of physical training. Her
utterance is true, if there is one possible world consistent with all of these propositions
in which I lift 200 pounds. Despite the fact that both utterances of "You can lift 200
pounds" involve modals with the same force, they express different propositions.

As we have seen, embedded infinitival questions with "how" and "where" typically are associated with something that has ability-like modal force. "John knows where to get good coffee in New York City" means that John knows a place where he can get good coffee in New York City, and "John knows how to swim" means that John knows a way in which he can swim. But this does not entail that the modal force is governed by the same parameter as any explicit use of a modal. As we have just seen, modals are highly context-sensitive. Even when distinct uses of the explicit modal "can" have the same force, the contextually salient modal parameter can, given a world of evaluation, yield differing sets of propositions as values.

Given this background, let us return to the phenomena that led Stanley and Williamson to posit practical ways of thinking. Stanley and Williamson noted that there is a felt difference in meaning between two distinct utterances. Suppose that Hannah doesn't know much about bicycles, and has certainly never ridden one. Susan points to John, and tells Hannah that John is riding his bicycle in a way in which Hannah could use to ride a bicycle. Since Hannah trusts Susan, it seems that Hannah thereby comes to know that that way is a way in which she could ride a bicycle, i.e. (15a) is true. Nevertheless, it seems that Hannah does not know how to ride a bicycle, i.e. (15b) is false:

(15)   a. Hannah knows that that way is a way in which she could ride a bicycle.

       b. Hannah knows how to ride a bicycle.

Stanley and Williamson (2001) appeal to practical ways of thinking to explain this contrast.

However, the contrast can be explained without appeal to ways of thinking. The difference in meaning between (15a) and (15b) is due to the different modal parameters governing the uses of the modal constructions in these sentences. Though the modals in (15a) and (15b) have the same force – they are kinds of dispositional, or ability modals – they are interpreted via distinct modal parameters. In (15a), the modal parameter is one that takes the world of evaluation, and yields a set of propositions that characterize Hannah's physical state after training for some time with a bicycle. In contrast, the natural modal parameter for the envisaged utterance of (15b) is one that takes the world of evaluation, and yields a set of propositions that characterize Hannah's physical state at the moment. That is why the two utterances express different propositions – because the modals in the two sentences are interpreted via distinct modal parameters.

There is a significant question about the modal parameter that is relevant for ascriptions of knowing how. I have described it as a "dispositional or ability" modal, because knowing how to do something seems to require that the agent *can*, in some sense of "can", perform the task. But, as a range of problem cases have shown over the years, the modal associated with knowing how is subtly different than the one associated with ordinary language ascription of abilities. As Katherine Hawley has persuasively argued (2003), the modal force associated with ascriptions of knowing how can be described as *counterfactual success* – success under some contextually deter-mined range of circumstances. The difference between explicit ability modals and ascriptions of knowing how is that the former typically (but, as we have seen, not always) require success in conditions like those obtaining at the actual world. In contrast, ascriptions of knowing how tolerate cases in which there is counterfactual success only in more distant situations. Let us see how this account deals with various problem cases.

Kieran Setiya (2008: 405) argues that knowing how to do something is not knowledge of ability by considering someone with the irrational true belief that they have been cured of their paralysis. According to Setiya, this person knows how to clench his fist, but does not know that he is able to clench his fist, since his belief that he is able to clench his fist is not properly justified. That knowledge how requires knowledge of counterfactual success in Hawley's sense explains this case. The person does know how to clench his fist, because this involves knowing that she can clench her fist in those worlds in which she is not paralyzed. Being paralyzed does not affect knowledge of counterfactual success. He does not know that he is *able* to clench his fist, because this would involve knowing that he can clench his fist in worlds very close to the actual world. While he truly believes that he can clench his fist in worlds very close to the actual world, his true belief is not justified, and therefore is not an instance of knowledge.

There are examples that show that knowing how to do something does not entail being able to do it. Carl Ginet (1975: 8) ably summarizes the case that knowing how to Φ does not entail the ability to Φ as follows:

in the case of every ability that I can think of with respect to which it is clear that there can be a case of a person who lacks that ability but knows all the same truths about how to do the thing as one who has the ability knows, it would sound very odd to characterize the difference between such a person and one who has the ability by saying that the latter *knows how* to do the thing but the former does not. For example, it would not be right to report the fact that I am able to lift a hundred pounds off the floor but my eight-year-old son is not by saying that I know how to do this but he does not know how. Insofar as there is any knowing how involved he knows how as well as I; he just doesn't have the strength to do it.

The other consideration is very similar. When someone knows how to . . . and has the ability to . . . (for example, ski expertly, play the violin well, read English, parallel park a car) but then suddenly loses the ability to . . . through a cause that clearly cannot change (at least not immediately) the truths he knows about how to do . . . (for example, he suffers a sudden paralysis or takes a drug that disturbs his muscular control or becomes blind) it would certainly not be right to report this sudden loss of ability to . . . by saying that this person suddenly no longer knows how to . . . An expert skier who in the course of a downhill run gets a bad case of stomach cramps and is able to complete the run only very clumsily still knows how to ski very well even while temporarily unable to do so.

Here is how one can account for Ginet's cases, using the semantics I have provided.

First, take the difference between Ginet in 1975 and his (then) 8-year-old son. There is a clear reading of "Ginet's son knows how to lift one hundred pounds off the floor" where it is true relative to the envisaged context. It is one in which the PRO is meant as PRO$_{arb}$ – i.e. Ginet's son knows how *one* could lift one hundred pounds off the floor, relative to a modal parameter that takes the world of evaluation to the set of propositions specifying the physical capacities of a normal adult. As we have seen, cases involving PRO$_{arb}$ are generic constructions, and generics are not universal quantifications. Ginet's then 8-year-old son knew how generally one could lift one hundred pounds off the floor. But knowing how to lift one hundred pounds off the floor in this sense does not entail that Ginet's son can lift one hundred pounds.

Something different is going on in the second kind of consideration discussed by Ginet. Take Ginet's example of an expert skier who gets a bad case of stomach cramps. He still knows how to ski well; he is just temporarily unable to do so. In this case, PRO is not PRO$_{arb}$ – the expert skier certainly still knows a way in which *he* could ski well. The modal parameter takes the world of evaluation, and yields a set of propositions specifying that skier's physical condition *under normal circumstances*. Knowing how to ski requires only (as Hawley would put it) counterfactual success under normal circumstances. The modal parameter relevant for Ginet's envisaged utterance of "he knows how to ski" is one that takes the world of evaluation, and yields a set of propositions that characterize the skier's physical state under normal (non-ill) circumstances. What is required for the skier to know how to ski is that the skier is aware of a way of skiing that he can use to ski well in at least one of those worlds, and furthermore that the skier know this. This does not require that the skier can ski well in that range of worlds in which his physical condition is what it actually is, i.e. a range of worlds in which he is ill.

This is also the right account of the felt gap between knowing how to do something and being able to do it in similar cases, such as that of a master pianist who loses her arms in a car accident. She is no longer able to play the piano, since explicit ability modals involve a modal parameter that is determined by how things are at the actual world. But she still knows how to play the piano, since there is a way of piano-playing with which she is acquainted and she knows that it is a way that she could use to play the piano in situations in normal situations in which she had arms.

Here is a third case, due to Jeff King (p.c.). Suppose there is a certain complex ski maneuver, which only the most physically gifted of athletes can perform. A ski instructor might know how to do that maneuver, without being able to perform it herself. The natural explanation of this kind of case has to do more with the *modal force*, rather than with the interpretation of PRO. Teachers are supposed to know how one *ought* to do things – not how one *could* do things. The teacher may even know how *he* ought to do that maneuver. But clearly, I can know either how I ought to do something, or how one ought to do something, without being able to do it myself.

Ascriptions of knowing how are modal constructions; knowing how to do something amounts to knowing some modal fact, either about oneself, or persons generally.

As we have seen, modal constructions are highly context-sensitive. Even when we focus on some kind of ability or dispositional reading of a modal, a particular utterance of "N knows how to ride a bicycle/solve a problem/etc/" may involve a modal parameter that determines a somewhat different range of worlds than explicit ability modals, such as "could" or "able". The variability explains the lack of entailment between attributions of knowing how to do something and attributions of ability. Furthermore, if one is hostile to ways of thinking, one could appeal to the contextual variability in modal constructions to explain the data that led Stanley and Williamson to adopt practical ways of thinking.

However, as we have seen, there are in fact practical ways of thinking of objects. As Peacocke and Heidegger point out, it is a *straightforward* matter to construct Frege puzzles concerning something presented to one practically and that very same thing presented to one visually. The only objections one could possibly have to practical ways of thinking of objects come from misunderstandings about the ontology of ways of thinking generally, misunderstandings that I have thoroughly addressed in the previous chapter and this one. It is also natural for a Fregean to take attributions of knowing how to involve practical ways of thinking of ways of doing things.

It is natural simultaneously to acquire a practical way of thinking of a way of Φ-ing, and sufficient evidence that it is a way to achieve counterfactual success at Φ-ing. So, often my knowledge of how to Φ comes at the same time as my successful thinking of a way of Φ under a practical way of thinking. But it is certainly possible to think of a way of Φ-ing under a practical way of thinking, and even entertain the proposition that it is a way to Φ, yet not know enough to know how to Φ. Katherine Hawley (forthcoming) considers a case in which "I master a sequence of moves on my skateboard, and I wonder whether showing this off will impress the kids at the local park. As it happens, they will be very impressed if they see me perform this sequence". As Hawley points out, the theory in Stanley and Williamson (2001) provides a natural explanation of what is occurring here:

I entertain the proposition that performing my routine is a way for me to impress the kids, and I entertain this proposition under a practical way of thinking (i.e. differently from the way in which a nonskating spectator would entertain this thought), but I do not know whether the proposition is true, and so I don't know how to impress the kids at the skate park. The appeal of this verdict is that it simultaneously acknowledges both my shortcomings (I don't know how to impress the kids) and my achievements (I can now entertain the relevant proposition under a practical way of thinking, a feat which has required hours of practice and acres of bruising).

As Hawley (forthcoming) also explains, the view also makes sense of the difficulties involved in learning how to do something by testimony. If someone shows me how to do something, before I learn how to do it from their demonstration, I must acquire a practical way of thinking of that method of doing it. This requires more than does acquiring knowledge of facts that can be described purely descriptively by testimony.

Practical ways of thinking are not necessary to explain the difference between the cases Stanley and Williamson discuss. However, they are necessary to explain the acquisition of skill on the basis of knowledge of facts, which are true propositions. What happens when I acquire skill in the activity of catching fly balls? What happens is that I come to the realization that a certain way of catching a fly ball, which I think of practically, is a way that will give me counterfactual success in fly ball catching. That the acquisition of a skill is due to the learning of a fact explains why certain acts constitute exercises of skill, rather than reflex. A particular action of catching a fly ball is a skilled action, rather than a reflex, because it is guided by knowledge, the knowledge of how to catch a fly ball. In order to know how to catch a fly ball, one must amass enough of the right *kind* of evidence to know, of a certain way of moving that one thinks of practically, that it is a way that will yield counterfactual success in fly-ball catching. Once this realization has been made, practice leads to direct action, action without the necessity for reflection.

6

Ascribing Knowledge How

My view of the nature of knowing how to do something is a view about the metaphysical nature of these states, and not a view in semantics. But the way I have developed the view of the nature of knowing how is by investigating properties of its ascriptions. I have defended views about the grammar and meaning of the elements of such ascriptions, and then built a view of knowing how simply by combining these elements. What has resulted is an intellectualist account of knowing how to do something, according to which knowing how to do something consists in knowing the answer to a question, an answer that involves first-person information about the knower.

The discussion thus far raises two sources of dissent, one empirical and the other foundational. The empirical objection concerns whether states of knowing how to do something, in the sense I have explained, are plausibly expressed by ascriptions of knowing how to do something in languages other than English. This concern has been pressed forcefully by Rumfitt (2003) and Wiggins (forthcoming). This in turn raises several distinct worries. First, if ascriptions of knowing how are sufficiently semantically distinct in other languages, this provides evidence for an ambiguity in English knowledge ascriptions. For example, it may suggest that "know" is ambiguous, and means one thing in ascriptions of knowing how, and another in ascriptions of other kinds of knowing-wh. Second, it would be a significant objection to the view of knowing how I have endorsed if it could not be plausibly taken to be what is expressed by ascriptions of knowing how in other languages. I would then be advocating an error theory of such ascriptions for speakers of such languages.

The second objection is more foundational in character. Why is it a virtue of my favored view of the nature of knowing how that it is plausible to take it as what is expressed by natural language ascriptions of knowing how? Why are natural language ascriptions of knowing how to do something relevant *at all* to inquiry into the nature of knowledge how? One might naturally hold that it is *science* that will discover the nature of states of knowing how to do something. It may be that science will discover that knowing how to do something has a certain nature, as a consequence of which it follows that these states are not expressed by certain natural language sentences. If so, then so much the worse for those languages in which the expressive resources are restricted to what one can non-scientifically assert.

In this chapter, I address both the empirical and the foundational concerns. I begin with the empirical one. As we will see in section 2, there is cross-linguistic variation in ascriptions of knowing how. However, it is hopeless to base an argument on such variation against either the methodology I have employed, or the view of knowing how I have defended. As I show in section 1, all parties to the debate agree that the philosophical motivations for holding that knowing how to Φ is not a kind of propositional knowledge extend smoothly to the view that other ascriptions of knowledge-wh also do not ascribe propositional knowledge. But there is no such cross-linguistic variation with any other kind of ascription of knowing-wh; for example, languages are uniform in ascriptions of knowing where to Φ. In section 3, I will show that in any case it is straightforward to give a semantics that assigns states of knowing how in my favored sense to all the different ways of ascribing knowing how. In section 4, I turn to a discussion of the foundational objection. Even if one accepted some version of the foundational objection, it would of course raise no worry whatsoever for my view of the nature of states of knowing how. At best, it would render superfluous some of the excursion through the semantics of various ascriptions. Nevertheless, it is worthwhile to see what in the foundational objection is confused, and what is worthy of serious consideration, as the discussion will pave the way for the topic of the subsequent chapter.

1.

The way English speakers ascribe practical knowledge is not the only method languages use. Just as Russian lacks the definite article, certain languages, such as German, lack direct translations of the English construction. More worrisomely, other languages employ subtly different means to translate sentences of the form 'x knows how to Φ', and it is not obviously clear how one could plausibly take them to express states of knowing how, in my favored sense. If there is no natural compositional semantics that links the account of knowing how I defend to these other ways of expressing practical knowledge, then it will lack a virtue that we should expect an account of the nature of practical knowledge to possess. To show that the view of knowing how I advocate has the virtues I claim for it, I must show that it is the best account of the uniform meaning expressed cross-linguistically by ascriptions of practical knowledge.

While ascriptions of knowing how appear syntactically to be embedded question constructions in English, there are a wide variety of languages in which they appear differently. There are many concerns this raises. First, perhaps the existence of these other languages shows that knowing how is not a species of knowing-wh after all. Second, perhaps my favored view of the nature of states of knowing how to do something cannot to be taken to be what is expressed by ascriptions of knowing how in languages in which they do not superficially take the form of embedded question constructions.

Ian Rumfitt (2003) has used the fact that ascriptions of knowing how differ syntactically across languages as a premise in an argument that knowing how to Φ is a different kind of state than that expressed by other ascriptions of knowing-wh to Φ, such as knowing where to Φ, knowing when to Φ, etc. (see also Wiggins forthcoming). This is too hasty. Insofar as there is an intuitive basis for thinking that knowing how to do something is not a species of propositional knowledge, it survives as an intuitive basis for thinking that knowing where to do something, knowing when to do something, and knowing what to do are not species of propositional knowledge. For example, one reason to think that knowing how to do something is not a species of propositional knowledge is that, while it is obvious that animals do know how to do various things, it is highly controversial that they have propositional knowledge. As Noë puts the point, in response to the theory in Stanley and Williamson (2001):

> The point is not that dogs can't grasp propositions. The point is that whether or not they can grasp propositions is an open question, one that is debated in cognitive science. The problem for Stanley and Williamson is that their analysis commits them to the strong consequence that dogs *can* grasp propositions, at least if it is to have any hope of being true. For if one thing is clear, it is that Pip does know how to catch a Frisbee (even though he is getting old). (2005)

However, if it is obvious that Pip knows *how to catch a Frisbee*, then it is equally obvious that Pip knows *when to leap at a Frisbee to catch it*, and *where to find his bone*.

Similarly, one might think that an outfielder knows how to catch a fly ball, and that this knowledge has an automatic quality that is inconsistent with being a manifestation of propositional knowledge. But the same automaticity is present when the outfielder manifests his knowledge of when to raise his mitt when a fly ball approaches. If the automaticity of an action based on it shows that *knowing how to catch a fly ball* is not propositional knowledge, then it also shows that *knowing when to raise one's mitt when a fly ball approaches* is not propositional knowledge. Psychologists who write on motor skills certainly do not restrict their attributions of knowledge to ascriptions of knowing how. For example, Reed et al., in an article on implicit knowledge and motor skill, write:

> In this paper we investigate what people can report about the knowledge they use when they decide to remain stationary, or to move forwards or backwards to catch a ball thrown directly towards them. That is, how they know whether, if they did not move, the ball would hit them or fall in front of them or fall behind. (2010: 64)

Here, Reed et al. describe the knowledge underlying the possession of the motor skill of catching a ball as involving *knowing whether a ball would hit them or fall in front of them or fall behind them.*

As far as considerations from animal cognition, or the automaticity of action go as arguments that knowing how to do something is not a species of propositional knowledge, they are equally arguments that knowing where, knowing when, and knowing what, and knowing whether are not species of propositional knowledge.

Knowing-wh stands or falls together – either they are all species of propositional knowledge, or none of them are. Some very recent defenders of Ryle have admirably emphasized this point. In fact, Michael Devitt (forthcoming) goes as far as to argue that the philosophical and scientific motivations that lead one to deny that knowing how to Φ is a kind of propositional knowledge lead one to deny that many kinds of knowing-wh are instances of propositional knowledge, even when the embedded questions occur with tensed complements:

> The foraging desert ant wanders all over the place until it finds food and then always heads straight back to its nest (described in Gallistel 1990). On the strength of this competence, we feel no qualms about saying that it "knows where its nest is." But to attribute any propositional attitudes to the ant simply on the strength of that competence seems like soft-minded anthropomorphism. Cognitive ethologists might lead us in that direction, of course . . . but we don't seem to get knowledge-that *for nothing* with knowledge-where. Stanley and Williamson next consider ascriptions that are like [ascriptions of knowing how to Φ] and the first group except that they are tensed and refer to another person; for example, 'Hannah knows how Bill rides a bicycle' (p. 418). Again none of these ascriptions, except the ascription of knowledge-why, seems "*clearly*" to ascribe propositions. Thus mightn't Hannah demonstrate this knowledge-how *simply* by imitating Bill riding a bicycle? And consider the western scrub jay. One of these, *X*, may observe another, *Y*, caching food, and later raid the cache (Clayton *et al* 2006). We are inclined to say that X knows where Y cached the food. Ethologists think that these jays are pretty smart but *must* they say that this knowledge-where is propositional?[1]

It should be widely acknowledged that the philosophical and scientific motivations that motivate the view that knowing how is not a kind of propositional knowledge also would lead one to conclude that many ascriptions of knowing-wh, *even ascriptions of knowing whether one of several options obtains*, do not ascribe propositional knowledge.

However, unlike translations of knowing how to Φ, languages are remarkably *uniform* in their ascriptions of knowing where, knowing when, and knowing whether. Only ascriptions of knowing how to Φ are cross-linguistic outliers. The felt semantic uniformity between ascriptions of knowing-wh does not extend to a cross-linguistic syntactic uniformity. This suggests that the variation between languages in the expression of knowing how has to do with grammatical rather than semantic facts.

Considerations from the automaticity of action and animal cognition apply generally to all varieties of knowing-wh. In contrast, only ascriptions of knowing how differ across languages. It is therefore not coherent to combine facts about the automaticity of action and animal cognition with facts about cross-linguistic variation of ascriptions of knowing how in an argument that knowing how is special and distinctive. The philosophical

---

[1] And even Ryle seems to have recognized this point: "to say that a soldier obediently fixed his bayonet, or fixed it in order to defend himself, does imply that he has learned some lessons and not forgotten them. The new recruit, on hearing the order to fix bayonet, or on seeing an enemy soldier approaching, does not know what to do with his bayonet, how to do it, or when to do it and when not to do it" (1949: 146). Thanks to Bengson and Moffett (forthcoming) for bringing this passage to my attention.

arguments that have been levied against the thesis of this book go in a dramatically different direction than the linguistic arguments that have been levied against the thesis of this book. Since all of the philosophical considerations suggest that states of knowing-wh are of the same kind, we should seek an explanation of the cross-linguistic diversity in ascriptions of knowing how that is consistent with this conclusion.

My purpose here is to broaden the scope of our investigation of ascriptions of knowing how to include ascriptions of knowing how in other languages. I will argue that the best overall account of ascriptions of knowing how in all languages is one that takes them to express states of knowing how in the above sense. I thereby preserve the felt uniformity between states of knowing-wh, while simultaneously removing the potential objection to the account of practical knowledge I favor.

2.

In this section, I describe some of the different patterns one finds in ascriptions of practical knowledge across languages. First, there are languages that are like English, such as Afrikaans, in which knowing how constructions are obviously embedded questions (the Afrikaans infinitive is formed by "om te" + Verb):

(1) John knows how to ride a bicycle.
     Jan weet hoe om fiets te ry.
     John knows how bicycle to ride.

(2) John knows how to swim.
     Jan weet hoe om te swem
     John knows how to swim

(3) John knows how to cook risotto.
     Jan weet hoe om risotto te kook.
     John knows how risotto to cook.

(4) John knows that Barack is the nominee.
     Jan weet dat Barack die genomineerde is.
     John knows that Barack the nominee is.

(5) John knows that he ought to ride a bicycle.
     Jan weet om fiets te ry.
     John knows bicycle to ride.

The second kind of language pattern, and perhaps the most common, is exemplified by a Romance language such as French, in which know how is most naturally expressed with the use of the propositional knowledge verb and the bare infinitive:

(6) Pierre knows how to swim.
(7) Pierre sait nager.
(8) Pierre sait comment nager.

In French (8) is fully grammatical. But it is an utterance of (7) that is synonymous with an English utterance of (6). The example in (8) communicates something different than (7). Most Romance languages pattern like French, in which the propositional knowledge verb takes what appears to be a bare infinitive as its complement. Some of the dialects of these languages differ from French in that while the bare infinitive is completely natural, it is synonymous and in roughly equal distribution with the form with the added question word that translates "how".

The third class of languages are ones such as Russian, in which it is far more natural to use a verb other than the propositional knowledge verb to translate a sentence like "I know how to swim":

(9) я умею плавать.
     I know how to swim

These languages appear to use a special word for practical knowledge. In some of these languages, though not Russian, it is also natural to use the explicit translation of English ascriptions of knowing how, with the full question morphology.

The fourth class of languages are ones such as German that do not allow direct grammatical translations of sentences like "Hannah knows how to swim", for the accidental syntactic reason that they do not allow *any* infinitives in embedded questions. As Wurmbrand writes in a recent study of infinitive constructions, "In general, German does not allow wh-infinitives" (2001: 107).[2] So German does not allow direct translations of any sentence of the form 'x knows wh to Φ'. Other languages, such as Swedish, pattern similarly.

The fifth class of languages are Niger-Congo languages like Defaka, in which embedded questions are relative clause constructions (see Akinlabi et al. forthcoming). In Defaka, the verb for "know" is "jiri".

(10) Bòmá jírí-mà Bruce á ésé-mà.
      Boma know-Tns Bruce her see-Tns
      "Boma knows that Bruce saw her."

In Defaka, instead of wh-words like "where", "who", or "what", nouns are used signifying the domain over which such wh-words intuitively quantify. For translations of sentences like "she knows how to do it", Defaka uses the noun "kaa", which means "way":

(11) á yè yáà káà jírí-mà.
      She it do way know-Tns

---

[2] Wurmbrand notes that there is a highly restricted class of cases in which wh-infinitives are marginally acceptable, as in "Ich weiss nicht was tun", but "there are strong limitations on the verb that appears in the infinitive". Wurmbrand concludes that German wh-infinitives in general "are not productive wh-constructions" (ibid.).

"She knows how to do it"
('She knows the how-do-it way')

Similarly for other embedded question constructions:

(12)   Tónyé Bòmá à átákí mbeí-mà dòm jírí?
        Tonye Boma the money take-Tns place know-?
        "Does Tonye know where Boma took the money (from)?"
        ('Does Tonye know the where-Boma-took-the-money place?')

(13)   á ísò ílà-mà kíá ì jírí-mà.
        She come reach-Tns time I know-Tns
        "I know when she arrived"
        ('I know the when-she-arrived time')

(14)   Bòmá à ébéré báá-mà tí ?óm jírí-mà.
        Boma the dog kill-Tns person body know-ma
        "Boma knows who killed the dog."
        ('Boma knows the who-killed-the-dog person')

There are also a number of other languages patterns. Finnish allows for grammatical embedded question syntax:

(15)   Jussi tietää mitten ajaa pyorää
        John knows how ride bicycle.

But Finnish also has the verb "osaa" that is much more naturally used in such constructions, which takes a bare infinitive:

(16)   Jussi osaa ajaa pyorää.
        John can ride bicycle.

So Finnish is English-like in allowing grammatical embedded question syntax, and Russian-like in having a special verb. Hungarian, in contrast, has both a German and Swedish pattern, and a French pattern. The propositional knowledge verb "tud" when it occurs with an explicit question word such as "hogyan" ("how"), must occur with a finite clause (as in "János tudja, hogyan kell úszni", John knows how he ought to swim). But knowledge how can also be expressed by "tud" together with the bare infinitive, as in "János tud úszni".

According to the analysis I have favor, "how" differs from "who", "where", and "when" only in introducing *ways* rather than persons, places, and times. We have seen in previous chapters that languages such as English fit smoothly with the analysis I have defended. Languages such as Defaka also provide good evidence for this analysis, since they bear this analysis on their sleeves. But we have yet to see how to account for other ways in which languages express practical knowledge.

3.

The most common cross-linguistic pattern of expressing practical knowledge is that exemplified by French and other Romance languages, which exploit the propositional knowledge verb together with the bare infinitive. Here is the challenge raised by such languages to my favored view of knowing how (Rumfitt 2003). In order for knowing how ascriptions to express my favored view of knowing how, the complement of the propositional knowledge verb "know" in constructions such as "Pierre knows how to swim" must denote the semantic value of an embedded question, namely a function from possible worlds to propositions. But there is no overt question word in the sentence "Pierre sait nager". So it appears that the complement of "savoir" in "Pierre sait nager" cannot be an embedded question, since it contains no question words. So either "Pierre sait nager" (implausibly) does not provide a translation of "Pierre knows how to swim", or the complement of "know" in "Pierre knows how to swim" does not after all denote the semantic value of an embedded question.

However, this argument is not sound. Even if there is no question word in constructions such as "Pierre sait nager", it is simple to give a compositional semantics that takes the complement of "savoir" to be an embedded question denotation. Consider the Groenendijk and Stokhof semantics for mention-all readings I explained in Chapter 2, and the related semantics for mention-some readings I have proposed in Chapter 5. On this account, the question word is semantically vacuous. An embedded question denotes, in the first instance, a property. The construction then induces a type-shift to a function from possible worlds to propositions. In both cases, the semantic type before the type-shift is a property. Nothing in the semantic derivation of the meaning of an embedded question depends upon the presence of a question word, either overtly or covertly.

Here is how one can straightforwardly obtain the embedded question semantics for examples such as "Pierre sait nager" using the second account of mention-some readings sketched in the previous chapter. The structure of a sentence such as "Pierre sait nager" involves two unobvious elements. First, the infinitive "nager" contains an occurrence of the unpronounced pronoun PRO in its subject position. Second, the verb "nager" is associated with a free variable. So the syntactic structure of "Pierre sait nager" is:

(17)   Pierre$_i$ sait PRO$_i$ nager x.

Just as we take explicit question words to contribute to semantic content certain associated properties – "where" with the property of being a place, "why" with the property of being a reason – so we take the argument of "savoir" in a construction such as (17) to express a semantic content that restricts the value of the variable "x" to *ways*.[3]

---

[3] I remain neutral on which element of "PRO$_i$ nager x", if any, contributes the property of being a way to the semantic content of the whole construction. Those who do not have a phobia of construction-specific composition rules may take it to be the result of a composition rule. Those who do can trace it either to the verb or the variable.

Abstracting from the complexities of the treatment of the *de se*, "PRO$_i$ nager x" therefore expresses (18), a function that takes a possible world to the property of being a way in which Pierre could swim in that world:

(18) $\lambda j \lambda x$(Pierre can swim at j in way x)^4

Following the analysis in the previous chapter (though abstracting from complexities involving question domains) (18) then type-shifts to:

(19) $\lambda j \lambda i (\exists p[$(Pierre can swim in way p at j) & (Pierre can swim in way p at i)])

Then one can apply the same semantics for "know" to "savoir" as in previous chapters to obtain the right semantics for "Pierre sait nager":

(20)   "Pierre sait nager" is true at a world w if and only if Pierre knows at w that $\lambda i (\exists p[$(Pierre can swim in way p at w) & (Pierre can swim in way p at i)])

In short, without any question word occurring either overtly or covertly, it is simple to give the embedded question semantics for languages in which knowledge how is expressed with a bare infinitive. Even if we take the apparent structure of languages such as French at face value, where "savoir" takes an infinitive complement, one can easily give my favored account of their meaning of ascriptions of knowing how.

An objection still remains to the treatment just proposed. For all I have said so far (21) and (22) express the same proposition:

(21)   Pierre sait nager.
(22)   Pierre sait comment nager.

However, French speakers do perceive a strong difference between "savoir + infinitive" and "savoir comment + infinitive", though the difference varies between dialects. An utterance of (22) communicates that Pierre has read about a way of swimming, but probably has not himself employed that way of swimming. In contrast, an utterance of (21) communicates what "Pierre knows how to swim" communicates in English. One would use the latter construction to communicate that a person has a discursive description of a way of doing something, and probably couldn't use it to swim. If (21) and (22) express the same proposition, why should there be such a perceived difference between the two constructions?

There are at least three possible accounts of the felt difference in what is conveyed between utterances of (21) and utterances of (22) that are consistent with the semantics I have given of (21). The first is purely pragmatic in character. According to it, utterances of (21) and utterances of (22) semantically express the same proposition. However, they communicate distinct propositions. The reason they communicate distinct propositions is because of Grice's *maxim of manner*. The second is semantic in

---

^{4} Of course, on the full account, one that incorporates the semantics of PRO suggested in Chapter 3, (18) contains an ordered pair of a third-person way of thinking of Pierre and Pierre, instead of just Pierre.

character. According to it, utterances of (21) and utterances of (22) semantically express distinct propositions. The reason that they express distinct propositions is because use of the explicit "comment", by violating the maxim of manner, signals a distinct domain associated with the property of being a *way*. Since domains affect the proposition semantically expressed, and not merely the proposition communicated, the propositions expressed by utterances of (21) and (22) are distinct. The third is also semantic in character. According to it, utterances of (21) and utterances of (22) semantically express distinct propositions. But the reason they do so is not because of a difference in the domains associated with the property of being a way, but because use of the explicit "comment" signals a distinction in the respective modal bases associated with the infinitive.

Here is how one can use Grice's maxim of manner to justify a purely pragmatic account of the felt distinction between utterances of (21) and (22). Paul Grice's conversational *maxim of manner* (1989: 28) states that one can "expect a partner to make it clear what contribution he is making and to execute his performance with reasonable dispatch". In French, it has become typical to use only the bare infinitive to express knowing how. Therefore, pronouncing the question word becomes a useless addition – someone who does so has not chosen "to execute his performance with reasonable dispatch". It clearly follows from the maxim of manner that one ought to utter (21) rather than (22). Grice's maxim of manner would therefore predict that use of the overt question word would flout the maxim of manner. By flouting the maxim of manner, it would thereby give rise to an *implicature*, no doubt of the generalized conversational variety. One might also expect that the implicature would vary between languages that allow the bare infinitive with the knowledge verb. In the case of French, the implicature seems to be to the effect that the agent acquired the knowledge by some discursive means.

Here is the second account of the felt distinction between utterances of (21) and (22), one that explains it in terms of a distinction between the propositions thereby expressed. It is possible that the occurrence of "comment" signals a distinction in the *question domain* for (21) and (22). On this account, the question domain associated with an utterance of (22) is one that only contains ordered pairs whose first constituent is a thing of which the person only has a discursive description (and presumably, the second member of the ordered pair would be a way of thinking that is characterized by a discursive description). So, when someone utters (22), they express a proposition true at a world w if and only if Pierre stands in the knowledge relation at w to a proposition that involves existential quantification only over ways of which Pierre only has a discursive description. In contrast, uses of the bare infinitive do not involve any such special restriction.

Here is the third account of the felt distinction between utterances of (21) and utterances of (22), one that, like the second account, also explains it in terms of a distinction between the propositions thereby expressed. It is possible that the occurrence of "comment" in (22) signals a difference in the *modal base* associated with the infinitive. An utterance of (21) is associated with a modal base that entails (say) that the agent can swim. In contrast, an utterance of (22) is associated with a distinct kind of modal base. On both the second and the third accounts of the distinction between (21) and (22), (21) and (22) would *express* distinct propositions.

It is clear that in a language in which it is possible to drop the overt question word in expressions of knowing how, Grice's maxim of manner predicts that one ought to drop the question word. By familiar Gricean reasoning, this entails that when one *does* use the question word one does so for a purpose. One purpose might be conversationally to implicate something that is not expressed. Another purpose might be to indicate that either the question domain or the modal base has changed, or both.

It is straightforward to give a compositional semantics for languages such as French that assigns to ascriptions of knowing how the account I have defended. Independently predicted pragmatic factors explain the difference in use between sentences like (21) and (22). *Contra* Rumfitt (2003) and Wiggins (forthcoming), there is no argument from such languages against the view that knowing how to do something is a species of propositional knowledge. But more can be said. We are now in a position to recognize that the best overall account of ascriptions of practical knowledge across languages takes them to express the view I have developed in previous chapters.

The alternative view of knowing how treats knowing how to do something as a relation to an *activity*, rather than as a relation to a *question-meaning*. One might think that this is what we generally mean when we ascribe knowing how, since the majority of the world's languages appear to employ the propositional knowledge verb together with the bare infinitive in so doing. But this conclusion is unwarranted. As we have seen, the kinds of philosophical and scientific considerations that would lead us conclude that knowing how to Φ is not a species of propositional knowledge would also lead us to conclude that knowing where to Φ is not a species of propositional knowledge. But there is no language known to me where the propositional verb together with the bare infinitive means *knowing where*. So the fact that in many languages ascriptions of knowing how do not superficially appear to take the form of an embedded question should not lead us to analyze them as relations to activities. So doing would lead to an unwarranted asymmetry between states of knowing how to do something and states of knowing when to do something and knowing where to find something, asymmetries that all parties to the debate about the nature of practical knowledge should reject.

Finally, the fact that ascriptions of knowing how take the form of embedded questions in many languages is not a syntactic illusion in those languages. In English, it is clear that in "knows how + infinitive", the occurrence of "how" is a distinct question word, and not part of the verb "know". For example, one can conjoin "how" with other question words, as in:

(23) An airman knows how and why to achieve essentials such as air superiority.
("Air Force Doctrine and Leadership", *Aerospace Power Journal* (summer, 2001)

(24)   Make sure your whole family knows when and how to call emergency telephone numbers. *http://www.usfa.dhs.gov/citizens/all_citizens/home_fire_prev/alarms/*

(25)   You will enjoy the safety of travelling with a knowledgeable local, who knows where and how to find the birds you want to see. *http://www.birdingpal.org/tours/*

If "know how" were a constituent in "know how + infinitive", none of these constructions should be possible. Finally, the following inference is valid:

(P1)   John knows how to surf.
(P2)   John knows when to surf.
(C)   John knows when and how to surf.

But if, in (P1), "knows how" were a single constituent, then this inference would not be valid.

It is true that "how" has somewhat different syntactic behavior than other question words. As (26) shows, the question word "how" permits some wh-words to take scope over it that are blocked by its close cousin "when":

(26)   What does John know how to do?
(27)   *What does John know when to do?

One might be tempted to use these facts to support the case that "know how" is a constituent in many ascriptions of knowing how in English. But this would be mistaken.

First, "know how" in such constructions is in fact a scope island. For example, "how" prevents quantifiers from taking scope over it. There is no *de re* reading of the indefinite "a mountain" in (28). The first sentence of (28) can only be read as attributing to John knowledge of how to climb mountains. In contrast (29), which does not contain a question word, clearly allows a *de re* reading, as is evidenced by the fact it supports singular anaphora:

(28)   *John knows how to climb a mountain. It is over there.
(29)   John plans to climb a mountain. It is over there.

Though "how" lacks some of the properties of other scope islands, allowing more phrases to move over it, it is a scope island nevertheless.

Second, "how" differs in this manner from other question words such as "why" and "when" in all of the constructions in which it occurs, as attested by the following:

(30)   What does John wonder how to do?
(31)   *What does John wonder why to do?
(32)   What did John figure out how to do?
(33)   *What did John figure out why to do?
(34)   What did John ask how to do?
(35)   *What did John ask why to do?

So unless the Rylean is prepared to argue that there is a non-propositional sense to all question-embedding verbs, akin to her non-propositional sense of "knows", she cannot use this difference between "how" and other question words in support of her claim.

Finally, "whether" patterns with "how" in being a weak scope island. A sentence such as "What does John know whether to do?" is considerably better than a sentence like "What does John know when to do?" If the fact that "how" generates very weak scope islands is taken as evidence that "know how" is a constituent, the fact that "whether" generates very weak scope islands should be taken as evidence that "know whether" is a constituent. But surely the Rylean does not want to defend the thesis that "know whether" expresses a single relation to an activity. Therefore, the Rylean cannot take the fact that "how" generates very weak scope islands as evidence that "know how" expresses a single relation to an activity.

In languages where ascriptions of knowing how take the surface form of embedded questions, it is because they genuinely have the syntactic structure of embedded questions. There is no hope of basing an argument for a Rylean semantics on the scope properties of "how". Furthermore, given that we can smoothly conjoin "how" with other question words, the only straightforward account of languages in which ascriptions of knowing how take the surface form of embedded questions is one in which "know" has a uniform meaning in all knowing-wh constructions.

The philosophical considerations that support the view that knowing how to Φ is not a kind of propositional knowledge also entail that knowing where to Φ and when to Φ are not kinds of propositional knowledge. Given the uniformity languages have in ascriptions of these latter kinds, the lack of uniformity languages exhibit in ascriptions of knowing how to Φ cannot provide any evidential weight in an argument that knowing how to Φ is not a kind of propositional knowledge. Furthermore, as we have seen, there is a perfectly plausible account of ascriptions of knowing how to Φ across languages that involves assigning such ascriptions states of knowing how to Φ, in my favored sense. So there are no empirical concerns for the account of knowing how I have defended – it is perhaps the most plausible cross-linguistic account of the content of ascriptions of knowing how to Φ. Still, however, one might worry that the fact that it is the most plausible such account does not count in its favor. Why does it constitute evidence *at all* for an account of the nature of states of knowing how that it is plausible to take that account to be what is expressed by ascriptions of knowing how?

4.

Why would one expect it to be a virtue of an account of knowing how that it is plausibly taken to be what is expressed by ascriptions of knowing how in natural language? Shouldn't we be open to the possibility that science could show us that states of knowing how are very different in kind from what ordinary speakers use sentences like "Ana knows how to swim" to express? If so, then although it might be a virtue of an account of the meaning of ascriptions of knowing how that it is plausibly correct for natural language, it is not a virtue of an account of the nature of states of knowing how. And it is the latter that concerns the philosopher, and not the former. In various forms and versions, this is the foundational objection to the methodology I have employed.

Even if one accepted that an account of ascriptions of knowing how was irrelevant to issues about the nature of states of knowing how, this would constitute no objection whatsoever to my view of the nature of these states. It is not even clear how much of the discussion in previous chapters it would render otiose. Discussions of semantics are often in fact discussions of metaphysics, carried out in the formal mode. When semanticists give accounts of sentences containing embedded questions, are they giving an account of what it is to bear a relation to a question, or are they giving an account of the meaning of certain sentences? The right answer is that they are doing both tasks at once; this is why so often linguistic semanticists treat philosophical discussions as contributions to formal semantics. For this reason, even if one chooses to ignore ascriptions of states of knowing how, the work in previous chapters is still directly relevant. The theories discussed in Chapter 2 are both explanations of the meaning of sentences containing embedded questions as well explanations of the nature of what it is to stand in the knowledge relation to a question. As I emphasized in Chapter 3, the discussion there is as much about the nature of *de se* thought as it is about the semantics of *de se* pronouns. The ability to move smoothly between the material mode and the formal is a consequence of the fact that modern semantic theories take the form of inductive characterizations of truth in a language.

So, even if we somehow decided that natural language were irrelevant, we would still need a metaphysical account of the nature of states like knowing-who, knowing-what, etc., and their relation to states of knowing that. We would also need a metaphysical account of the contents of *de se* attitudes. The previous chapters could then be read in the material mode, as providing the details of such accounts.

Be that as it may, it is hard not to view the foundational objection as straightforwardly incoherent. The objection uses the English expression "knowing how to do something" in the metalanguage. It could *hardly be* that science could discover that knowing how to swim was a distinct state than is expressed by "knowing how to swim". After all, quite minimal principles governing the nature of the truth-predicate render this incoherent.

Some perhaps suitably restricted version of the following schema is widely considered to be an a priori truth:

(Truth) "S" is true if and only if S

Replacing the schematic letter "S" by "Ana knows how to swim", we obtain:

(Truth) "Ana knows how to swim" is true if and only if Ana knows how to swim.

This consequence is plainly incompatible with the possibility of scientists (or anyone else for that matter) discovering that the proposition expressed by the English sentence

"Ana knows how to swim" is not the same proposition as the proposition that Ana knows how to swim.

There are of course certain instances of (Truth) that are problematic. One class of problematic instances of (Truth) is those in which instances of "S" lead directly to paradoxes. Most famously, these occur when "S" contains self-referential vocabulary. For example, if we replace "S" by "This sentence is not true", minimal logical and semantic principles entail a contradiction. Another class of problematic instances of (Truth) is those in which "S" contains context-sensitive vocabulary. For example, if we replace "S" in (Truth) by "I am tired", the resulting instance is false. An utterance of "I am tired" can be true, even though I am not tired (since the person uttering the sentence is not Jason Stanley). So, where "S" is replaced by "I am not tired", the left hand side of (Truth) can be true, and the right hand side false. Perhaps the envisaged objection is that, where "S" is replaced by sentences containing "knowing how" (Truth) fails for these familiar reasons.

I am not at present aware of plausible minimal logical and semantical principles which would lead to paradox when "S" is replaced by a sentence like "Ana knows how to swim" in (Truth). For example, it does not seem that "Ana knows how to swim" involves the kind of self-reference that is typical of Liar-Paradoxical sentences. Perhaps additional scrutiny of the linguistic structure of such sentences will reveal such self-reference, but for the moment it seems rather a stretch to hypothesize its existence. Nor are there arguments from the cognitive neuroscience literature I am aware of at least that would lead one to expect that substituting sentences like "Ana knows how to swim" into (Truth) leads to a novel version of the Liar Paradox.

The more plausible view is that (Truth) fails when "S" is replaced by a sentence like "Ana knows how to swim" because sentences of this sort contain some kind of context-dependence. Presumably the idea would be that there is some indexical constituent in a sentence such as "Ana knows how to swim". Just as the context-insensitive meaning of the first-person pronoun "I" yields different contents in different contexts, so the context-sensitive meaning of this indexical yields different contents in different contexts. The context-insensitive meaning (or "character" in the sense of Kaplan 1989a) is such that, relative to a context in which it is uttered by a non-scientist, it expresses one proposition, and relative to a context in which it is uttered by a scientist, it expresses a different proposition.

It is not simple to see how to develop such an account of the context-sensitivity of ascriptions of knowledge how to support the view that scientists express different propositions from the folk by the use of sentences like "Ana knows how to swim". Suppose, for example, that the context-sensitive indexical element is the verb "knows" itself. When "knows how to swim" is used by a non-scientist, then "knows" expresses the propositional knowledge relation. When "knows how to swim" is used by a scientist, then "knows" expresses a relation to an activity. However, as I have argued, "how to swim" denotes an embedded question-meaning, a function from possible worlds to propositions. An embedded question-meaning is not in the same semantic category as an activity, which presumably is just a *property*. So if "knows" were an indexical that expresses the propositional knowledge relation in the mouths of non-scientists, and a relation to an activity in the mouths of scientists, the meaning scientists would express would be semantically defective. The verb "knows" in their mouths would express a relation between a person and an activity, but its complement would be an embedded question-meaning.

Suppose one could plausibly locate an indexical element in predicates such as "knows how to swim" that yields different semantic contents when used by scientists and non-scientists. It would remain difficult to see what the context-independent meaning of the element would be. What is the meaning of (say) "know" such that, when it is used by scientists, it denotes one kind of relation, and when used by non-scientists, it denotes another kind of relation? Rather than speculate further about the nature of this deep, hidden context-dependence, I will suppose that context-dependence too is not a plausible way to reject the relevant instances of (Truth).

The relevant instances of (Truth) are very plausible. Therefore, one cannot coherently argue that scientists have discovered that knowing how to do something is not what is expressed by ascriptions of knowing how to do something. The claim that states of knowing how to do something are expressed by ascriptions of knowing how to do something is as close to an *a priori* truth as we are likely to find in philosophy.

It is of course possible that cognitive scientists can discover that *there are no states of knowing how to do something*. Perhaps cognitive scientists, in researching the mind, will discover that what we ordinarily express by the use of folk notions like "knowing how to swim" does not correlate with any interesting natural kind. And perhaps it is this kind of consideration that Alva Noë has in mind when he writes, about the similar methodology employed in Stanley and Williamson (2001):

The biggest problem with [Stanley and Williamson's methodology] is that it directs our attention to considerations about language (how people talk) when theorists of mind (in philosophy or cognitive science) are interested in human nature and the nature of mind. (2005)

Somewhat speculatively, I will suppose that the idea here is that science could discover that the states that we express with our ordinary ascriptions of knowing how to Φ do not correspond to a natural kind, or perhaps do not even exist. When cognitive scientists use phrases that have pre-established ordinary usages, they intend to use them in technical senses that are unrelated to their previous uses. If so, then while it is a virtue of an account of the ordinary notion of knowing how to do something that it is plausibly taken to be what is expressed by ordinary ascriptions of knowing how, the ordinary notion is just not relevant for the cognitive sciences.[5]

---

[5] I am not sure if this is quite the point Noë is making, since, as we have seen earlier in the chapter, he also holds that "For if one thing is clear, it is that Pip [Noë's dog] does know how to catch a Frisbee". Presumably, what is clear is in the *ordinary* sense of ascriptions of knowing how, Pip knows how to catch a Frisbee. Nothing is "clear" when words are being used in some alternative technical sense.

   The correct attitude about the relation between the terminology of folk physics, and the terminology of the *physical* sciences, is that they are unrelated. In so far as the folk use the term "mass", it does not need to be connected to what physicists mean by that term. But it is far from clear that this is the correct attitude to have towards the *cognitive* sciences. If we were confronted by an account of our mental workings that had no place for notions like belief, desire, or knowledge, but only (say) concepts described in fundamental neurobiological terms, would that really be an acceptable account of the cognitive facts? Presumably, it is not accidental that physicists employ terminology that has no obvious relation to its ordinary use (if the relevant term even has an ordinary use), whereas so many of the crucial terms used in cognitive science have clear pre-established ordinary usages.

   Like most scientists, cognitive scientists and psychologists working on topics related to knowing how and knowing that – such as the implicit and explicit knowledge distinction, or the procedural and declarative knowledge distinction, or the distinction between knowing how and knowing that – only occasionally speak on a meta-level about their discipline. However, when they do address the relation between ordinary and technical usage, it is clear that many regard adherence to pre-established usage as a virtue. As Dienes and Perner write in an influential survey article on implicit and explicit knowledge:

Another advantage of our analysis is that it is grounded in the ordinary use of the terms "implicit" and "explicit" (e.g., "They didn't say so explicitly; it was left implicit"), whereas traditional definitions have depended on further related distinctions . . . These [other] definitions of implicit memory/learning raise the question of why the terms implicit/explicit are used at all . . . when using technical terms with an existing ordinary meaning, it seems to us, we should adhere to that existing meaning as far as possible and not impose some arbitrary "operational definition," or else we make it difficult for the scientific community to share the same meaning, because the natural meaning is likely to keep intruding. (Who still adheres – or ever adhered – to the operational definition of intelligence as that which the WAIS [Wechsler Adult Intelligence Scale] measures?) So it is not an unimportant feature of our use of the implicit-explicit distinction that it attempts to stay true to its natural meaning, which we believe was the unarticulated reason for introducing the distinction in the first place, and what partially motivated its acceptance and continued use. (1999: 736)

In Cohen and Squire, one of the classic articles on procedural and declarative knowledge, they conclude:

This distinction between procedural and rule-based information and declarative or data-based information, which is reminiscent of the classical distinction between "knowing how" and "knowing that", has been the subject of considerable discussion in the literature of cognition and artificial intelligence. The experimental findings described here provide evidence that such a distinction is honored by the nervous system. (1980: 209)

Similarly, Twila Tardif et al., in a paper on the relation between knowing that and knowing how:

In everyday understanding and in cognitive science (e.g. Cohen & Squire), knowing-how and knowing-that are certainly different (e.g., one can know that a computer boots up without knowing how to boot one up, and vice-versa). This distinction has been pervasive in the memory literature —in the distinction between declarative and procedural memory – and in discussions of types of knowledge in psychology and philosophy for the past century (see, e.g., Bergson, 1911; Ryle, 1949). (2005: 562–3)

It is clear that faithfulness to ordinary usage of the terms employed ("everyday understanding") is taken to be a virtue of a theory of the notion among cognitive scientists working directly on concepts related to knowing how and knowing that. It is therefore important even from the perspective of cognitive science to settle on what the folk notion of knowing how is – that is, the notion of knowing how to do something that is expressed by ordinary attributions of knowing how. Cognitive scientists are unprepared simply to jettison the folk notions of knowing how and knowing that. In fact, they seem to take the ordinary notions as guiding their inquiry.

However, though evidence from cognitive science should not lead us to jettison the ordinary notions, it could lead us to reject the view that knowing how is a species of knowing that. For it could turn out that evidence from cognitive science may lead us to the conclusion that the ordinary notion of knowing corresponds to two different kinds of relations between propositions – the knowing how kind, and the knowing that kind. As Glick emphasizes:

Intellectualism is a thesis about the relationship between two mental phenomena, and cognitive science is the field devoted to the study of mental phenomena. If we want to know whether emotional pain is a sort of physical pain, the obvious place to turn is to cognitive science. Similarly if we want to know whether working memory is a kind of long-term memory. And indeed, the field has delivered results on these questions, questions about whether a sub-type/ type relationship obtains between two mental phenomena. Working memory is not a kind of long-term memory, and although the distinction is not strictly tied to the length of time that a memory is retained, the empirical data vindicate the household distinction between short-term and long-term memory: The sort of memory one uses to get from the phone book to the phone keypad is not the sort of memory one uses to remember one's own phone number. The status of Intellectualism is also a question of the type/sub-type sort, so there is an obvious reason to think that an appropriate methodology for addressing it is to appeal to cognitive science. (Forthcoming)

Glick is right that evidence from cognitive science may show that the ordinary notion of knowing does not involve a "type/sub-type" relation between knowing that and knowing how, as I have maintained. Empirical investigation could reveal that the relation expressed by "know" is a non-natural kind, corresponding to two distinct relations to propositions – one the sort expressed in ascriptions of knowing how to do something, and the other in other kinds of knowledge ascriptions.

On the face of it, Glick's worry sits uneasily with the cognitive science literature. The same knowledge that can be described by ascriptions of knowing how can be described by other kinds of ascriptions as well. As we have seen, for example, the knowledge of how to catch the ball can be described as the knowledge whether the ball would fall in front of the agent, behind the agent, or hit the agent. But this only shows that the knowing how kind of relation to a proposition could be what is relevant with other ascriptions of knowledge as well. When we describe an agent as knowing that the ball would hit them if thrown, what makes our statement true is that agent stands in the knowing how kind of relation to a proposition. When we describe an agent as knowing that Obama is president, what makes our statement true is the agent is standing in the knowing that kind of relation to a proposition. The various natural language words for "know" do not discriminate between these relations, because in the nature of a scientific discovery that knowledge has this disjunctive status.

Here are the two challenges that might be posed to the project from work in the cognitive sciences. First, it might be that such work shows that knowing how is the phlogiston of folk psychology. Though, as I have indicated, this is a conclusion cognitive scientists themselves would be reluctant to draw, we must nevertheless be open to it as a possibility. The second challenge is that it might turn out that while research in cognitive science is consistent with knowing how to do something being a state with propositional content, it is inconsistent with knowing how to do something involving the propositional knowledge *relation*. We must now look more closely at the sort of evidence from cognitive science to see if it warrants either of these drastic conclusions.

7

The Cognitive Science
of Practical Knowledge

I have argued that knowing how to do something is a kind of propositional knowledge, a kind of propositional knowledge that guides skilled actions. I have, however, been silent thus far on the voluminous literature on the psychology and cognitive science of skilled action. The silence is potentially troubling. On the surface, at least, there seems to be relatively straightforward ways of using this literature to raise problems for my central claims.

My purpose in this chapter is to show that what we know so far about the cognitive science of skilled action is consistent with my views about the nature of knowing how. In section 1, I argue that one could identify the notion of procedural knowledge as it is discussed in the cognitive science literature with knowing how in the sense I have defended – there is nothing in the literature that precludes this. If so, then declarative knowledge is but one species of propositional knowledge. In section 2, I evaluate and reject an argument for the view that all propositional knowledge is declarative knowledge in the cognitive scientific sense, an argument based on the premise that propositional knowledge is capable of being verbalized. In section 3, I consider and reject some arguments that exploit epistemic principles about propositional knowledge to show that procedural knowledge is not propositional knowledge. In section 4, I consider various arguments for the view that knowing how to do something is non-conceptual in nature, which, if sound, would also raise problems for the view that knowing how to do something is a kind of propositional knowledge. In section 5, I look at the literature of the verbal overshadowing effect, which provides evidence that verbalization impedes skilled performance.

1.

In response to Stanley and Williamson (2001), a number of philosophers have argued that there is a straightforward argument from cognitive science against a propositional knowledge view of knowing how. For example, Michael Devitt writes:

The folk distinction between knowledge-that and knowledge-how is commonly thought to be the same as the psychological one between "declarative" and "procedural" knowledge. That distinction originated in AI but is widely acknowledged, frequently applied, and very important in psychology. (Forthcoming)

If so, then the fact that procedural knowledge is not a species of declarative knowledge entails that the folk notion of knowing how is not a species of the folk notion of knowing that. One might use this as a premise to argue that knowing how to do something is not a kind of knowing that.

As Devitt correctly notes, the distinction between procedural and declarative knowledge "originated in AI" and was subsequently borrowed by psychologists. As Dienes and Perner write:

The procedural-declarative knowledge distinction was introduced in artificial intelligence . . . and later taken over in psychological modeling . . . It concerned how best to implement knowledge: Should one represent the knowledge that all men are mortal as a general declaration "for every individual it is true that if that individual is human it is also mortal"? Whenever knowledge of a human individual was introduced in the database this general information would be consulted to infer by general inference rules that that individual must also be mortal. The alternative would be to have a specialized inference procedure: "Whenever an individual is introduced that is human, represent that individual is mortal." (1999: 743)

The distinction between procedural and declarative knowledge was not introduced as a distinction between two types of states of knowledge. It was rather intended as a distinction between ways in which one could generate a given state of knowledge – via either declarative methods or procedural methods. Unfortunately, relating this to a putative distinction between knowing how to do something and knowing that something is the case confuses matters, as the latter is a putative distinction between *two kinds of states*, rather than a distinction between *two ways of implementing a state*.

It is clear in the original discussions of the procedural/declarative distinction in artificial intelligence that the distinction between declarative and procedural knowledge is not a distinction between two kinds of states – either states with non-truth-evaluable contents versus states with truth-evaluable contents, or even different relations to truth-evaluable contents. Here is a quote from Terry Winograd's classical article "Frame Representations and the Declarative–Procedural Controversy":

First, let us look at the superficial lineup of the argument. It is an artificial intelligence incarnation of the old philosophical distinction between "knowing that" and "know how". The procedur-alists assert that our knowledge is primarily a "knowing how". The human information processor is a stored program device, with its knowledge of the world embedded in the programs. What a person (or robot) knows about the English language, the game of chess, or the physical properties of his world is coextensive with his set of programs for operating with it . . .

The declarativists, on the other hand, do not believe that knowledge of a subject is intimately bound with the procedures for its use. They see intelligence as resting on two bases: a quite general set of procedures for manipulating facts of all sorts, and a set of specific facts describing particular knowledge domains. In thinking, the general procedures are often applied to the domain-specific data to make deductions. Often this process has been based on the model of axiomatic mathematics. The facts are *axioms* and the thought process involves *proof procedures* for drawing conclusions from them . . .

From a strictly formal view there is no distinction between the positions. Anyone who has programmed in languages like LISP has been forced into believing that "programs are data". We can think of the interpreter (or the hardware device, for that matter) as the only program in the system, and everything else as data on which it works. Everything, then, is declarative.

From the other end, we can view everything as a program . . . A fact is a simple program which accepts inputs equivalent to questions like "Are you true?" and commands like "Assume you are true!". It returns outputs like "true" and "false", which have lasting effects which will determine the way it responds in the future (equivalent to setting internal variables). Everything is a procedure. Clearly, there is no sharp debate on whether a piece of knowledge *is* a program or a statement. We must go below these labels to see what we stand to gain in *looking at* it as one or the other. (1975: 186–7)

The distinction Winograd is drawing here is certainly *not*, as he states, an "incarnation" of the old philosophical distinction between knowing that and knowing how. The "old philosophical distinction" between knowing how and knowing that is a distinction between *kinds of states*. Those who endorse the distinction, such as Ryle, think that states of knowing how do not have contents that are true or false, whereas states of knowing that do have contents that are true or false. It would be sheer madness to assert, as Winograd does, that "from a strictly formal view", there is no distinction between a state with a truth-evaluable content and a state without a truth-evaluable content. Similarly, it would be sheer madness to assert that "there is no sharp debate" about whether a piece of knowledge has truth-evaluable content or lacks truth-evaluable content.

The debate about declarative knowledge and procedural knowledge does not concern the existence of states of knowledge that lack truth-evaluable content. It is rather a dispute about how to *implement knowledge*, i.e. how best to derive propositional knowledge states, procedurally or declaratively. As Winograd writes, solving the debate requires deciding whether it is best to think of humans (or best to program machines) as deriving their knowledge via declarative methods, or rather deriving their knowledge via procedural methods.[1] This is not a distinction between kinds of knowledge – it is a distinction between ways of implementing (or deriving) the knowledge we have. Indeed, Winograd treats with skepticism the idea that we should seek a "synthesis", by admitting knowledge that is best implemented procedurally, and knowledge that is best implemented declaratively:

At this point it is tempting to look for a synthesis – to say "You need both. Some things are better represented procedurally, others as declarative facts, and all we need to do is work on how these

---

[1] "We must examine the mechanisms which have been developed for dealing with these representations, and the kind of advantages they offer for epistemology. In this entire discussion, we could divide the question into two aspects: 'What kind of representation do people use?' and 'What kind of representation is best for machine intelligence?'" (1975: 187).

can be integrated." This reaction misses what I believe is the fundamental ground for the dispute. It is not simply a technical issue of formalisms, but it is an expression of an underlying difference in attitude towards the problems of complexity. (1975: 191)

According to Winograd, the declarative/procedural dispute is a difference in attitude about the most efficacious way to implement possession of information. Proceduralists think that all information, including information that can be represented in the form of simple declarative generalizations, is at bottom derived from procedures. Declarativists think that all information, including information that is hard to state in the form of simple declarative generalizations, is implemented ultimately by sentence-like representations. Winograd himself thinks a "synthesis" should be reached by describing a method for implementing knowledge that has both procedural and declarative *aspects*. Clearly, Winograd is thinking of the distinction as one between ways knowledge is derived, not kinds of knowledge states. As researchers in artificial intelligence use the distinction, it is irrelevant to the question of whether knowing how to do something is a state with a truth-evaluable content.[2]

So, as the expressions are used in artificial intelligence, the propositional knowledge that p could be arrived at via procedural means, and the knowledge of how to Φ could be arrived at via declarative means. The distinction is not one between states with different kinds of content, but between ways of arriving at states with that content. But perhaps cognitive neuroscientists, despite appropriating the terminology from artificial intelligence, mean something quite different. That is, perhaps when cognitive neuroscientists use "procedural knowledge", they do not refer to knowledge that is arrived at by procedural means, but rather mean what Ryle and his followers think of as knowing how, i.e. knowledge the content of which is an activity, rather than a proposition. And perhaps when cognitive neuroscientists use "declarative knowledge", they do not refer to knowledge that is arrived at by declarative means, but rather mean knowledge the content of which is a proposition, i.e. something truth-evaluable.

At first glance, cognitive neuroscientists seem explicit that the distinction they draw between declarative knowledge and procedural knowledge is a distinction that has to do with the method by which knowledge is implemented in a system, rather than with its content. As we have seen above, in Cohen and Squire's classic 1980 article, they speak of the distinction as one "between procedural and rule-based information and declarative or data-based information". In the first instance, this distinction does not have to do with the content of the knowledge that is either rule-based or data-based; it has to do with how that knowledge is derived by the system. Similarly, in Dienes and

---

[2] If we are thinking of procedural knowledge *simply* as knowledge implemented in a certain way, knowledge derivable by procedural methods, then it is straightforwardly irrelevant to the knowing how–knowing that debate. Very simple mechanical objects can have procedural knowledge in this sense. But one would be loath to declare that calculators have knowledge how. It sounds very odd indeed to point at my calculator and say, "like me, this calculator knows how to add". Being *merely* procedurally implemented cannot be sufficient for knowing how.

Perner (1998: 743), they use the example of the knowledge that all men are mortal to make the distinction between declarative and procedural knowledge – describing declarative ways of implementing this knowledge, and procedural ways. But the knowledge that all men are mortal is clearly propositional knowledge. Without further argument, it is difficult to see how this directly bears on the question whether knowing how to do something has propositional content.[3]

However, this is not the only way the procedural knowledge–declarative knowledge distinction is characterized in cognitive neuroscience. Here is a description of the distinction between declarative and procedural memory from a fairly recent review article on the cognitive neuroscience of human memory (Gabrieli 1998). We can use it to extract a somewhat different characterization of the distinction between declarative and procedural knowledge, one that, unlike the distinction drawn in artificial intelligence, is not one defined in terms of implementation (I have omitted only the references to relevant literature):

> Declarative memory encompasses the acquisition, retention, and retrieval of knowledge that can be consciously and intentionally recollected ... Such knowledge includes memory for events (episodic memory) or facts (semantic memory) ... Episodic memories are measured by direct or explicit tests of memory, such as free recall, cued recall, or recognition, that refer to a prior episode ... In contrast, nondeclarative or procedural kinds of memory encompass the acquisition, retention, and retrieval of knowledge expressed through experience-induced changes in performance. These kinds of memory are measured by indirect or implicit tests where no reference is made to that experience. Skill learning, repetition priming, and conditioning are classes of implicit tests that often reveal procedural memory processes dissociable from declarative memory. (Ibid.: 90)

So, declarative knowledge is "knowledge that can be consciously and intentionally recollected", and procedural knowledge is "knowledge expressed through experience-induced changes in performance". Is there an argument from these characterizations of the distinction that procedural knowledge is *a fortiori* not genuine propositional knowledge?

It is true, as Gabrieli writes, that declarative knowledge is taken by neuroscientists to include as a sub-species what they call "knowledge of facts". If facts are identified with true propositions, then it will turn out that all propositional knowledge is declarative knowledge. Since procedural knowledge is not declarative knowledge, one could use this argument to conclude that procedural knowledge is not propositional knowledge.

However, this argument is far too quick. If we take the cognitive neuroscientists' talk of "facts" to refer to true propositions, it also follows that not all declarative

---

[3] Brian McLaughlin has pointed out to me an analogous point with regard to the connectionist literature. Connectionists often claim that certain things are implicitly represented in the patterns of connectivity among units, rather than being explicitly represented by activated units or patterns of activation over units. But even when connectionists describe what is implicitly represented in the patterns of connectivity, they typically use that-clauses.

knowledge is genuine propositional knowledge. For some declarative knowledge is not (in the cognitive neuroscientific vernacular) "knowledge of facts". Consider the distinction between episodic memory and semantic memory:

Episodic memory... deals with unique, concrete, personal temporally dated events that the rememberer has witnessed, whereas semantic memory involves general, abstract, timeless knowledge that a person shares with others. (Tulving 1986: 307)

Episodic memory is one kind of declarative memory. Episodic memories are memories that involve experiences of mine, memories whose content involves propositions I would express via the use of *indexicals*, such as the first-person English pronoun "I". Let us say that an "episodic content" denotes the kind of proposition that is associated with episodic memory, and likewise for "semantic content". Episodic knowledge is knowledge of episodic contents; semantic knowledge is knowledge of semantic contents. But episodic knowledge, such as the knowledge that I was in Jena last month, or the knowledge that it is cold here, is not in cognitive neuroscientific terms "knowledge of facts". Only semantic knowledge is "knowledge of facts". Nevertheless, my knowledge that I was in Jena last month is propositional knowledge. By "facts", cognitive neuroscientists mean to refer only to the contents of what they call "semantic knowledge". But these contents do not exhaust all propositional contents. They are, at best, the contents expressed by sentences containing no context-sensitive vocabulary – contents like *that doctors sometimes carry pins in their hands*. Factual knowledge in this sense is a *sub-species* of propositional knowledge, as philosophers use the terms.

Declarative knowledge is "knowledge that can be consciously and intentionally recollected", and procedural knowledge is "knowledge expressed through experience-induced changes in performance". Putting aside the misleading talk of "facts", nothing in this quote entails or even suggests that procedural knowledge is not propositional. Procedural knowledge is knowledge that is typically expressed through an increase in skill. But knowledge of propositions could easily be expressed through an increase in skill. My belief that I should catch a fly ball by positioning my body in a certain way could become knowledge by practicing catching fly balls in that manner. The practice of catching fly balls in that manner would give me proprioceptive evidence that my belief is true. Unless one thought (absurdly) that proprioception is not a source of evidence, it is obvious that propositional knowledge can be expressed through an increase in skill.

Differences in implementation may typically correlate with differences in content. It has been established that episodic memory and semantic memory are disassociable. There are amnesias that target them differentially. I may suffer damage that results in intact memory for things like *that doctors sometimes hide pins in their hands*, but no intact memory for propositions like *that I was stuck by such a pin recently*. Both episodic knowledge and semantic knowledge are clearly forms of propositional knowledge. They are forms of propositional knowledge that have as their contents *different kinds of propositions*. The ability to acquire and retain episodic knowledge is the ability to acquire and retain knowledge of propositions expressed by certain kinds of egocentric vocabulary – vocabulary involving indexicals like "I" and "here".[4] The ability to acquire and retain semantic knowledge is the ability to acquire and retain knowledge of propositions expressed in non-egocentric vocabulary (or at least vocabulary that does not include certain egocentric terms). This is not a distinction between *kinds of knowledge*, but rather a distinction between *kinds of propositional contents*. It appears that just as the brain has specific mechanisms governing place and person names, the brain has specific mechanisms governing indexical propositions and non-indexical propositional contents.

Just as episodic knowledge is not another *kind* of knowledge, but rather garden-variety knowledge of certain kinds of propositions, the most obvious way to think of procedural knowledge is as garden-variety knowledge of certain kinds of propositions. In particular, the procedural knowledge that an amnesiac can acquire is garden-variety knowledge of a special class of propositions, those describing *activities*. For example, an amnesiac who can acquire a pattern-analyzing skill can acquire knowledge of propositions involving ways of doing that skill, but cannot acquire knowledge of many other kinds of propositions, such as propositions about her past experiences. Even if differences in how knowledge is implemented *do* correlate with kinds of content, the contents of procedural knowledge are still propositions. They are just propositions about activities – exactly the kinds of propositions that, on my favored analysis, are the contents of states of knowing how to do something.

Thus, if we take the cognitive neuroscientists to refer to knowledge with different kinds of content, when they discuss the declarative–procedural knowledge distinction, it simply does not follow that the content of procedural knowledge is non-propositional. The obvious way to take the neuroscience literature is in the terms I have described. The content of procedural knowledge is propositional, but involves different *kinds* of propositions than stock cases of declarative literature. That is, it is completely consistent with a strong reading of the neuroscience distinction between declarative and procedural knowledge – that it concerns states of knowledge with different kinds of content, and not merely points about implementation – that procedural knowledge is propositional knowledge of the sorts of propositions that I take states of knowing how to do something to have as their contents. In fact, given that the other types of memory – episodic and semantic – clearly seem to be propositional in character, this is the most natural way to take the distinction between procedural and declarative knowledge.

---

[4] Tulving's description of the potential contents of semantic memory as the kind of information "that one shares with others" reflects the long tradition of thinking about indexical propositions about oneself as non-communicable (Frege 1918). More recently, some have argued that the exact information expressed by sentences containing demonstratives and indexicals is not sharable (Heck 2002).

In short, there is nothing in cognitive neuroscience that entails that procedural knowledge is not a species of genuine propositional knowledge. Even if we were to identify procedural knowledge with knowing how, the account I have given of the nature of knowing how is a perfectly natural account of procedural knowledge, in the sense relevant in neuroscience. The fact that knowledge of propositions about ways of engaging in activities is dissassociable from knowledge of propositions that are not about ways of engaging in activities is no more and no less surprising than the fact that propositions about my experiences are dissassociable from knowledge of propositions that are not about my experiences. So, even if we take the unnecessarily controversial step of identifying procedural knowledge with knowing how, there is no evidence in cognitive neuroscience that is incompatible with the claim that the relation of knowing how to knowing that is that of a species to a genus.

It is no part of my aim to defend the thesis that procedural knowledge is co-extensive with knowing how. It may very well be the categories of knowing how and knowing that cross-cut the categories of procedural knowledge and declarative knowledge. All I have argued is that, even if procedural knowledge is co-extensive with knowing how to do something, that is fully consistent with my account of the nature of the latter states.

2.

We have seen that, even on the assumption that knowing how to do something is co-extensive with procedural knowledge in the sense of cognitive neuroscience, the view that knowing how is a species of knowing that is consistent with the main discussions in cognitive neuroscience. My purpose in this section is to address a distinct argument that all propositional knowledge is declarative knowledge, which must ultimately rely on various philosophical views about propositional knowledge. Here is the argument. Declarative knowledge is knowledge the content of which is somehow capable of being verbalized. If all propositional knowledge must be capable of being verbalized, then propositional knowledge is declarative knowledge.

I argue that this argument is not sound. In the sense of "capable of being verbalized" in which all propositional knowledge has content that is capable of being verbalized, procedural knowledge too is knowledge with content that is capable of being verbalized. In fact, I go further than necessary in this chapter. I also argue that "capable of being verbalized" cannot be a criterion of declarative knowledge, because procedural knowledge has content that is capable of being verbalized in the very same way as *episodic knowledge* has content that is capable of being verbalized. But episodic knowledge is a kind of declarative knowledge.

One feature of declarative knowledge is that it is *explicit*, which we can take provisionally at least to mean that it is available in the form of a conscious representation. Devitt (forthcoming) concludes from this fact that it is co-extensive with the folk notion of knowledge-that:

What is declarative knowledge? The key thing to note for our purposes is that there is a consensus in psychology that it involves a *conscious representation* of what is known. Thus, psychologists think that a subject has declarative knowledge of the processing rules for a task only if she consciously represents the rules. So the person who has declarative knowledge that R is a rule of arithmetic must represent that fact in her central processor. So, if we adopt the popular, and in my view correct, representational theory of the mind ("RTM"), declarative knowledge can indeed be identified with the folk's knowledge-that.[5]

Charles Wallis, in using the psychological discussions of the distinction between procedural and declarative knowledge to conclude that knowing how is not knowing that, makes a similar claim about the conditions under which knowledge is propositional:

the brain areas operant in the elicitation and generation of such contextually reliable complexes of dispositions are strongly dissociable from areas of the brain responsible for propositional knowledge. Neurological evidence regarding such behavior clearly implicates areas of the brain other than those associated with propositional knowledge (hippocampus and inferior temporal lobe) in the causal generation of such behavior (e.g. the basal ganglia and the motor areas) ... This last point proves very significant since the claim that knowledge-how reduces to propositional knowledge has always, and rightly, been understood as requiring that (1) The knowledge itself be propositional knowledge or at least encoded explicitly as particular linguistic or quasi-linguistic expressions that were (2) causally operant in the manifestation of the knowledge ... These are likewise the claims of relevance to epistemologists and to such programs in the philosophy of mind as belief–desire psychology. (2008: 141)

Wallis here seems to think that epistemologists view propositional knowledge by definition as knowledge that is "at least encoded explicitly as particular linguistic or quasi-linguistic expressions that were ... causally operant in the manifestation of knowledge."

Devitt and Wallis are arguing that propositional knowledge is, by its nature, somehow capable of being presented in explicit form. This is their argument that propositional knowledge is declarative knowledge, in the psychologist's sense. It is because they think that propositional knowledge is explicit that it is "identical to the folk's knowledge-that".

Devitt and Wallis's argument that the cognitive scientific notion of declarative knowledge is co-extensive with the philosophers' notion of propositional knowledge relies on their assumption that propositional knowledge is co-extensive with explicit knowledge. This raises two questions. First, are Devitt and Wallis correct that all and only declarative knowledge is explicit? Second, are Devitt and Wallis right that there are sound philosophical reasons to think that all propositional knowledge is explicit?

---

[5] I take it that both declarative knowledge and the folk's knowledge-that encompass not only conscious knowledge, but also dispositional states of knowledge. I knew that sofas don't bake gingerbread five minutes ago, even though I was not consciously representing that knowledge. The wording of Devitt's quote suggests otherwise, but I assume he was just being careless.

Devitt and Wallis each commit themselves to the view that propositional knowledge requires something like a language of thought. We have already seen that this is contentious. A number of philosophers reject the view that propositional attitudes require a language of thought (e.g. Matthews 2007). As we have seen in Chapter 1, an anti-representationalist view of the mental is completely consistent with the fact that we have propositional knowledge states. Nevertheless, even if we accept that propositional attitudes require stored symbolic states, Devitt and Wallis are wrong that there is anything in cognitive neuroscience that would lead one to the conclusion that knowing how is not a species of propositional knowledge.

Devitt and Wallis's discussions conflate several related but orthogonal distinctions in cognitive neuroscience. First, there is a distinction between declarative knowledge and procedural knowledge. Second, there is a distinction between explicit knowledge and implicit knowledge. Third, there is a distinction between being represented by means of linguistic or quasi-linguistic symbols, and not being so represented.

There are different characterizations of the distinction between implicit and explicit knowledge, and different characterizations of the distinction between procedural and declarative knowledge. But on all such characterizations, the distinctions are not the same. For example, Reed et al. write:

If a dissociation can be demonstrated between the knowledge that controls someone's behavior and their ability to report how that behavior is controlled, the knowledge is said to be implicit. (2010: 63)

Given this characterization, it is clear that some procedural knowledge is explicit. It is true that many people have skills that they cannot describe. But it is certainly not essential to possessing a skill that one cannot verbalize one's mastery. As any physician in training knows, some physicians who are skilled at a procedure are poor at describing how they do what they do, and other physicians who are skilled at a procedure are very good at describing how they do what they do. Physicians skilled at a procedure who are also very good at describing to others how they do it possess explicit procedural knowledge. The category of explicit procedural knowledge is both practically and theoretically important. Awareness of how one is doing what one is doing is important not just in educating, but also in correcting oneself when one encounters obstacles in performance.[6]

---

[6] The phenomenon of verbal overshadowing shows that verbalizing one's performances may lead to worse success in performance, as the verbalization seems to interfere with the execution of the skilled activity. Flegal and Anderson (2008) even provide evidence that verbalizing one's performances may lead to a decrease in performance even subsequent to the verbalization. All of this is consistent with the fact that some people can describe in detail the ways in which they perform various procedures. The existence of leading medical schools shows that, contrary to the provocative title of Flegal and Anderson (ibid.), some of those who can verbalize their performances are also very skilled at those performances. For more on verbal overshadowing, see section 5 below.

Conversely, there can be implicit knowledge that is not procedural. My memory of seeing the word "cat" before might control my behavior in a word stem completion task, even though, because I have ingested alcohol, I am not consciously aware that I have seen the word "cat" before (Duka et al. 2001). My memory of seeing the word "cat" before is implicit, but not procedural, and so is my knowledge. There can be explicit knowledge that is procedural and implicit knowledge that is not procedural. The implicit/explicit distinction should not be conflated with the procedural–declarative distinction.

As we have seen, in the AI literature, the procedural–declarative distinction concerns the way knowledge is implemented, rather than the type of knowledge it is. Cognitive neuroscientists have borrowed this vocabulary to describe a distinction between kinds of retention based upon double dissociations. The different kinds of retention are associated with different areas of the brain. But cognitive scientists do not speak with one voice about the representation of procedural knowledge and declarative knowledge. It is consistent with the fact that procedural information can be retained while declarative information cannot, and vice versa, that both are represented by representational, and even symbolic representational mechanisms. Though the fact that the vocabulary is borrowed from an implementation distinction in AI no doubt confuses the matter, in principle one should nevertheless distinguish conceptually between procedural and declarative knowledge as categories in cognitive neuroscience, on the one hand, and claims about how those categories are ultimately represented, on the other.

Some prominent researchers deny that the implicit/explicit distinction is binary. Karmiloff-Smith (1986) breaks this binary distinction into four distinct levels, "implicit", "primary explication", "secondary explication", and "tertiary explication", all of which she believes need to be distinguished to explain child linguistic development. The first is knowledge that is not explicitly represented at all. The second is when the first level is represented in the same representational code in which it is merely implicitly represented. The third is when it is conscious but not verbalizable. The fourth is when it is both conscious and verbalizable. Dienes and Perner (1999: 748) agree with Karmiloff-Smith that "there is no simple dichotomy between implicit and explicit knowledge", though they deny that there is a distinction between Karmiloff-Smith's third and fourth levels.

Just as it is an open question how to characterize the notions of "implicit" and "explicit" knowledge, it is equally an open question how to characterize the somewhat technical notion of declarative knowledge as it occurs in cognitive neuroscience. Devitt and Wallis both think that it is in the nature of propositional knowledge to be implemented via representations. Perhaps the reasoning behind their identification of propositional knowledge with declarative knowledge is that declarative knowledge is that knowledge that is implemented by representations, and procedural knowledge is that knowledge that is not implemented by representations. Therefore, propositional knowledge is not procedural knowledge.

Even if we grant the controversial philosophical claim that propositional knowledge is by its nature implemented by representations, the argument is not sound. As Fodor (1968) makes clear, if one is convinced by the arguments that show that propositional knowledge is implemented via symbolic representations, one should be swayed by parallel arguments for the conclusion that procedural knowledge is implemented via symbolic representations. It is true that the AI distinction between procedural knowledge and declarative knowledge is an implementation distinction of this sort. But it is at best a speculative hypothesis that this is an accurate description of the double disassociations found in certain kinds of amnesia. So even if propositional knowledge requires symbolic representations, it does not follow that procedural knowledge is not propositional knowledge.[7]

Devitt and Wallis add further conditions to what is necessary for propositional knowledge aside from the propositional content of the state being implemented symbolically. Devitt and Wallis hold that knowing that p requires the availability of an explicit, conscious representation of the proposition that p. What are the grounds for this additional requirement?

It is hard for me to speculate what the argument would be for the view that propositional knowledge requires all the features that neuroscientists associate with declarative knowledge. Part of the problem is that it is not particularly clear how to describe what neuroscientists mean by "declarative knowledge" in qualitative terms, that is, terms other than the kind of knowledge lacking in subjects with a certain kind of brain injury. One is tempted to describe declarative knowledge as knowledge the content of which one can characterize in words, i.e. knowledge that is *capable of being verbalized*. But there is a serious problem with this characterization. It is not clear what words the agent is allowed to use in verbalizing the agent's knowledge.

Consider a punch-drunk boxer, who still retains the skill of boxing against a southpaw, though he isn't particularly skilled in describing it. He can still verbalize his knowledge of how to box against a southpaw, by showing how to box against a southpaw, and simultaneously uttering the sentence "This is the way I fight against a southpaw". This is certainly a verbalization, and it is a verbalization of something he knows in virtue of which he possesses a skill. But presumably one would not want to grant that the boxer has declarative knowledge, in the neuroscientist's sense. The capacity *merely* to verbalize one's knowledge is not sufficient for declarative knowledge.[8]

Words such as "this" and "that" are *demonstrative* expressions, part of a class of context-sensitive singular terms that include the personal pronouns "he", "she", and

---

[7] It could also be that procedural knowledge could be identified with Karmiloff-Smith's "primary explication level", it which case it would be represented, albeit not consciously.

[8] Fodor suggests that "the criterion of accessibility [is] the availability for explicit report of the information that these representations encode" (1983: 56). I see no reason why the punch-drunk boxer is not giving an explicit report of his knowledge how.

"it", and indexicals such as "I", "here", "now", and "today". The function of these terms is to allow us to refer to things for which we lack convenient labels. To take an extreme example, perhaps I have amnesia and have forgotten who I am. I can still say that *I* am confused. This is the class of words Bertrand Russell (1950: ch. VII) calls *egocentric particulars*.[9] There is a philosophical tradition of thinking of truly scientific discourse as lacking egocentric particulars. As Russell writes:

A physicist will not say "I saw a table", but like Neurath or Julius Caesar, "Otto saw a table"; he will not say "A meteor is visible now", but "A meteor was visible at 8h. 43. G.M.T.", and in this statement "was" is intended to be without tense. (Ibid.: 108–9)

Perhaps this philosophical tradition reflects something about the organization of knowledge. Perhaps declarative knowledge is knowledge that is capable of being verbalized without the use of egocentric vocabulary.

The problem with this suggestion is that *episodic memory* is a kind of declarative memory (Gabrieli 1998: 89–90). Presumably, then, episodic knowledge is a kind of declarative knowledge. But as we have seen in the previous section, episodic knowledge is knowledge the content of which can only be stated with the use of egocentric words. My episodic memory is my memory of events in which *I* was a participant. Therefore, declarative knowledge *does* include knowledge the content of which can only be stated with the use of egocentric words.

Perhaps one way to think of the kind of knowledge that neuroscientists describe as declarative is that it is the kind of knowledge of which one can give an accurate and informative description. This is not a particularly helpful characterization of the kind of knowledge in question, because the notion of an "informative description" is context-sensitive; what may be an informative description in one context, may not be in another context. Nevertheless, one can fasten onto a sense of the notion of an informative description in which the punch-drunk boxer's statement of his knowledge, that this is a way he boxes against a southpaw, while being a perfectly accurate description, does not constitute an informative description of his knowledge of how to box against a southpaw.[10]

However, it is thoroughly unclear why it should be a condition on propositional knowledge that knowing that p requires that one possess an accurate informative verbal description, in the required sense, of the content that p. First, the condition is *intuitively* unmotivated. The natural description of the case of the punch-drunk boxer is that the boxer knows that he can box against a southpaw in that way, i.e. that the boxer has

---

[9] Because Russell thought that "all egocentric words can be defined in terms of 'this'" (e.g. "'I' means "the biography to which this belongs"), he in fact confines his discussion of this entire class of terms to the case of demonstratives (ibid.: 108).

[10] One way to think of the punch-drunk boxer case is in terms of Karmiloff-Smith's distinction between *secondary explication* and *tertiary explication*. The boxer is consciously aware of his procedural knowledge, but cannot verbalize it in the sense required to qualify as declarative knowledge. This would suggest, *contra* Dienes and Perner (1999), that we need the distinction after all.

propositional knowledge. Second, the condition is *epistemologically* unmotivated. What theory of knowledge imposes the additional condition that one has an accurate and informative verbal description of the proposition that p, in order to know that p? What puzzles in epistemology would this fifth condition on knowledge resolve? I have no idea how one would even begin to mount an argument that there is such a fifth condition on knowledge.

3.

Even if one abandons the task of arguing that propositional knowledge is co-extensive with declarative knowledge, there are still other ways to marry principles about propositional knowledge with the neuroscience literature to argue that knowing how to do something is not propositional knowledge, at least on the assumption that procedural knowledge is co-extensive with knowing how. In this section, I consider several such arguments. I then argue against the epistemic principles that are required to support these arguments.

Here is one such principle that one could use to argue that procedural knowledge is not propositional knowledge. There are cases in which brain-damaged subjects know how to do certain tasks, but are not aware that they know how to do those tasks. In other words, some subjects know how to do a task, without knowing that they know how to do that task. But one might think that propositional knowledge is governed by the *KK principle*: if x knows that p, then x knows that x knows that p. If the KK principle is valid, the existence of subjects who know how to Φ but do not know that they know how to Φ shows that knowledge how is not propositional knowledge.

Thus stated, the KK principle is false. An objection to the KK principle is that if one accepts it, one must accept that knowing that p requires having the concept of knowledge. But it seems plausible that small children can have knowledge about the world, before they possess the concept of knowledge. However, one can evade this objection by appeal to a less drastic version of the KK principle – if one knows that p, then one is in a position to know that one knows that p. One might think that these amnesiacs know how to do various tasks, but are in principle incapable of knowing that they know how to do these tasks. Therefore, if knowing how to do a task is a kind of propositional knowledge, amnesiacs who are in principle incapable of coming to know that they know how to do a task would be counterexamples to the less drastic version of the KK principle.[11]

However, all versions of the KK principle are widely (though not universally) rejected in contemporary epistemology. It has been accepted by many epistemologists that knowledge that p requires that one's belief that p is in some sense *reliable*. There are

---

[11] I will grant for the sake of argument that in the relevant cases, the amnesiacs are not in principle capable of coming to know that they know how to perform the relevant task, though I do not see this as a plausible reading of the relevant literature.

of course many theories of what reliability consists in. One natural construal of a reliability condition on knowledge is due to Timothy Williamson, "one avoids false belief reliably in a case α if and only if one avoids false belief in every case similar enough to α" (2000: 124). The claim that knowing that p requires one's belief to be reliable, on this construal, means that knowledge that p requires one's belief track the truth in all possible situations similar to the actual one. If one knows that p, then in similar situations, one believes that p if and only if p is true. But knowing that one knows that p is more demanding – it requires that one's belief that one knows that p track the truth in all possible situations similar to the actual one. But that in turn requires one's belief that p to track the truth in all situations similar to any possible situation similar to the actual one. In short, knowing that one knows that p requires that one is *reliably reliable*. It is straightforward to give a model in which one's belief that p can track the truth in all similar situations, without it being the case that one's belief that p tracks the truth in all situations similar to situations similar to the actual one. As Williamson writes, "One can be reliable without being reliably reliable. Since knowledge requires reliability, it is hardly surprising that one can know without knowing that one knows" (2000: 125). The KK principle is hardly unobjectionable in contemporary epistemology.

There are brain-damaged patients who deny that they know how to perform a certain task, but still know how to do that task. Using the existence of such patients to conclude that knowing how to do something is not a kind of propositional knowledge requires appeal to the KK principle. But it is not even *sufficient* to appeal to the KK principle for this kind of argument against the view that knowing how is a kind of propositional knowledge. One might think that reliable true belief formation is sufficient, not only for knowledge, but knowledge of knowledge. If so, one would accept the KK principle. But one would not then take the envisaged patient to be someone who knows how to do a task, but doesn't know that she knows how to perform the task. Instead, one would take the fact that her knowledge how was reliably formed to entail that she does in fact know that she knows how to do that task, despite her explicit denials to the contrary. So if one wanted to use these sorts of cases to raise a problem for the view that knowing how is a kind of propositional knowledge, one requires not only the KK principle, but also a certain kind of defense of that principle that is not based on the externalist epistemologies that have become so dominant in recent years.

Here is another way to use the neuroscience literature to argue that knowing how to do something is not a kind of propositional knowledge, one that also depends on internalist theses in epistemology. The neuroscience literature shows that one can know how to do something, without remembering how one acquired that knowledge. One can know how to do something, without being able to proffer any grounds at all for one's knowledge. Suppose one thought that knowing that p requires that one has access (in some sense of "access") to the essential grounds of one's knowledge – the grounds that make it the case that one knows that p. If so, one would be in possession of an argument that knowing how to do something is not a kind of propositional knowledge. Indeed, one does not need something as exotic as the neuroscience literature to make the point that one can know how to do something without having access to the grounds that make it knowledge. I know how to ride a bicycle, but I have no memory whatsoever of learning how to ride a bicycle.

However, the premise that knowing that p requires that one has access to the essential grounds of one's knowledge is widely disputed; its denial is the defining feature of the externalist theories of knowledge and justification that dominate the landscape of contemporary epistemology. For example, according to a prominent theory of knowledge proposed by Alvin Goldman, for a true belief to count as knowledge, it must be caused by a generally reliable process. My true belief can be caused by a reliable process, without my having any inkling whatsoever that it is. Virtually all externalists hold that someone can know a proposition at least partly in virtue of grounds that are consciously inaccessible to her.[12] No argument based on the internalist premise that knowledge requires that one has access to its essential grounds will be compelling to contemporary epistemologists who embrace a robust externalism about knowledge.[13]

It is in any case intuitively quite clear that there are cases in which I know that p, but lack access to the essential grounds of my knowledge. Furthermore, these are cases that precisely parallel the example of my knowledge of how to ride a bicycle. These are the cases that provided the original intuitive motivations for externalist theories of knowledge. As Goldman writes in his classic paper, "A Causal Theory of Knowing":

I know now, for example, that Abraham Lincoln was born in 1809. I originally came to know this fact, let us suppose, by reading an encyclopedia article. I believed that this encyclopedia was trust-worthy and that its saying Lincoln was born in 1809 must have resulted from the fact that Lincoln was indeed born in 1809. Thus, my original knowledge of this fact was founded on a warranted inference. But now I no longer remember this inference. I remember that Lincoln was born in 1809, but not that this is stated in a certain encyclopedia. I no longer have any pertinent beliefs that highly confirm the proposition that Lincoln was born in 1809. Nevertheless, I know this proposition now. My original knowledge of it was preserved until now by the causal process of memory. (1967: 370)[14]

Goldman's classic example parallels the above example of knowing how to ride a bicycle. Just as I no longer recall the grounds of my knowledge of how to ride a bicycle, I may no longer recall the grounds of my knowledge that Abraham Lincoln was born

---

[12] One can imagine an externalist who holds that knowledge that p requires access to the states that in fact are the grounds for one's belief that p, but does not require that one have access to the fact that they are in fact one's grounds for one's belief that p. I am not aware of any externalist who holds this particular version of externalism, however (thanks to Brian Weatherson for discussion).

[13] Even if one is attracted to the view that knowledge essentially involves justification by *reasons*, states with propositional content, as Harman (1973) has made vivid, it does not follow that these reasons must be *consciously accessible*.

[14] Goldman credits this example to Gilbert Harman.

in 1809. But since my knowledge was originally acquired from a reliable source, it is propositional knowledge nevertheless.

Charles Wallis fails to keep the morals of the philosophical literature in mind when bringing to bear the neuroscience literature against the conclusions of Stanley and Williamson (2001). Wallis writes:

Stanley and Williamson's claim that such beliefs are necessary for knowledge-how is clearly empirically false. I conclude that literature from four distinct fields of inquiry undermine the existence of the sorts of beliefs hypothesized by Stanley and Williamson (2001). As noted above: (1) Cognizers often perform tasks without any conscious experiences of remembering that they know how to perform the task, perceiving that they are performing the task, identifying the task they are performing, or knowing that they can perform the task. (2) Cognizers often cannot articulate the information or indicate the complexes of dispositions which would constitute the content of their supposed beliefs when explicitly questioned about such information and dispositions. (3) Cognizers often exhibit no conscious awareness of environmental factors or information shown by analysis to have importantly influenced their responses, and hence exhibit no basis for supposing that they believe that the information is relevant to their performance. (4) Cognizers often offer demonstrably false or highly implausible accounts of the reasoning underlying their performance inconsistent with any beliefs regarding how they actually perform the task, and hence cannot be supposed to have true beliefs regarding how they, in fact, perform a task. (2008: 140)

As we have just seen, someone can have propositional knowledge, without recognizing that they have propositional knowledge. Therefore, it is consistent with the thesis that knowing how is propositional knowledge that cognizers can know how to do something, without knowing that they know how to do something. In short, Wallis's (1) is consistent with knowing how being a kind of propositional knowledge.[15] We have already seen that there is no "fifth condition" on knowledge defended by epistemologists that would lead one to use Wallis's (2) to deny that knowing how to do something is a kind of propositional knowledge.

That Wallis thinks (3) has bearing on the status of a state as propositional knowledge again shows that he has less than adequate grasp of the literature in epistemology over the last half-century. As we have seen, externalist theories of justification and knowledge do not require that I am consciously aware of the processes that gave rise to my beliefs (or even implicitly aware of them, or even capable of being made aware of them). Such theories are fully consistent with one's knowing that p, without being aware of the environmental factors that have importantly influenced the formation of their belief. Indeed, that is the point of externalist theories of knowledge.

Wallis's last point is that someone may know how to Φ, and on that basis Φ, yet falsely describe the way they employ to Φ. It is simply not clear why Wallis thinks this

---

[15] Wallis's claim that cognizers can know how to do a task without knowing that they can do a task is not warranted by the neuroscience literature, and seems rather to be based on combining facts from the neuroscience literature with misconceptions about epistemology.

shows that the person in question lacks the propositional knowledge that is knowing how to Φ, according to the account I have defended. Wallis thinks that if someone has false beliefs about the nature of a thing then they cannot have *de re* knowledge about that thing. But this view is absurd on the face of it. Suppose I falsely believe that what is in fact just the sofa in my living room is an alien from Mars. I can still know that that object is grey, despite my false beliefs about its nature. The fact that I would falsely describe the sofa does not undermine the fact that I have knowledge about it. Similarly, I might very well have false descriptive beliefs about a certain way of Φ-ing, while retaining my knowledge about that way of Φ-ing, thought of demonstratively or practically, that it is a way to Φ.[16]

4.

As we saw in Chapter 1, Hubert Dreyfus is one of the major opponents of the intellectualist view that skilled action is action guided by propositional knowledge. As Dreyfus puts his view, "embodied skills, when we are absorbed in enacting them, have a kind of content which is non-conceptual, non-propositional, non-rational (even if rational means situation specific) and non-linguistic" (2007: 360). Dreyfus is clearly an opponent of the intellectualist position I defend, according to which an agent's action is skilled in virtue of the agent's propositional knowledge of how to do it.

A defining feature of skilled action, according to Dreyfus, is that it is *non-conceptual*, by which I take him to mean that its content is different in kind than the content of propositional attitude states. There are neuroscientists who hold that procedural knowledge is similarly non-conceptual:

> We do not believe that people have an implicit symbolic representation "Run so as to keep the angle of gaze increasing at a decreasing rate" . . . The rule is represented in a non-conceptual way; that is, the rule is not constituted of representations that can be freely recombined with any other representation . . . The rule cannot be reported because verbal report requires the use of concepts. It may be that some people object to calling this 'knowledge' or a 'representation' but we see no reason to restrict the notion of knowledge to conceptual, symbolic representations. (Reed et al. 2010: 74)

There is thus a way a proponent of Dreyfus's view could use the literature in cognitive neuroscience to establish that knowing how to Φ is not a kind of propositional knowledge, given the assumption that procedural knowledge is knowing how. If knowing how to Φ consists of non-conceptual representations, then on one way of

---

[16] Wallis's second "difficulty" for Stanley and Williamson is that "knowledge-how often involves complexes of dispositions so elaborate and so diverse in their temporal and environmental contexts as to make the notion that individuals have single beliefs indexically identifying these "ways," Russellian or otherwise, implausible in the extreme" (ibid.: 140). This is such a bizarre objection, it is hard to evaluate. Russia is also quite diverse in its temporal and environmental context, but I seem to have no problem having single beliefs about it.

dividing the conceptual terrain, Dreyfus would be right that it is not a propositional attitude. It would rather be an attitude towards something else – the content of a non-conceptual state.

The literature on non-conceptual content has been excessively opaque. Advocates of non-conceptual content have failed to distinguish between what Jeff Speaks (2005) calls "absolute non-conceptual content" and "relatively non-conceptual content".[17] As Speaks defines it, *absolute* non-conceptual content, is content that is different in *kind* from the content of beliefs – perhaps beliefs have propositions as their content, whereas states with non-conceptual content in this sense have something other than propositions as their content. In contrast, *relatively* non-conceptual content is content that has constituents that are not grasped by the agent. A mental state may have a proposition as its content, but be relatively non-conceptual, because the person having the state does not grasp some of the constituents of that proposition.[18] It is not clear whether Reed et. al. (2010) think of procedural knowledge as absolutely or relatively non-conceptual. But I take Dreyfus's view to be the view that knowing how has non-conceptual content in the absolute sense, and not the relative sense. After all, Dreyfus clearly holds that knowing how does not have the kind of content that propositional attitudes possess.

However, the assumption that states of knowing how to Φ lack conceptual content in either sense is contradicted by the fact that ascriptions of knowing how create *opaque contexts*. An opaque context is a linguistic context in which substitution of co-referring expressions fails (opaque contexts are also called *non-extensional*). Characteristically, propositional attitude verbs create opaque contexts. Intuitively, John can believe that Hesperus is a planet, even though John believes that Phosphorus is a planet is false, even though "Hesperus" and "Phosphorus" refer to the same object, viz. the planet Venus. "Hesperus" and "Phosphorus" cannot be substituted for one another in the scope of a propositional attitude verb, despite the fact that they have the same referent. It is widely assumed that something like concepts are required to individuate the contents of such states.

The important point for our purposes is that ascriptions of knowing how create opaque contexts (see Stanley and Williamson 2001: 416). David Carr brings out this fact by the use of an elegant example:

Suppose a famous dancer was to perform before an audience, an item from his repertoire to which he has himself given the following title:

(12)   A performance of Improvisation No. 15

---

[17] As Speaks acknowledges, the distinction between absolute and relatively non-conceptual contents is due originally to Richard Heck (2000), who labels it the distinction between *content* non-conceptual content and *state* non-conceptual content.

[18] As Speaks (2005) shows in detail, most arguments for non-conceptual content are in fact only arguments for relatively non-conceptual content.

THE COGNITIVE SCIENCE OF PRACTICAL KNOWLEDGE   169

To the astonishment of a member of his audience who just happens to be an expert on communications, the movements of the dancer turn out to resemble an accurate (movement perfect) semaphore version of Gray's "Elegy", though the dancer is quite unaware of this fact. We may describe what is seen by the audience member as follows:

(13)   A semaphore recital of Gray's 'Elegy'.

Although we can describe the dancer as knowing how to bring about (12) we cannot reasonably suppose that he also knows how to bring about (13). Even though (12) and (13) are … but different characterizations of the same action, we cannot safely switch these characterizations in knowing how contexts. So it appears that sentences about knowing how, unlike those about ability, are truly non-extensional. (1979: 407–8)

A performance of Improvisation No. 15 is the same event as a semaphore recital of Gray's "Elegy". But knowing how to do one does not entail knowing how to do the other. Carr's example shows that one may know how to Φ without knowing how to Ψ, even though Φ-ing and Ψ-ing are the same actions. If knowing how to do something is non-conceptual, as Dreyfus maintains, it would be utterly mysterious why attributions of knowing how create opaque contexts.

If the contents of states of knowing how to do something involve concepts, why is it the case that it is so hard to verbalize these states? We have already answered this question. It is not hard to verbalize these states. One just needs to exploit *demonstrative* concepts in describing the contents of states of knowing how. As John McDowell has emphasized in response to Gareth Evans's argument for the non-conceptual content of color experience:

why should we accept that a person's ability to embrace color within her conceptual thinking is restricted to concepts expressible by words like "red" or "green" and phrases like "burnt sienna"? It is possible to acquire the concept of a shade of color, and most of us have done so. Why not say that one is thereby equipped to embrace shades of color within one's conceptual thinking with the very same determinateness with which they are presented in one's visual experience, so that one's concepts can capture colors no less sharply than one's experience presents them? In the throes of an experience of the kind that putatively transcends one's conceptual powers – an experience that *ex hypothesi* affords a suitable sample – one can give linguistic expression to a concept that is exactly as fine-grained as the experience, by uttering a phrase like "that shade", in which the demonstrative exploits the presence of the sample. (McDowell 1994: 56–7)

As we have seen in the punch-drunk boxer case, even if he could not describe the way in which he boxes with the use of context-insensitive vocabulary, he still could exploit demonstratives to verbalize his knowledge of how to box against a southpaw.

An alternative way to think of the sense in which states of knowing how to Φ are non-conceptual is similar to the sense in which Tyler Burge thinks of *de re belief* as non-conceptual. As Burge writes:

From a semantical viewpoint, a *de dicto* belief is a belief in which the believer is related only to a completely expressed proposition (dictum). The epistemic analogue is a belief that is fully conceptualized. That is, a correct ascription of the *de dicto* belief identifies it purely by reference to a "content" all of whose semantically relevant components characterize elements in the believer's conceptual repertoire." (1977: 345–6)

In contrast, "A *de re* belief is a belief whose correct ascription places the believer in an appropriate non-conceptual, contextual relation to objects the belief is about" (ibid.) Burge's idea is that a *de re* belief is one that contains a nonconceptual representation of its object, its *res*.[19] Assuming that knowing how to Φ is a *de re* attitude in Burge's sense entails that it contains non-conceptual representations. But thinking of the contents of states of knowing how as non-conceptual in Burge's sense would not aid Dreyfus. The fact that the content of states of knowing how would, on Burge's account, contain non-conceptual representations does not preclude them from being propositional attitudes. After all, even on Burge's account, *de re* beliefs are propositional attitudes *par excellence*.[20]

I do not have to have an accurate *descriptive* conceptualization of my way of Φ-ing, in order to know how to Φ. But I do need to have the concept associated with the activity of Φ-ing. I cannot be said to know how to ride a bicycle if I have no clue what a bicycle is. Furthermore, the fact that I need to have the concept associated with the activity of Φ-ing in order to know how to Φ is not contradicted by the existence of brain-damaged patients who cannot remember having engaged in Φ-ing in the past, absent an overly demanding epistemologically internalist condition on the possession of concepts.

There are other ways to use the psychology of skilled action to argue that knowing how to do something is a non-conceptual state. Sean Kelly (2000, 2002) uses the psychology of motor-intentional behavior to argue that "many of our most basic ways of relating intentionally to the world are precisely not in the form of having thoughts about it" (2000: 163). Following Merleau-Ponty, Kelly holds that reflection upon the psychology of skilled action provides evidence for the view that "perceiving and acting upon the objects in the world are more basic modes of intentionality… and these perceptions and actions have an intentional content that is, as Merleau-Ponty says, 'pre-predicative'" (ibid.). Kelly's target is what he calls the "cognitivist", and I am not sure the theses I defend count as cognitivist in his sense. However, as an intellectualist about skilled action, I hold that skilled action is explained by propositional mental states – i.e. our most basic ways of interacting with the world are guided by our propositional

---

[19] In later work, Burge characterizes the intuitive basis of the distinction he was trying to draw as follows: "*De re* attitudes are ascribed by indicating representational contents that contain successfully applied demonstrative or indexical elements. *De dicto* attitudes are ascribed by indicating representational contents that contain no demonstratives or indexicals" (2007: 68). So perhaps by "non-conceptual" Burge means something closer to what, following McDowell, I would call the content of a demonstrative content.

[20] "I have heard interpretations of the paper according to which there is a 'hole' in the representational aspects of the proposition, where the hole corresponds to the object (which completes the proposition). I regard these interpretations as rather silly" (Burge 2007: 75).

knowledge. So it is important for my purposes to show that the kind of considerations Kelly adduces against the cognitivist do not tell against the central thesis of this book.

Kelly's argument against the cognitivist position appeals to the fact that there is a distinction between *pointing* and *grasping*. In a now classic paper, Goodale and Milner describe a patient DF, who, due to carbon-monoxide poisoning, acquired a "profound inability to recognize the size, shape and orientation of visual objects" (1992: 22). Despite this inability, "DF showed strikingly accurate guidance of hand and finger movements directed at the very same objects." As they write:

> when presented with a large slot that could be placed in one of a number of different orientations, she showed great difficulty in indicating the orientation either verbally or manually (i.e. by rotating her hand or a hand-held card). Nevertheless, she was as good as normal subjects at reaching out and placing her hand or the card into the slot, turning her hand appropriately from the very onset of the movement. (Ibid.)

In fact, as Goodale and Milner point out, there is a double disassociation between accurate visual indication or description and grabbing. While DF has an inability to point accurately, patients with optic ataxia "are unable to reach accurately towards visual targets they have no difficulty recognizing" (ibid.: 21).[21] According to Kelly, these results confirm Merleau-Ponty's view that "pointing and grasping are based on two different kinds of understanding of place" (2000: 171).

One can use Kelly's point to raise a worry for my view of knowing how, using Goodale and Milner's results. DF's action of placing the card into the slot is an intelligent action, one accomplished with skill. On my view, therefore, it is guided by propositional knowledge. But prior to reaching out, DF does not know what the orientation of the slot is. How, then, could her action be guided by propositional knowledge? I take it that is Kelly's challenge. In fact, Josefa Toribio explicitly uses Goodale and Milner's results to mount this exact challenge against the view of knowing how in Stanley and Williamson (2001):

> DF knows how to w (place a letter through an oriented rectangular slot) because she entertains the proposition that w is a way for her to w. w must thus appear to DF as being a way to w, and DF must grasp this property as bearing upon what ought to be done to w. However, DF couldn't possibly entertain such a proposition because she cannot grasp one of its constituents – she cannot perceive the features, e.g. the orientation, that govern her motor behavior in the posting task, and hence couldn't recognize them as in any way constituting a reason for her action. DF lacks the kind of phenomenal experience that would underwrite an appreciation of her own behavior as suited to solving the problem. (2008: 43–4)

Suppose we take Goodale and Milner's results to show that DF does not know what the orientation of the slot is. That does not entail that DF's action is not guided by knowledge how, in my sense. At most, it would show that possession of the knowledge

---

[21] The classic source for the results concerning optic ataxia is Perenin and Vighetto (1988).

how to fit cards into slots, in my favored sense, does not require knowledge of what the orientation of the slot is. In short, *at most* what DF shows is that one can know how to post a card into a slot, without knowing what the orientation of the slot is. Given my account of knowledge how, this result raises no problem whatsoever for the view that DF's action of posting the card into the slot is guided by propositional knowledge. All it shows is that one can have propositional knowledge concerning a way of putting a card into a slot, without knowing the orientation of that slot. DF shows that propositional knowledge concerning a way of putting a card into a slot, *contra* Toribio, does not require perceiving all the features of that way.

What is the relation between DF and the normal agent? Here is a hypothesis. In posting a card into a slot, both act on their propositional knowledge of how to get a card into a slot. But DF cannot accurately report on the orientation of the slot, whereas the normal agent can. DF's knowledge of how to put a card into a slot is propositional knowledge that is based on a non-conceptual understanding of the orientation of the slot, understood here in the sense of an understanding of the orientation of the slot that is not available to conscious apprehension. She is able to have propositional attitudes about a way of posting a card into a slot in virtue of this non-conceptual understanding of orientation, yielded by her intact dorsal stream. In contrast, the normal agent does have consciously available knowledge of the orientation of the slot before she acts. This is a difference between DF and the normal agent, but not one that can be used to deny that DF's action is guided by propositional knowledge of how to put a card into a slot.[22]

A final argument for the non-conceptual content of knowing how to do something is due to Richard Heck (2007). Heck argues that certain representations take the form of cognitive maps, and according to Heck:

having a cognitive map of one's environment is quite different from having a collection of explicit beliefs about it. One manifestation of this fact is that one can "know how to get somewhere" and yet have no idea how to give someone directions for getting there – except, perhaps, by imagining the route one would take, thus putting one's cognitive map to use in imagination. (Ibid.)

The fact that some representations take the form of cognitive maps does not mean that they are non-conceptual. A cognitive map can determine one kind of mode of presentation of a way of getting somewhere. Modes of presentation do not need to be characterized in descriptive terms. Knowing how to get to Boston is knowledge of a

---

[22] Interestingly, Kelly (2002: 388) reports that Goodale has communicated to him that DF does use demonstratives in apparent reports of the orientation of the slot – she says things, moving her hand in a certain way, "I believe the slot is oriented *this* way". The fact that DF in fact can use a demonstrative to express her knowledge of the orientation straightforwardly vitiates many of the philosophical uses of her case (which is why Kelly argues, I think unconvincingly, that her demonstrative does *not* denote the orientation). Regardless, my response does not depend upon ascribing to DF knowledge of orientation that is capable of verbal articulation.

proposition concerning a way of getting to Boston, where the functional role of that way is specified via features of the cognitive map.

It should be clear from the foregoing that I am not, in this section, denying the existence of a level of non-conceptual content. I have absolutely no stake in the issue. Perhaps we need non-conceptual content to explain *why* I have the visual demonstrative concepts I do, and perhaps we need non-conceptual content to explain some of the ways of thinking that constitute the content of my knowledge of how to grasp a doorknob, or my knowledge of how to get to Boston. It may be that non-conceptual content is needed to have the propositional attitudes that are required to guide an action, in order for that action to be skilled. This role of non-conceptual content, as enabling propositional mental states, raises no problem at all for the thesis that an action is skilled, or intelligent, in virtue of being a manifestation of propositional knowledge.

5.

It is fairly well established that high-level skill execution is impaired when subjects are asked to monitor and report on the methods they employ during execution. For example, in one representative study, Beilock et al. asked skilled golfers "to attend to a particular component of their golf-putting swing. Specifically, individuals were instructed to monitor the swing of their club and at the exact moment they finished the follow-through of their swing, bringing the club head to a stop, to say the word 'stop' out loud" (2002): 8). The task significantly impeded performance. Exercise of procedural knowledge seems to be impaired by verbalization. If procedural knowledge is knowledge how, and knowledge how is a species of propositional knowledge, why would being forced to attend consciously and deliberative to the content of the knowledge inhibit performance?

We have already answered this question in Chapter 1. The view that skilled action is an exercise of propositional knowledge does not require that one has to engage in a distinct mental action of considering that proposition when acting. As Peter Railton emphasizes in his work, skilled action often requires acting automatically on the basis of one's propositional attitude states. It is therefore no surprise whatsoever that being forced to engage in an additional intelligent action of contemplation or reflection (and yet an additional action of *verbalizing* said reflection) would impede performance. This fact has no bearing on whether or not the state guiding the action has propositional content.

If reflection impedes or distorts the manifestation of procedural knowledge in the way I have suggested, then we should expect it also to have a similar effect on the manifestation of other kinds of knowledge. And it does. The phenomenon of verbal overshadowing is certainly not local to procedural knowledge. In fact, the classic study of the verbal overshadowing effect (Schooler and Engstler-Schooler 1990) has to do with the retrieval of declarative knowledge, and not procedural knowledge. In that paper, Schooler and Engstler-Schooler asked subjects to look at a video involving a bank robbery. One group was asked to describe the face of the robber on paper, and the other group was given another unrelated task. The group that was *not* asked to write up a description of the robber had a much higher success in subsequently identifying the face of the robber. As one should expect if propositional knowledge guides without preaching, verbalizing and presumably even actively entertaining its content can impede and distort its manifestation.

There are all sorts of automatic mechanisms that operate in a genuine sense sub-personally. The human (and animal) capacity for skilled action is based upon these mechanisms. However, behavior that is a consequence solely of these processes is mere reflex. What makes an action an exercise of skill, rather than mere reflex, is the fact that it is guided by the intellectual apprehension of truths.

8

Knowledge Justified

If Derek is a skilled fielder of fly balls, then he knows how to field a fly ball; if Michael is a skilled swimmer, then he knows how to swim. That someone skilled at an activity knows how to do that activity is as good a candidate as any to be a conceptual truth. It is therefore no surprise that everyone who discusses skilled action, from Ryle forwards, agrees that skilled action requires knowledge how. The debate has been about the nature of knowledge how. I have argued that skilled action is action guided by knowledge how, and that knowing how to do something amounts to knowing a fact. Skilled action is action guided by knowledge of facts.

My aim in the final chapter of the book is to address residual discomfort with its conclusions. Knowledge is a standard more demanding than justified true belief. In section 1, I justify the more demanding standard in the face of apparent Gettier-style counterexamples. In section 2, I return to the case of expert performance. One might worry that if knowing how to do something is a kind of propositional knowledge, it should take the form of codified maxims that provide clear instructions for action in every situation. But expert knowledge-how often requires adjusting appropriately to novel situations, ones not covered by previously codified instructions. In section 3, I turn to the role knowledge-how has in explaining knowledge of action.

1.

That an action is skilled only if it is guided by knowledge of facts about ways of performing it explains why calling an action "skilled" is one kind of approval. Unskilled action is subject to the same kind of internal opprobrium qua action as action based on ignorance. Unskilled action is like acting without knowing. Of course, sometimes I must act, though I lack the skill – the ship is sinking, and I must try to swim though I do not know how. Here too there is an analogy with action based on obvious propositional knowledge. Expediency may demand that I must act without gathering all the facts. The ship is sinking; I am in the water, and I do not know in which direction land is closest. Expediency demands that I choose one.

Recall the view that an action is done for a proper reason only if it is knowledge. Some have replied that proper action requires only that one's reasons for acting are justified beliefs, or that proper action requires only that one's actions are based on justified beliefs that one knows (Neta 2009). Jessica Brown (2008) argues for the position that whether or not knowledge is the norm of practical reasoning depends upon context. Her position is not the position of the contextualist about knowledge ascriptions, who argues that one can accommodate an intuitive link between knowledge and proper reasons for acting by the view that "know" changes its standards accordingly. Her position is rather that neither knowledge nor ascriptions of knowledge co-vary with proper reasons for acting or ascriptions thereof. Relative to some situations, the proper reasons for acting require only knowledge, relative to other situations proper reasons for acting require more than knowledge, and relative to other situations they require less than knowledge.[1]

In a similar vein, one might agree that skilled action is action guided by propositional attitude states, but disagree that it is action guided by the propositional attitude of knowledge. One might, for example, think of the requirements for skill as a relation to a proposition that is more similar to justified belief than knowledge. Or perhaps, with Brown, one thinks that the conditions for skilled action vary with the situation. In some cases, a relation less strict than knowledge is required for skilled action, whereas in other situations a relation more strict than knowledge is required for skilled action. But there is an additional implausibility in arguing that skilled action does not rely on propositional knowledge.

It is a (near enough) conceptual truth that acting with skill requires knowledge how. This near enough conceptual truth is more entrenched than the view that acting with proper reason requires knowledge. To argue that a condition weaker than knowledge is sufficient for skilled action one must not only argue that knowledge is more demanding than is required for skill, but one must also make the case that we use the verb "know" to pick out both the more and the less demanding relation. For example, Yuri Cath (forthcoming) holds that the knowing how relation is like the *seeming* relation. So Cath holds that "know" is ambiguous. Furthermore, the ambiguity is not one that can plausibly be explained in terms of some kind of indexicality. The seeming relation and the propositional knowledge relation are not plausibly different values of the same context-invariant meaning or indexical character. In short, those who deny that skill requires propositional knowledge must endorse a genuine ambiguity claim. This is a cost that those such as Brown (2008) and DeRose (2009), who reject even the intuitive case for the knowledge condition on proper reasons, must not bear.

One reason to think that a less demanding relation than knowledge is required for skilled action is that there are cases that suggest that one can acquire skill without having the attendant propositional knowledge. Reflection on Gettier cases provides a

---

[1] Keith DeRose (2009: 254–7) is a contextualist who does not pursue a contextualist account that would preserve the claim that proper reasons for acting must be known. DeRose (ibid.) argues, like Brown (2008), that there are intuitive cases in which one can sometimes properly act on the basis of motivating reasons that are not known. However, DeRose is slightly more inclined that Brown to endorse a contextualist account of the view that (DeRose ibid.: 264): "If an agent knows that p, then she is well enough positioned with respect to p to appropriately treat p as a reason for acting."

rich source of such examples.[2] Here is a classic example of a Gettier case. Suppose that Bill sees his colleague Fred driving in a Porsche. Believing on this basis that Fred owns a Porsche, Bill then infers that a colleague of his owns a Porsche. Unbeknownst to Bill, his other colleague Hannah owns a Porsche, which she had lent to Fred for the day. So Bill has a justified true belief that a colleague of his owns a Porsche, but it is not a case of knowledge.

The reason that Bill's belief is not a case of knowledge is a matter of theoretical controversy. For example, according to Goldman (1967), the reason that Bill's belief is not a case of knowledge is that there is not an appropriate causal connection between the fact that a colleague of Bill's owns a Porsche and his belief that a colleague of Bill's owns a Porsche. According to Harman (1973: 120ff.), the reason that Bill's belief is not a case of knowledge is that it is based on reasoning that essentially involves a false intermediate step. The correct theoretical account of Gettier cases is irrelevant here; all that is required to pose a problem for the view that knowing how to do something is a kind of propositional knowledge is the assumption that Gettier-type situations undermine propositional knowledge.

Ted Poston (2009) provides a general argument, directed against Stanley and Williamson (2001), that there are no Gettier cases for knowledge how. His argument involves two premises:

(P1) Gettier cases for know how, if they exist, require that the subject intelligently and successfully F, where F ranges over actions.
(P2) If one can intelligently and successfully F, then one knows how to F.

Poston's argument entails that there can be no Gettier cases for knowing how. I do not wish to dispute Poston's (P1). The problems are rather with (P2). First, exploiting (P2) as a premise seems rather unfair in an argument against the view that there are Gettier cases for knowing how. As Poston himself recognizes, the intelligence condition and the success condition "are analogous to the justified belief condition and the truth condition in Gettier cases of knowledge that". So appealing to (P2) in an argument that one can possess knowledge how just in virtue of these conditions begs the question.

Given that (P2) begs the question, one cannot simply appeal to it – one must provide an argument. Presumably, Poston's argument for (P2) is based on intuitions about cases, to the effect that intuitively each instance of (P2) is true. Arguments based on appeal to intuitions are difficult to assess, because the line between what is intuitive and

---

[2] Brown's arguments (2008: 171–2) against the view that a proper reason for acting must be known also involve Gettier cases (see also Littlejohn 2010). As I have tried to make clear, the pre-theoretical plausibility of the view that skilled action requires knowledge how is higher than the pre-theoretical plausibility of the claim that proper reasons must be known. For this reason, Cath uses Gettier cases to argue, not that knowing how isn't required for skilled action, but that propositional knowledge is not required for knowing how. This requires the additional claim that "know" can express something other than the propositional knowledge relation.

what is theoretical is, to say the least, vague. However, even taking the methodology at face-value, it is simply false that each instance of (P2) is intuitively true.

Bengson et al. (2009) present 138 subjects with the following case:

Irina, who is a novice figure skater, decides to try a complex jump called the Salchow. When one performs a Salchow, one takes off from the *back inside* edge of one skate and lands on the *back outside* edge of the opposite skate after one or more rotations in the air. Irina, however, is seriously mistaken about how to perform a Salchow. She believes incorrectly that the way to perform a Salchow is to take off from the *front outside* edge of one skate, jump in the air, spin, and land on the *front inside* edge of the other skate. However, Irina has a severe neurological abnormality that makes her act in ways that differ dramatically from how she actually thinks she is acting. So, despite the fact that she is seriously mistaken about how to perform a Salchow, whenever she actually attempts to do a Salchow (in accordance with her misconceptions) the abnormality causes Irina to unknowingly perform the correct sequence of moves, and so she ends up successfully performing a Salchow.

The subjects "were asked both whether Irina knows how to do the Salchow and whether Irina is able to do the Salchow." Only 12 percent of the participants in the study reported that Irina knows how to do the Salchow. In contrast, 86 percent of the participants in the subject judged that Irina is able to do the Salchow, but does not know how to do the Salchow.

In one sense of "intelligent", Irina's act of doing the Salchow is intelligent. It was the result of a conscious decision. So in one sense of "intelligent", Irina can intelligently and successfully do the Salchow. However, if ordinary reactions about cases are granted evidential weight, one must concede that Irina does not know how to do the Salchow. Therefore, Poston's (P2) is false.[3]

Yuri Cath (forthcoming) has given another argument that there are cases of knowledge how that are not Gettier-susceptible. The example is as follows:

The Lucky Light Bulb: Charlie wants to learn how to change a light bulb, but he knows almost nothing about light fixtures or bulbs (as he has only ever seen light bulbs already installed and so he has never seen the end of a light bulb, nor the inside of a light fixture). To remedy this situation Charlie consults *The Idiot's Guide to Everyday Jobs*. Inside, he finds an accurate set of instructions describing the shape of a light fixture and bulb, and the way to change a bulb. Charlie grasps these instructions perfectly. And so there is a way, call it '$w1$', such that Charlie now believes that $w1$ is a way for him to change a light bulb, namely, the way described in the book. However, unbeknownst to Charlie, he is extremely lucky to have read these instructions, for the disgruntled author of *The Idiot's Guide* filled her book with misleading instructions. Under every entry she intentionally misdescribed the objects involved in that job, and described a series of actions that would not constitute a way to do the job at all. However, at the printers, a computer error caused the text under the entry for "Changing a Light Bulb", in just one copy of

---

[3] There is a sense of "intelligent" in which Irina's action is intelligent – it is guided by a conscious decision. But, as Harman (1976) points out, the fact that one does something intentionally does not entail that one intends to do it. Irina intentionally performs the Salchow, but does not intend to perform the Salchow.

the book, to be randomly replaced by new text. By incredible coincidence, this new text provided the clear and accurate set of instructions that Charlie would later consult.

Cath's case is meant to put pressure on the analysis of knowledge how proposed in Stanley and Williamson (2001) and here because, in the envisaged case Charlie lacks the propositional knowledge that my favored account says constitutes knowledge how – that is, Charlie believes, but does not know, that $w1$ is a way for him to change a light bulb. But he does not know that $w1$ is a way for him to change a light bulb. However, according to Cath intuitively Charlie does know how to change a light bulb. Cath uses this to argue that "knows how" does not express the knowledge relation between a person and a proposition, but rather expresses the *seeming* relation. In short, for Cath, knowing how is a propositional attitude. But it is not the propositional attitude relation of *knowledge*.

The problem with Cath's argument is that it is too general – if sound, it applies to many kinds of knowing-wh. For example:

The Lucky Light Bulb II: Charlie wants to learn where to purchase light bulbs, but he knows almost nothing about stores in his city of Syracuse. To remedy this situation Charlie consults *The Idiot's Guide to Stores in Syracuse*. Inside, he finds an accurate description of directions to a store at which one can buy light bulbs. Charlie grasps these directions perfectly. And so there is a place, call it 'p', such that Charlie now believes that p is a place he can buy light bulbs, namely the place described in the book. However, unbeknownst to Charlie, he is extremely lucky to have read these instructions, for the disgruntled author of *The Idiot's Guide* filled her book with misleading instructions. Under every entry she intentionally misdescribed the stores, and described a series of directions that would lead to parking lots and residential homes. However, at the printers, a computer error caused the text under the entry for "Purchasing Light Bulbs", in just one copy of the book, to be randomly replaced by new text. By incredible coincidence, this new text provided the clear and accurate set of instructions that Charlie would later consult.

Charlie believes, but does not know, that p is a place he can buy light bulbs. But the intuition that Charlie knows where to buy light bulbs is as strong in this case as is the intuition that Charlie knows how to change light bulbs in The Lucky Light Bulb.

It would be good to have more data on folk intuitions about Gettier cases and knowing-wh. But from the armchair at least, it seems that many types of uncontroversial propositional knowledge ascriptions are not intuitively Gettier susceptible. Suppose Mary learns to play tennis from a generally reliable tennis coach. The coach teaches her what is in fact a way to ace her regular opponent, a way that involves twisting her body to the left at a certain point in the arc of her movement. However, the coach did not in fact intend to teach her this – he meant to deceive her, but because of incompetence in fact taught her correctly. Suppose, watching Mary ace her opponent using this method for the first time, I say "Mary knew when to twist her body to the left in hitting that shot". This ascription seems perfectly true, even though Mary only had a justified true belief, and lacked genuine knowledge.

What these examples reveal is that, in the case of knowledge-wh, Gettier intuitions are less robust than in the case of ascriptions of explicit knowledge-that, if present at all. As John Hawthorne writes:

Suppose I ask in an ordinary setting whether someone knows whether Boston is the capital of Massachusetts. Suppose it turns out that he does truly believe this though the epistemic credentials of his path to that belief are decidedly shaky. Perhaps he got it from a book that misprinted most of the state capitals though not this one. Perhaps he got the information from someone that he had good reason to distrust (who happened to be sincere on this occasion or else who tried to lie and accidentally told the truth on this occasion). Would your acceptance of the statement "Boston is the capital of Massachusetts" fail to be knowledge in such cases? Not so, or not clearly so. (2000: 202)

Hawthorne is undeniably correct that many Gettier cases involving know-whether *seem* like knowledge. Despite the fact that ascriptions of knowledge-where and knowledge-whether are propositional knowledge ascriptions *par excellence*, the Gettier intuition is often weak or non-existent. Since ascriptions of knowing how are ascriptions of knowing-wh, we should therefore expect Gettier intuitions for such cases also often to be weak or non-existent. But this has nothing whatever to do with whether they are propositional knowledge ascriptions. As Hawthorne emphasizes, ascriptions of knowing-whether often do not appear Gettier-susceptible, despite clearly being ascriptions of propositional knowledge.

The phenomenon that features of the conversational context can lead us to accept false knowledge ascriptions is familiar even with explicit propositional knowledge ascriptions of the form "x knows that p." Consider ascriptions of propositional knowledge to quiz show contestants who make correct lucky guesses. With no trouble at all, we find ourselves saying things like "He knew the answer", or "That contestant was the only one who knew that Moscow is the capital of Russia", even when we are fully aware that it was a lucky guess. This is because, given the pragmatics of reporting on game show situations, we are focused only on who gave the true answer – not even whether they believed it.

Why is it that knowledge-wh ascriptions seem less Gettier-susceptible than cases like "John knows that someone in his office drives a Ford?" The explanation involves the pragmatics of situations in which we ascribe such knowledge. Typically, when we make ascriptions like "John knows where to find the nearest chip shop", we are only interested in the truth or falsity of John's belief about the location of the nearest chip shop. We want to know whether, were John to set off on a search for chips guided by his belief, he would successfully obtain chips. Similarly, when we ask whether John knows how to ride a bicycle, we are typically only interested in whether, were John to set off on a bicycle guided by his belief about how to ride a bicycle, he would successfully be able to achieve his goal (perhaps of getting us chips). The reason we do not hear many ascriptions of knowledge-wh as Gettier susceptible is not because they are non-propositional. Rather, it is because the pragmatics of situations in which we ascribe knowledge-wh often places the focus on true belief, rather than justification.[4]

When we are asking someone where to go, are how to get somewhere, we typically do not care how they have arrived at their belief – we care only whether it is true. The point that often someone with a true belief can be just as good a guide in action or direction as someone who has knowledge is as old as Plato's *Meno*. Of course, the fact that our conversational purposes lead us often to be satisfied with mere true belief does not obscure for a moment the fact that knowledge of how to do something is more valuable than true belief. Suppose that John has formed a true belief about how to fly a plane from an unskilled flight instructor who has, by luck, given John the correct instructions. We would not be as happy with John as our pilot as we would be with someone trained by a skilled flight instructor even if we were antecedently assured that their beliefs about how to fly the plane are the same. We still find ourselves choosing the surgeon trained at the better institution, even if we were antecedently convinced that the two surgeons had the same beliefs about how to perform the surgery, and the mechanisms that govern their execution equally fluid.

2.

A mark of expertise is the ability to respond efficiently to novel situations. The expert surgeon is able to adjust her scalpel to a surprising complication in a way that the novice surgeon, even one with the same knowledge of what has been published in the journals, is not. An expert outfielder is able to adjust to an unusually hit fly ball better than a novice. And, as Taylor Carman (forthcoming) brings out, we are *all* experts at the art of conversation, an activity expertise which demands fluidly adjusting to subtleties of novel situations. If skilled action is action guided by reasons, how could it be that expertise demands responding to particularities for which no previously codifiable rules could plausibly provide instruction?

The point that skilled action requires responding to novel situations is similar to a point made by a certain group of moral theorists about ethical principles. *Moral particularists*, such as Jonathan Dancy and John McDowell, hold that moral agents do not employ general, exceptionless moral principles in guiding their behavior; indeed they hold that there are no such exceptionless moral principles. They argue that the variability and novelty of the situations that the moral agent encounters entails that there are no exceptionless moral principles that apply to all cases. The moral agent must navigate the particularities of each situation without them. This is analogous to the argument from skilled action to the conclusion that skilled action is not guided by principles.

---

[4] I also think such pragmatic factors are at work in explaining the pattern of intuitions about Gettier cases Brown (2008) employs against the view that proper reasons for acting must be known. But I will not make the case for this here.

However, moral particularists do *not* conclude, from the premise that moral agents encounter novel situations that cannot be covered by exceptionless, codifiable moral principles that acting morally is not acting on a reason. Moral particularists do not think that moral behavior is guided by the same set of exceptionless reasons, and they do not think that the reasons that are relevant in a particular situation can be expressed in non-demonstrative terms. But moral particularists nevertheless *do* tend to accept that moral behavior is behavior that is responding to reasons. What moral particularists reject is, as McDowell puts it, "the assumption that to involve reason in action could only be to apply to the situation in which one acts some content fully specifiable in detachment from the situation" (2007: 340).

The debate about moral particularism shows that the fact that expertise requires fluid responses to novel situations has no bearing on the thesis that skilled action is acting on the basis of reasons. Skilled action may involve fluid *acquisition* of reasons for acting in novel situations, reasons that are only accessible to one when one is in that situation. The fact that some reasons for acting can only be entertained when one is in the situation is fully consistent with the agent's acting for those reasons.

However, the route of the moral particularist is not the only way to account for the fact that expertise requires fluidly reacting to novel situations, and it is not the route I will take in responding to the challenge. Instead, I will argue that these facts about expertise are explicable on other grounds. First, one must recognize, as we have seen in detail in this book, that not all propositions are codifiable in fully descriptive terms. Second, one must recognize that propositional knowledge of maxims or rules is not, as Dreyfus would have it, "detached" from behavior. Third, one must be sensitive to the interplay between the standing epistemic states of the speaker and the automatic mechanisms that structure her behavior accordingly.

Someone skilled at fielding fly balls knows, of a way of fielding fly balls, that it is a way for him to achieve counterfactual success in fielding fly balls. This knowledge is *de re* knowledge about a way of doing something. Since *de re* knowledge is in general not reducible to *de dicto* knowledge, their knowledge does not consist in a relation to a set of propositions whose content can be given purely descriptively. Understanding what it is to be able to know a proposition of this kind explains why an expert at fielding fly balls can respond swiftly to novel situations.

As we have seen in Chapters 3 and 4, we have a capacity to think about an object in the world as ourselves in virtue of possessing a complex of dispositions towards that object. I think of an object as myself only if I am disposed to take information as guiding my behavior in a distinctively first-person way. When the object that is in fact myself is placed in novel situations, the fact that I think about that object in a distinctively first-person way explains my ability to react fluidly to those situations. In a similar manner, the fact that a skilled outfielder has *de re* knowledge of a way of thinking of fielding a fly ball, and thinks of that way practically, explains why he is able to react fluidly to the occasional unusual fly ball. One can only have the right kind of propositional knowledge of a way of doing something if one's dispositional structure is sufficiently complex to accommodate novel situations. Otherwise, one merely has *de dicto* knowledge of a descriptive instruction manual.

Of course, when we say that a skilled outfielder knows how to field a fly ball, we do not mean that he knows, of at least one way to field a fly ball, that it gives him counterfactual success in fielding fly balls. That is, we do not intend the *mention-some* reading of the embedded question, "how to field a fly ball". Rather, in such a case, we mean the mention-all reading of the embedded question. What we assert when we assert of a skilled outfielder that he knows how to field fly balls is that he knows *all* of a range of relevant ways that give him counterfactual success in fielding fly balls. Hence, to say of an outfielder in baseball that he knows how to catch a fly ball is to impart to him knowledge of *many* propositions of the form 'w is a way for him to field a fly ball'. For each of these propositions, knowledge of it structures his behavioral dispositions in manifold ways. Experts have knowledge of many propositions about ways of performing the same task. Each propositional knowledge state results in what Ryle would call a *multi-track* disposition. It is the apprehension of truths by the intellect that explains why a professional outfielder is able to adapt to field fly balls hit in novel ways, and that we are able to adapt so smoothly to novel conversational situations.

I have argued that in acquiring a skill, we first learn various rules. Practice allows us to move from the initial situation in which we repeatedly have to consult these rules, to skilled action, where we can act directly upon them. Hubert Dreyfus has challenged this picture, arguing that it conflicts with the intuitive phenomenology of expertise. Dreyfus suggests an analogy that makes vivid the confusion he sees in it:

> our experience suggests that rules are like training wheels. We may need such aids when learning to ride a bicycle, but we must eventually set them aside if we are to become skilled cyclists. To assume that the rules we once consciously followed become unconscious is like assuming that, when we finally learn to ride a bike, the training wheels that were required for us to be able to ride in the first place must have become invisible. The actual phenomenon suggests that to become experts we must switch from detached rule-following to a more involved and situation-specific way of coping. (2005)

Dreyfus is correct that, were this analogy apt, it would pose a problem to the view of skilled action I have been defending. Learning to ride a bicycle starts with training wheels. But once one knows how to ride a bicycle, there is no sense in which one is still being guided by the training wheels. The training wheels give one access to the knowledge of how to ride a bicycle, which then takes over. Explaining why Dreyfus's analogy is not apt provides an opportunity for me to say more about the relation between the propositional knowledge that guides skilled action, and the automatic mechanisms that are responsible for its implementation in expert performance.

Here is the relation between a novice and an expert that is suggested by the picture of skilled action I have argued for in this book. The novice who is just acquiring a skill learns a method by which she can accomplish that skill – this involves the acquisition of propositional knowledge. But in the novice, the automatic mechanisms that apply the propositional knowledge to specific situations are not in place. The novice must repeatedly engage in distinct actions of "consulting" the propositional knowledge she has acquired in performing. These distinct actions interfere with the smooth application of the propositional knowledge she has acquired to the situations she confronts when engaged in the activity. The novice basketball player must tell herself repeatedly how to shoot a jump shot – she must remind herself to bend her knees, to follow through on her shot, etc. If placed in a game, the fact that she has to engage in distinct actions of "telling herself" things will significantly impede her performance.

In the expert agent, by contrast, the automatic mechanisms that, as Fodor (1983: 9) puts it, "bring the organization of behavior into conformity with the propositional structures that are cognized" are smoothly functioning. The expert does not need to "tell herself" things.[5] She does not need to engage in distinct actions of consulting the propositional knowledge that guides her in acting. She just *implements* that knowledge in her actions. Practice has allowed the automatic mechanisms that are responsible for executing epistemic states (whether dispositional or not) to take over.

Dreyfus maintains that in the case of the expert there are no guiding propositional states. Such states merely play the role of "training wheels" that are no longer required by the expert. But this entails that the automatic mechanisms contain *all* the content necessary to guide the expert's actions. And this simply cannot be right.

The automatic mechanisms that bring the organization of behavior into conformity with propositional attitudes are *perfectly general*. There is not one set of automatic mechanisms for catching a fly ball, and another for throwing a baseball from the outfield to the infield – it would be preposterous to multiply automatic mechanisms in this fashion. Perhaps there is just one automatic mechanism responsible for applying one's standing epistemic states, or perhaps there are several distinct classes of such automatic mechanisms – ones governing propositional states concerning actions like jumping, catching, and leaping, and others governing propositional states concerning (say) language use. But the difference between an expert's knowledge of how to catch a fly ball and an expert's knowledge of how to throw out a runner from the outfield lies solely in the propositional states that guide the action, and not the automatic mechanisms employed to place their behavior in conformity with standing epistemic states. The move from being a novice to being an expert involves bringing these automatic mechanisms to bear on the propositional knowledge that one has acquired. Once one achieves expertise, one therefore no longer needs to engage in a distinct action of *consulting* the propositional knowledge, since one is in a position to apply the propositional knowledge directly to the situation at hand.

Toribio describes expertise in golf as follows, a description that she takes to be problematic for a propositional view of knowing how:

---

[5] "In general, as Aristotle says, one does not deliberate about an acquired skill; the description of what one is doing, which one completely understands, is at a distance from the details of one's movements, which one does not consider at all" (Anscombe 1963: 54).

To be an expert at e.g. playing golf is to be able, under certain circumstances, and without any further training, to automatically adjust and respond appropriately to all kinds of variations and difficulties as presented by the game. What golf training does is to change the functional poise of certain perceptual inputs by engendering a skill that allows the subject to automatically and unreflectively make certain body, grip and balance adjustments such as may promote a successful, efficient – and, ideally, legal – way of getting the ball to the green. (2008: 49)

But Toribio's description of expertise is fully consistent with the picture of expertise I have sketched in this book. The expert golf player knows *many* propositions of the form 'w is a way to get a ball to the green'. Knowledge of each of these propositions structures her behavior in a certain way, i.e. knowledge of each such proposition entails the possession of what Ryle would call a "multi-track disposition". Her expertise consists not just in the possession of this large body of propositional knowledge, but also in the fact that the automatic mechanisms responsible for applying standing epistemic states of an agent are well-aligned to her propositional knowledge about golf. It is because, unlike the novice, she has a large body of propositional knowledge about the activity, and that she can bring it directly to bear on it, that she can smoothly and unreflectively adjust to new situations.

Nor, as we have already seen in the first chapter, is it plausible to identify the workings of the automatic mechanisms that apply standing epistemic states to concrete situations with any kind of knowledge how. First, as we have just discussed, these mechanisms do not concern any particular activity. In contrast, knowing how to ride a bicycle (for example) does concern a particular activity – its content is about that activity. Second, it is undeniable that knowledge of how to do something is a standing epistemic state of an agent; both those who deny and those who accept its propositional nature agree with this truism. But for *any* of the standing epistemic states of the agent, she needs to possess automatic mechanisms that are responsible for applying them to particular situations. Even if knowing how to do something were an ability or a complex of dispositions, an agent needs to have automatic mechanisms that are responsible for the application of the ability or the complex of dispositions to the particular situation at hand. In short, the automatic mechanisms that do the work of bringing behavior into conformity with standing epistemic states of the speaker cannot be identified with knowledge how, *no matter what* one's views of the nature of knowledge how.

3.

Famously, according to G.E.M. Anscombe, we have *non-observational knowledge* of what we are doing:

Say I go over to the window and open it. Someone who hears me moving calls out: What are you doing making that noise? I reply "Opening the window". I have called such a statement knowledge all along; and precisely because in such a case what I say is true – I do open the window; and that means that the window is getting opened by the movements of the body out of whose mouth those words come. But I don't say the words like this: "Let me see, what is this body bringing about? Ah yes! the opening of the window!" (1963: 51)

Anscombe's theoretical account of the non-observational knowledge we have of what we are doing is controversial, resting as it does upon Aquinas's thorny notion of practical knowledge, "the cause of what it understands" (ibid.: 87). But the phenomenon to which she draws our attention must nevertheless be explained.

There are well-known sources of resistance to the thought that we have non-observational knowledge of what we are doing. First, in *Intention*, Anscombe maintains that I know what I am doing, even when I do not manage to do it.[6] One might be misled into thinking that Anscombe therefore has in mind some strange notion of knowledge. But as Falvey (2000) has emphasized, I can easily be Φ-ing, even though I do not manage to Φ – indeed, that is the point of the progressive. So even if I do not manage to Φ, I still may know that I am Φ-ing. However, even if we are in fact sometimes wrong about what we are *doing*, and not just what we manage to do, we should not be misled into adopting either a strange notion of knowledge, or rejecting the obvious fact that we do in fact come to know what we are doing without observing our actions. As David Velleman writes:

claims about an agent's self-knowledge aren't meant to be proof against radical skepticism. When I say that you usually know what you're doing, I don't mean that you're absolutely and incorrigibly certain; I mean that you know by ordinary standards of evidence. And when other philosophers say that you know your actions without observation, they mean – or, at least, ought to mean – that observation isn't necessary for knowledge that meets equally ordinary standards. By stricter standards, observation wouldn't be sufficient. (1989: 19–20)

Some philosophers may be tempted to deny that we have non-observational knowledge of what we *will* do, on the grounds that all sorts of unintended obstacles may arise. But Velleman's point is relevant here too. The resistance such philosophers have to allowing non-observational knowledge of what we will do is nothing other than the resistance some philosophers have to allowing knowledge based on inferences from observation about future contingent statements generally. There is no *special* kind of skepticism here about knowledge of our future actions – there is just the familiar kind of skepticism about knowledge of the future.

Second, there is the large body of literature descending from or related to the objection in Davidson's classic paper, "Intending", that purports to show that one can intend to Φ without believing that one will Φ:

---

[6]   For example, in speaking of the action of writing "I am a fool" on the blackboard with her eyes shut, she writes, "The intention for example would not have been executed if something had gone wrong with the chalk or the surface, so that the words did not appear. And my knowledge would have been the same even if this had happened" (1963: 82).

in writing heavily on this page I may be intending to produce ten legible carbon copies. I do not know, or believe with any confidence, that I am succeeding. But if I am producing ten legible carbon copies, I am certainly doing it intentionally. (1980: 92)

If one can be Φ-ing intentionally without believing that one is Φ-ing, then there will be cases in which one does something intentionally, without believing that one is doing it, and hence without knowing that one is doing it. If we take Anscombe's claim to be that in every case of intentionally Φ-ing, I know without observation that I am intentionally Φ-ing, then Davidson's case raises a problem for Anscombe's claim.

There are many responses to Davidson's argument. For example, Harman (1976) distinguishes between doing something intentionally and intending to do it, and argues that the latter, but not the former requires belief.[7] It could be in Davidson's case that he intentionally produced the copies, without intending to produce the copies. There are many other response strategies (for a summary, see Velleman 1989: 114ff.). Even if we reject all of these strategies, and accept that there are some instances of intended actions that do not involve belief, we must explain not only what Sarah Paul calls "the pervasive presence of non-observational belief in intentional action" (2009: 6), but also the pervasive presence of non-observational *knowledge*. It is in the service of this project that a propositional notion of knowing how plays a central role.[8]

It is because knowing how to do something is propositional knowledge that knowledge of intention leads to knowledge of action. There are in fact distinct accounts of the role of knowing how in bridging this gap. Here is one. Suppose that I know that I have the intention to wash the dishes tonight. Suppose I also know how to wash the dishes. As long as I know that the conditions tonight will be conducive to washing the dishes, and I know that I generally do what I intend, then (as long as I do in fact end up washing the dishes) I know that I will be washing the dishes.

Anscombe herself rejected the view that knowledge of what we are or will be doing is based on inference:

in so far as one is observing, inferring etc. that Z is actually taking place, one's knowledge is not the knowledge that a man has of his intentional actions. (1963: 50)

As usual, Anscombe is correct about the phenomenology; where she errs is in the conclusion she draws from her observations. As Gilbert Harman writes about arguments of this kind:

A difficulty with such arguments is that they require the assumption that we have an independent way to tell when inference has occurred and when it has not. It is not clear why that assumption

---

[7] von Wright also argues that "One must distinguish between intentional acting and intention to a certain thing" (1971: 89).

[8] Anscombe was aware of the connection of knowing how and the cases she described as exercises of practical knowledge – as she writes, "A man has practical knowledge who knows how to do things..." (1963: 88).

is any more acceptable than the skeptical assumption that we know ahead of time what the valid principles of inference are. (1973: 20)

Harman argues, for example, that even perceptual beliefs that do not seem to involve inference in fact involve inference, albeit not conscious, fully specifiable inference.[9] The view that inference leaves canyons that lend themselves to discovery by purely phenomenological exploration is specious.[10]

According to one account of how we know what we are or will be doing, it rests upon knowledge of intention, or "will" (Grice 1971; Paul 2009). According to others, most notably the well-known theory of Velleman (1989), it rests upon the self-justifying status of the intention itself. For Velleman, the intention to perform an action is the belief that one is going to do the action as the result of forming the belief. The belief formed depends for its justification on two bits of background knowledge – first, knowledge that one will be able to do the action, and second, knowledge that beliefs of this sort do typically lead to their own fulfillment. The intention cannot justifiably be formed without such background knowledge in place. So on Velleman's view as well, knowledge of ability is a necessary precondition for knowledge of action.

I have no stake in choosing between these different positions on the role of intention in an account of knowledge of action. The view of knowing how defended here provides a straightforward explanation of why something like knowledge of ability is crucial to so many otherwise *different* accounts of knowledge of action. The subtle distinctions drawn at the end of Chapter 5 between ability-talk and ascriptions of knowing how should not obscure the fact that when philosophers use the awkward construction "knowledge of ability", it is really just the ordinary notion of knowing how that they have in mind.[11] It is because knowledge how is garden-variety propositional knowledge, knowledge of counterfactual success, that knowledge of action is knowledge in the ordinary sense of the term.

Kieran Setiya argues that any view of intentional action must accommodate the truth of (K):

(K) If A is doing Φ intentionally, A knows how to Φ, or else he is doing it by doing other things that he knows how to do. (2008: 404)

---

[9] Harman points out that inductive reasons cannot be fully specified, as "it is unlikely that anyone could specify the relevant total evidence in any actual case" (ibid.: 29).

[10] Sarah Paul writes, "Merely noting that our knowledge of what we are doing seems to be directly accessible upon reflection does nothing to demonstrate that it is non-inferential. Evidence-based information processing can take place rapidly and automatically at a non-conscious level, without the mindful entertaining of premises or feeling of drawing a conclusion" (2009: 10).

[11] According to Kieran Setiya (2008), knowing how must *supplement* knowledge of ability in an account of why I am entitled to form intentions to act and beliefs about what I will do. As we have seen in Chapter 5, he is right that ascriptions of ability and ascriptions of knowing how do not always involve the same modal base, and so can come apart from one another. But he is wrong to think that knowledge of ability is required *in addition* to knowledge how in an account of the epistemology of decision (see below).

However, Setiya (ibid.: 405) argues that (K) is not consistent with a notion of knowing how that is similar to propositional knowledge of ability. I have argued in the past for a principle that is even stronger than (K), viz. that intentional action requires knowledge how (Stanley and Williamson 2001: 415; Stanley forthcoming). So I certainly accept (K). Since I hold that knowing how is similar enough to propositional knowledge of ability, and I accept (K), I must respond to the challenge.

Setiya's argument involves an example of his we have discussed already in Chapter 5. Recall that Setiya's case involves someone who is recently paralyzed, but has irrational optimism that she is cured. On this basis, she clenches her fist, and does so successfully. According to Setiya, she intentionally clenches her fist, despite lacking knowledge of ability. The worry is that this person lacks knowledge of how to clench her fist in my sense, knowledge of counterfactual success, but nevertheless, *contra* (K), intentionally clenches her fist.

As I discussed in Chapter 5, Setiya's particular example does not pose a worry for my view of knowing how. The person *does* possess the required knowledge of how to clench her fist, though she lacks knowledge of ability. Knowledge of counterfactual success does not entail knowledge of ability. So this particular example poses no threat to (K). However, closely related examples do pose a worry for the conjunction of (K) with my favored view of knowing how. These examples are familiar from the first section of this chapter.

Consider a case in which someone acquires a true belief about how to fly a plane from an otherwise faulty instruction manual. They decide to fly an airplane, and on this basis enter the cockpit of an airplane and start flying it. It seems that the person is intentionally flying the airplane. However, on the view of knowing how I have defended, they do not know how to fly the airplane. This case is one that places pressure, in the way Setiya envisages, on the consistency of (K) and the view of knowing how defended in this book.

This kind of case is just like the challenge from Gettier cases we discussed in section 1. A natural reaction in Gettieried cases of knowledge how is to conclude that the agent knows how, despite lacking the relevant propositional knowledge. In such cases, I argued that the agent in fact does not know how to do the relevant action, but we easily allow the attributions because of the pragmatics of attributions of knowledge how. This version of Setiya's challenge places additional pressure on this response. Given the truth of (K), it may appear that I must also deny that the Gettieried agent *intentionally performs* the action in question.

However, it is no accident that Setiya uses examples of basic actions, like clenching one's fist, in the statement of his example. As Setiya notes, there are some worries with a version of (K), such as that endorsed in Stanley and Williamson (2001: 415), that drops the modification "or else he is doing it by doing other things that he knows how to do."[12] The case of the Gettieried pilot is consistent with (K), because, though she

---

[12] "I am trying to defuse a bomb, staring with confusion at an array of colored wires. Which one to cut? In desperation, not having a clue what the wires do, whether they will trigger the bomb or not, I disconnect the

does not know how to fly the plane, she still did so intentionally, via other activities that she did know how to do. Raising a problem for the conjunction of (K) and the view of knowing how I have defended in this book would require an example of a Gettieried case of basic action, where the agent genuinely lacks knowledge of counterfactual success. It is not clear to me that there are persuasive cases of this kind, because I have a hard time imagining cases in which someone can reliably clench their fist on the basis of their intention to do so and yet lack the propositional knowledge in question. In the case of basic actions, such as fist-clenchings, it may be sufficient for possession of the propositional knowledge in question that the subject has the disposition to clench one's fist in the relevant manner when they form the intention to do so (as long as the agent possesses the relevant concepts, such as the concept of a fist). Certainly, as we have seen in previous chapters, the behavior of clenching one's fist in a certain manner on the basis of one's intention is a characteristic expression of the relevant propositional knowledge. Finally, if the agent lacks such a disposition, it is not clear to me that her action of clenching her fist would be best described as intentional.[13]

Knowing how to do something plays a crucial role in explaining how we come to know what we are doing without observation. This role is consistent with many otherwise different accounts of how we come to possess this knowledge. The fact that knowing how to do something is *propositional* knowledge shows that the realm of what we do does not require some altogether novel kind of epistemological framework to explain our access to it.

4.

Knowing how to do something amounts to knowing a truth. This explains both the human capacity for skilled action, as well as the fact that when we act with skill, we know what we are doing without observation. The obstacles to accepting this thesis came from confusions about the nature of truths, about what it is to know them, and about what it is to act upon such knowledge. We have required the full resources of Philosophy to dispel the errors, and are now finally in a position to see what should have been obvious all along: that it is only when our behavior is guided by intellectual recognition of truths that it deserves to be called "intelligent".

---

red wire – and the timer stops. Even though I did not know how to defuse the bomb, and managed to do so through dumb luck, I count as having defused the bomb intentionally" (ibid.: 404).

[13] I will not here explore a defense of the unmodified version of (K) proposed in Stanley and Williamson (2001). Such a defense would require making a distinction akin to Harman's distinction between acting intentionally and intending. In the Gettier cases I have just described, the person would be acting intentionally in flying the plane, without (at least initially) being capable of forming the relevant intention.

Bibliography

Akinlabi, A., B. Connell, Ozo-Mekuri Ndimele, W. Bennett, E. Obikudu, and I. Essien. (Forthcoming). "Documenting Defaka and Nkoroo". NSF.

Aloni, M. (2002) "Questions under Cover", in D. Barker-Plummer, D. Beaver, J. van Benthem, and P. Scotto de Luzio (eds.), *Words, Proofs, and Diagrams* (Stanford: CSLI Publications).

Anscombe, G.E.M. (1963) *Intention* (Oxford: Basil Blackwell).

—— (1981) "The First Person", in G.E.M. Anscombe, *Metaphysics and the Philosophy of Mind: Collected Philosophical Papers Volume II* (Minneapolis: University of Minnesota Press), 21–36.

Arpaly, N. (2003) *Unprincipled Virtue: An Inquiry into Moral Agency* (New York: Oxford University Press).

Bach, K. (1997) "Do Belief Reports Report Beliefs?", *Pacific Philosophical Quarterly* 78: 215–41.

Beck, Sigrid and Rullmann, H. (1999) "A Flexible Approach to Exhaustivity in Questions", *Natural Language Semantics* 7, 249–98.

Beilock, S., Carr, T., MacMahon, C., and Starkes, J. (2002) "When Paying Attention Becomes Counterproductive: Impact of Divided Versus Skill-Focused Attention on Novice and Experienced Performance of Sensorimotor Skills", *Journal of Experimental Psychology: Applied* 8(1): 6–16.

Belnap, N. and Steel, T.B. (1976) *The Logic of Questions and Answers* (New Haven: Yale University Press).

Bengson, J. and Moffett, M. (forthcoming) "Two Conceptions of Mind and Action: Knowing How and the Philosophical Theory of Intelligence", in J. Bengson and M. Moffett, *Knowing How: Essays on Knowledge, Mind, and Action* (Oxford University Press, forthcoming).

Bengson, J., Moffett, M., and Wright, J. (2009) "The Folk on Knowing How", *Philosophical Studies* 142(3): 24–50.

Bhatt, R. (2006) *Covert Modality in Non-finite Contexts* (New York: Mouton de Gruyter).

Boer, S. and Lycan, W. (1986) *Knowing Who* (Cambridge, MA: MIT Press).

Boghossian, P. (2003) "Blind Reasoning", *Proceedings of the Aristotelian Society, Supplementary Volume* 77: 225–48.

Bromberger, S. (1966) "Questions", *Journal of Philosophy* 63: 597–606.

Brown, D. (1970) "Knowing How and Knowing That, What", in O.P. Wood and P. George, *Ryle* (eds.) (London: Macmillan), 213–48.

Brown, J. (2008) "Subject-Sensitive Invariantism and the Knowledge Norm for Practical Reasoning", *Nous* 42(2): 167–89.

Burge, T. (1977) "Belief De Re", *Journal of Philosophy* 74(6): 338–62.

—— (2007) "Postscript to 'Belief De Re'", in T. Burge, *Foundations of Mind* (Oxford: Oxford University Press), 65–81.

Carman, T. (2001g) "Conceptualism and the Scholastic Fallacy", in J. Schear (ed.), *The Myth of the Mental* (New York: Routledge).

Carnap, R. (1952) "Meaning Postulates", *Philosophical Studies* 3: 65–73.

—— (1958) *Meaning and Necessity* (Chicago: University of Chicago Press).

Carr, D. (1979) "The Logic of Knowing How and Ability", *Mind* 88: 394–409.

Carroll, Lewis (1895) "What the Tortoise Said to Achilles", *Mind* 4(14): 278–80.

Cath, Y. (forthcoming) "Knowing How without Knowing That", in J. Bengson and M. Moffett (eds.), *Knowing How: Essays on Knowledge, Mind, and Action* (Oxford: Oxford University Press).

—— (ms) "Regarding a Regress".

Chalmers, D. (forthcoming) "Propositions and Attitude Ascriptions: A Fregean Account", in *Nous*.

Chierchia, G. (1984) "Topics in the syntax and semantics of infinitives and gerunds", Ph.D. dissertation, Amherst, MA: University of Massachusetts.

—— and McConnell-Ginet, S. (2000) *Meaning and Grammar: An Introduction to Semantics* (2nd edn, Cambridge, MA: MIT Press).

Chomsky, N. (1981) *Lectures on Government and Binding* (Dordrecht: Foris Publishing).

—— (1995) *The Minimalist Program* (Cambridge, MA: MIT Press).

Church, A. (1951) "A Formulation of the Logic of Sense and Denotation", in P. Henle, H.M. Kallen, and S.K. Langer (eds.), *Structure, Method, and Meaning: Essays in Honor of H.M. Sheffer* (New York: Liberal Arts Press).

Cohen, N. and Squire, L. (1980) "Preserved Learning and Retention of Pattern-Analyzing Skill in Amnesia: Dissociation of Knowing how and Knowing that", *Science* 210: 207–10.

Davidson, D. (1980) "Intending", in D. Davidson, *Essays on Actions and Events* (Oxford: Clarendon Press), 83–102.

DeRose, K. (2009) *The Case for Contextualism* (Oxford: Oxford University Press).

Devitt, M. (forthcoming) "Methodology and the Nature of Knowing How", *Journal of Philosophy*.

Dienes, Z. and Perner, J. (1999) "A Theory of Implicit and Explicit Knowledge", *Behavioral and Brain Sciences* 22: 735–808.

Documenting Endangered Languages program: grant number 0553971.

Dowty, D., Wall, R., and Peters, S. (1981) *Introduction to Montague Semantics* (Dordrecht: Reidel).

Dreyfus, H. (2005) "Overcoming the Myth of the Mental: How Philosophers Can Profit from the Phenomenology of Everyday Expertise", APA presidential address.

—— (2007) "The Return of the Myth of the Mental", *Inquiry* 50(4): 352–65.

—— and Kelly, S. (2007) "Heterophenomenology: Heavy-handed Sleight-of-Hand", *Phenomenology and the Cognitive Sciences* 6(1/2): 45–55.

Duka, T., Weissenborn, R., and Dienes, Z. (2001) "State Dependent Effects of Alcohol on Recollective Experience, Familiarity and Awareness of Memories", *Psychopharmacology* 153: 295–306.

Egan, A. (2009) "Billboards, Bombs, and Shotgun Weddings", *Synthese* 166(2): 251–79.

Evans, G. (1982) *Varieties of Reference* (Oxford: Clarendon Press).

—— (1985) "Understanding Demonstratives", in G. Evans, *Collected Papers* (Oxford: Oxford University Press), 291–321.

Falvey, K. (2000) "Knowledge in Intention", *Philosophical Studies* 99(1): 21–44.

Flegal, K. and Anderson, M. (2008) "Overthinking Skilled Motor Performance: Or Why Those Who Teach Can't Do", *Psychonomic Bulletin and Review* 15: 927–32.

Fodor, J. (1968) "The Appeal to Tacit Knowledge in Psychological Explanation", *Journal of Philosophy* 65(20): 627–40.

—— (1975) *The Language of Thought* (Cambridge, MA: Harvard University Press).

—— (1983) *The Modularity of Mind* (Cambridge, MA: MIT Press).

—— (1987) *Psychosemantics: The Problem of Meaning in the Philosophy of Mind* (Cambridge, MA: MIT Press).

Folescu, M. and Higginbotham, J. (forthcoming) "Two Takes on the De Se".

Frege, G. (1918) "Der Gedanke", *Beiträge zur Philosophie des deutschen Idealismus* 2 1918–1919, S. 58–77.

Gabrieli, J.D.E. (1998) "Cognitive Neuroscience of Human Memory", *Annual Review of Psychology* 49: 87–115.

Ginet, C. (1975) *Knowledge, Perception, and Memory* (Boston: Dordrecht Reidel).

Ginzburg, J. (1995a) "Resolving Questions: I", *Linguistics and Philosophy* 18: 459–527.

—— (1995b) "Resolving Questions: II", *Linguistics and Philosophy* 18: 567–609.

—— (1996) "Interrogatives", in S. Lappin (ed.), *The Handbook of Contemporary Semantic Theory* (Oxford: Blackwell Press), 385–422.

—— (forthcoming) "How to Resolve *How to*", in J. Bengson and M. Moffett (eds.), *Knowing How: Essays on Knowledge, Mind, and Action* (Oxford: Oxford University Press).

Glick, E. (forthcoming) "Two Methodologies for Evaluating Intellectualism", *Philosophy and Phenomenological Research*.

Goldman, A. (1967) "A Causal Theory of Knowing", *Journal of Philosophy* 64(12): 357–72.

—— (1976) "What is Justified Belief?"

Goodale, M. and Milner, D.A. (1992) "Separate Visual Pathways for Perception and Action", *Trends in Neuroscience* 15: 20–5.

Grice, P. (1971) "Intention and Uncertainty", Proceedings of the British Academy 57: 263–79.

—— (1989) "Logic and Conversation", in P. Grice, *Studies in the Way of Words* (Cambridge, MA: Harvard University Press), 22–40.

Groenendijk, J. and Stokhof, M. (1982) "The Semantics Analysis of WH-Complements", *Linguistics and Philosophy* 5: 175–233.

—— and Stokhof, M. (1997) "Questions", in *Handbook of Logic and Language* (Cambridge, MA: MIT Press), 1055–1124.

Hamblin, C.L. (1958) "Questions", *Australasian Journal of Philosophy* 36(3): 159–68.

—— (1973) "Questions in Montague English", *Foundations of Language* 10: 41–53.

Harman, G. (1973) *Thought* (Princeton: Princeton University Press).

—— (1976) "Practical Reasoning", *Review of Metaphysics* 29(3): 431–63.

Hawley, K. (2003) "Success and Knowing How", *American Philosophical Quarterly* 40(1): 19–31.

—— (forthcoming) "Testimony and Knowing How", *Studies in the History and Philosophy of Science*.

Hawthorne, J. (2000) "Implicit Belief and A Priori Knowledge", *Southern Journal of Philosophy*, supplement.

—— and Stanley, J. (2008) "Knowledge and Action", *Journal of Philosophy* 105(10): 571–90.

Heck, R. (2000) "Non-conceptual Content and the 'Space of Reasons'", *Philosophical Review* 109: 483–523.

—— (2002) "Do Demonstratives Have Senses?", *Philosophers' Imprint* 2.

Heidegger, M. (1962) *Being and Time*, translated by Macquarrie, J. and Robinson, E. (New York: Harper & Row).

Heim, I. (1994) "Interrogative Semantics and Karttunen's Semantics for *Know*", in R. Buchalla and A. Mittwoch (eds.), *Israel Association for Theoretical Linguistics 1*, (Hebrew University, Jerusalem), 128–44.

Higginbotham, J. (1992) "Reference and Control", in R.K. Larson, S. Iatridou, U. Lahiri, and J. Higginbotham (eds.), *Control and Grammar* (Dordrecht: Kluwer), 79–108.

—— (1993) "Interrogatives", in *The View from Building 20* (Cambridge, MA: MIT Press), 195–227.

—— (2003) "Remembering, Imagining, and the First Person", in A. Barber (ed.), *Epistemology of Language* (Oxford: Oxford University Press), 496–533.

—— and May, R. (1981) "Questions, Quantifiers, and Crossing", *Linguistic Review* 1: 41–80.

Hintikka, J. (1989) "Reasoning about Knowledge in Philosophy", in J. Hintikka and M. Hintikka (eds.), *The Logic of Epistemology and the Epistemology of Logic* (Dordrecht: Kluwer), 17–36.

—— and Hintikka, M. (1989) *The Logic of Epistemology and the Epistemology of Logic* (Dordrecht: Kluwer).

Hornstein, N. (1999) "Movement and Control", *Linguistic Inquiry* 30: 69–96.

Hyman, John (1999) "How Knowledge Works", *Philosophical Quarterly* 49(197): 433–51.

Karmiloff-Smith, A. (1986) "From Meta-Processes to Conscious Access: Evidence from Children's Metalinguistic and Repair Data", *Cognition* 23(2): 95–147.

Kaplan, D. (1989a) "Demonstratives" in Almog, J., Perry, J. and Wettstein, H. (eds.), *Themes from Kaplan* (Oxford: Oxford University Press), 481–564.

—— (1989b) "Afterthoughts" in Almog, J., Perry, J. and Wettstein, H. (eds.), *Themes from Kaplan* (Oxford: Oxford University Press), 565–614.

Karttunen, L. (1977) "Syntax and Semantics of Questions", *Linguistics and Philosophy* 1: 3–44.

Kelly, S.D. (2000) "Grasping at Straws: Motor Intentionality and the Cognitive Science of Skilled Behavior", in M. Wrathall and J. Malpas (eds.), *Heidegger, Coping, and Cognitive Science: Essays in Honor of Hubert L. Dreyfus – Vol. II* (Cambridge, MA: MIT Press), 161–77.

Kelly, S. (2002) "Merleau-Ponty on the Body," *Ratio* 15(4): 376–91.

King, J. (2002) "Designating Propositions", *Philosophical Review* 111(3): 341–71.

Korsgaard, C. (1997) "The Normativity of Instrumental Reason", in G. Cullity and B. Gaut (eds.), *Ethics and Practical Reason* (Oxford: Oxford University Press), 213–54.

—— (2008) *The Constitution of Agency* (Oxford: Oxford University Press).

—— (2008a) "Acting for a Reason", in C. Korsgaard, *The Constitution of Agency* (Oxford: Oxford University Press), 207–30.

Kratzer, A. (1977) "What *Must* and *Can* Must and Can Mean", *Linguistics and Philosophy* 1: 337–55.

Krifka, M. Carlson, G., Pelletier, F.J., ter Meulen, A., Chierchia, G., and Link, G. (1995) "Genericity: An Introduction", in G. Carlson and F. Jeffry Pelletier (eds.), *The Generic Book* (Chicago: University of Chicago Press), 1–124.

Kripke, S. (1972) *Naming and Necessity* (Cambridge, MA: Harvard University Press).

Lahiri, U. (2002) *Questions and Answers in Embedded Contexts*, Oxford Studies in Theoretical Linguistics (Oxford: Oxford University Press).

Landau, I. (2000) *Elements of Control: Structure and Meaning in Infinitival Constructions* (Dordrecht: Kluwer).

—— (2003) "Movement out of Control", *Linguistic Inquiry* 34(3): 471–498.

—— (2004) "The Scale of Finiteness and the Calculus of Control", *Natural Language and Linguistic Theory* 22: 811–77.

Lewis, D. (1979) "Attitudes De Dicto and De Se", *Philosophical Review* 88: 513–43.

—— (1982) "'Whether' Report", reprinted in D. Lewis, *Papers in Philosophical Logic* (Cambridge: Cambridge University Press, 1998), 45–56.

Littlejohn, C. (forthcoming) "Must We Act Only on What We Know?" *Journal of Philosophy*.

McDowell, J. (1994) *Mind and World* (Cambridge: Harvard University Press).

—— (2007) "What Myth?" *Inquiry* 50(4): 338–351.

Matthews, R. (2007) *The Measure of Mind: Propositional Attitudes and their Attribution* (Oxford: Oxford University Press).

Moltmann, F. (2003) "Propositional Attitudes without Propositions", *Synthese* 135(1): 77–118.

—— (2006) "Generic 'one', Arbitrary PRO, and the First Person", *Natural Language Semantics* 14(3): 257–81.

Montague, R. (1974) edited by Richmond Thomason, *Formal Philosophy* (New Haven: Yale University Press).

—— (1974a) "The Proper Treatment of Quantification in Ordinary English", in *Formal Philosophy* (New Haven: Yale University Press), 247–70.

Moss, S. (forthcoming) "Updating as Communication", *Philosophy and Phenomenological Research*.

Neta, R. (2009) "Treating Something as a Reason for Action", *Nous* 43: 684–99.

Noë, A. (2005) "Against Intellectualism", *Analysis* 65(4): 278–90.

Paul, S.K. (2009) "How We Know What We're Doing", *Philosophers' Imprint* 9(11): 1–24.

Pavese, C. and Stanley, J. (2011) "Speaking of Practical Knowledge", *Proceedings of Semantics and Linguistic Theory* 20.

Peacocke, C. (1981) "Demonstrative Thought and Psychological Explanation", *Synthese* 49(2): 187–217.

—— (1986) *Thoughts: An Essay on Content* (Oxford: Basil Blackwell).

Perenin, M.-T. and Vighetto, A. (1988) "Optic Ataxia: A Specific Disruption in Visuomotor Mechanisms" *Brain* 111: 643–74.

Perry, J. (1977) "Frege on Demonstratives", *Philosophical Review* 86(4): 474–97.

—— (2001) *Reference and Reflexivity* (Stanford: CSLI Publications).

Poston, T. (2009) "Know-how to be Gettiered?", *Philosophy and Phenomenological Research* 79(3): 743–7.

Pryor, J. (1999) "Immunity to Error through Misidentification", *Philosophical Topics* 26.

Quine, W.V. (1976) "Worlds Away", *Journal of Philosophy* 73(22): 859–63.

Railton, P. (2004) "How to Engage Reason: The Problem of Regress", in J. Wallace, M. Smith, S. Scheffler, and P. Pettit (eds.), *Reasons and Value: Themes from the Moral Philosophy of Joseph Raz* (Oxford: Clarendon Press), 176–200.

—— (2006) "Normative Guidance", in R. Shafer-Landau (ed.), *Oxford Studies in Metaethics* (Oxford: Clarendon Press), 3–33.

—— (2009) "Practical Competency and Fluent Agency", in D. Sobel and S. Wall (eds.), *Reasons for Action* (Cambridge: Cambridge University Press), 81–114.

Recanati, F. (2007) *Perspectival Thought: A Plea for Moderate Relativism* (Oxford: Oxford University Press).

Reed, N., McLeod, P., and Dienes, Z. (2010) "Implicit Knowledge and Motor Skill: What People Who Know How to Catch Don't Know", *Consciousness and Cognition* 19: 63–76.

Roberts, C. (2009) "*Know-how*: A Compositional Approach", in E. Hinrichs and J. Nerbonne (eds.), *Theory and Evidence in Semantics* (Stanford: CSLI Publications).

Rumfitt, Ian (2003) "Savoir Faire", *Journal of Philosophy* 100: 158–66.

Rumfitt, I. (forthcoming) "Inference, Deduction, Logic", in J. Bengson and M. Moffett (eds.), *Knowing How: Essays on Knowledge, Mind, and Action* (Oxford: Oxford University Press).

Russell, B. (1950) *An Inquiry into Meaning and Truth* (London: George, Allen & Unwin).

Ryle, G. (1946) "Knowing How and Knowing That", *Proceedings of the Aristotelian Society* 46.

—— (1949) *The Concept of Mind* (Chicago: University of Chicago Press).

—— (1971) *Collected Papers, Volume 2* (Hutchinson and Co.: London).

—— (1971a) "Unverifiability-By-Me", in Ryle, *Collected Papers, Volume 2*, 121–30 (first published in 1936).

—— (1971b) "The Verification Principle", in Ryle, *Collected Papers, Volume 2*, 287–93 (first published in 1951).

—— (1971c) "Knowing How and Knowing That", in Ryle, *Collected Papers, Volume 2*, 212–25 (first published in 1946).

—— (1971d) "A Rational Animal", in Ryle, *Collected Papers, Volume 2*, 415–34 (first published in 1962).

—— (1979) *On Thinking* (Oxford: Basil Blackwell).

Schaffer, J. (2007) "Knowing the Answer", *Philosophy and Phenomenological Research* 75(2): 383–403.

—— (2009) "Knowing the Answer Redux: Replies to Brogaard and Kallestrup", *Philosophy and Phenomenological Research*, 78(2): 478–500.

Schooler, J. and Engstler-Schooler, T. (1990) "Verbal Overshadowing of Visual Memories: Some Things are Better Left Unsaid", *Cognitive Psychology* 22: 36–71.

Setiya, K. (2008) "Practical Knowledge", *Ethics* 118: 388–409.

Sgaravatti, D. and Zardini, E. (2008) "Knowing How to Establish Intellectualism", *Grazer Philosophische Studien* 77(1): 217–61.

Shoemaker, S. (1968) "Self-Reference and Self-Awareness", *Journal of Philosophy* 65(19): 555–67.

Snowdon, P. (2003) "Knowing How and Knowing That: A Distinction Reconsidered", *Proceedings of the Aristotelian Society*.

Soames, S. (2003) *Philosophical Analysis in the Twentieth Century: Volume 2, The Age of Meaning* (Princeton: Princeton University Press).

Speaks, J. (2005) "Is There a Problem about Non-Conceptual Content?" *Philosophical Review* 114(3): 359–98.

Stalnaker, R. (1978) "Assertion", *Syntax and Semantics*, vol. 9 (New York: Academic Press), 315–32.

—— (1987) *Inquiry* (Cambridge, MA: MIT Press).

—— (1997) "Reference and Necessity", in B. Hale and C. Wright (eds.), *A Companion to the Philosophy of Language* (Oxford: Basil Blackwell), 534–54.

—— (1999) "Belief Attribution and Context", in R. Stalnaker, *Context and Content* (Oxford: Oxford University Press), 150–66.

—— (2008) *Our Knowledge of the Internal World* (Oxford: Oxford University Press).

Stanley, J. (1998) "Persons and their Properties", *Philosophical Quarterly* 48: 159–75.

—— (2005) *Knowledge and Practical Interests* (Oxford: Clarendon Press).

—— (2010) "'Assertion' and Intentionality", *Philosophical Studies* 151(1): 87–113.

—— (forthcoming) "Knowing (How)", *Nous*.

—— and Szabo, G.Z. (2000) "On Quantifier Domain Restriction", *Mind and Language* 15(2/3): 219–61.

—— and Williamson, T. (2001) "Knowing How", *Journal of Philosophy* 98: 411–44.

Stine, G. (1976) "Skepticism, Relevant Alternative, and Deductive Closure", *Philosophical Studies* 29: 249–61.

Tanney, J. (2005) "Ryle", entry in the *Stanford Encyclopedia of Philosophy*.

—— (2005) "Une Cartographie des Concepts Mentaux", in Gilbert Ryle's *La Notion d'Esprit* (Paris: Payot), 7–70 (quotes from the English translation).

Tardif, T., Wellman, H., Fong Fung, K., Liu, D., and Fang, F. (2005) "Preschoolers' Understanding of Knowing-That and Knowing-How in the United States and Hong Kong", *Developmental Psychology* 441(3): 562–73.

Toribio, J. (2008) "How Do We Know How?", *Philosophical Explorations* 11(1): 39–52.

Tulving, E. (1986) "What Kind of a Hypothesis Is the Distinction between Episodic and Semantic Memory?", *Journal of Experimental Psychology: Learning, Memory, and Cognition* 12 (2): 307–11.

Velleman, D. (1989) *Practical Reflection* (Princeton: Princeton University Press).

—— (1996) "Self to Self", *Philosophical Review* 105(1): 39–76.

von Fintel, Kai (1994) "Restrictions on quantifier domains", Ph.D. thesis, University of Massachusetts at Amherst.

von Wright, G.H. (1971) *Explanation and Understanding* (Ithaca: Cornell University Press).

Wallis, C. (2008) "Consciousness, Context, and Know-How", *Synthese* 160(1): 123–53.

Weatherson, B. (2007) "Doing Philosophy with Words", *Philosophical Studies* 135: 429–37.

Wiggins, D. (forthcoming) "Knowing How To and Knowing That", *Mind* [ ].

Williams, B. (1973) "Imagination and the Self", in Bernard Williams, *Problems of the Self* (Cambridge: Cambridge University Press), 26–45.

Williamson, T. (1999) Review of A.W. Moore, *Points of View*, *Philosophical Books* 40(1): 43–5.

—— (2000) *Knowledge and Its Limits* (Oxford: Oxford University Press).

—— (2003) "Understanding and Inference", *Proceedings of the Aristotelian Society, Supplementary Volume* 77: 249–93.

—— (2009) "Probability and Danger", *Amherst Lecture in Philosophy* 4: 1–35.

Winograd, T. (1975) "Frame Representations and the Declarative–Procedural Controversy", in D.G. Bobrow and A. Collins (eds.), *Representations and Understanding: Studies in Cognitive Science* (New York: Academic Press), 185–210.

Wittgenstein, L. (1958) *The Blue and Brown Books* (Oxford: Basil Blackwell).

Wurmbrand, S. (2001) *Infinitives: Restructuring and Clause Structure* (New York: Mouton de Gruyter).

Index